T0248210

Praise for
CONTAINING BIG TECH

"Tom Kemp's *Containing Big Tech* is very eloquently written and explains how we got to the point where our precise location and movements are constantly tracked and sold to unknown players globally. Kemp's thoughtful and detailed book shows us a clear path forward to ensure consumers have the right to privacy and how the excesses of today's technology behemoths can be contained and reined in."

—Rick Arney, co-author of the California Consumer Privacy Act (CCPA) and Proposition 24, the California Privacy Rights Act (CPRA)

"Tom Kemp's prescient *Containing Big Tech* arrives just as AI threatens to amplify all of the excesses of the tech industry—the consolidation of markets, the manipulation of people, the assault on privacy, and the loss of control over the technologies deployed. *Containing Big Tech* is essential reading to understand the challenges ahead and the solutions to pursue."

—Marc Rotenberg, president and founder of
the Center for AI and Digital Policy

"In *Containing Big Tech*, Tom Kemp presents a compelling case for reining in Big Tech, illustrating through powerful facts and narratives the unique threats from digital surveillance to privacy, addiction and exploitation of users, and competition and innovation. The impact on all of us, and our children, is both chilling and profound. A must-read to understand the threats and challenges posed by Big Tech on society."

—Nita Farahany, author of *The Battle for Your Brain: Defending the Right to Think Freely in the Age of Neurotechnology*; Robinson O. Everett Professor of Law & Philosophy at Duke University

"Concerned about violations to your online privacy and the impact of AI on society? Tom Kemp's *Containing Big Tech* will demystify what the large tech players are doing with your personal information and how you can better protect yourself and your kids."

—**Debra J. Farber,** host of the *Shifting Privacy Left* podcast

"Tom Kemp's *Containing Big Tech* is a refreshing and insightful look at how Big Tech is over collecting our data, using AI in problematic ways, and dominating key digital markets. If you want to learn more about the impact of Big Tech on our society, read this book."

—**Christopher A. Smith,** author of *Privacy Pandemic*

"Tom Kemp is an expert in cybersecurity and privacy. His eloquent writing and detailed knowledge of the tech space provide a clear road map to protect against the overcollection and misuse of your data."

—**Debbie Reynolds,** host of the *Data Diva Talks Privacy* podcast

CONTAINING BIG TECH

CONTAINING BIG TECH

How to Protect Our
CIVIL RIGHTS, ECONOMY,
and DEMOCRACY

TOM KEMP

FAST
COMPANY
Press

Fast Company Press
New York, New York
www.fastcompanypress.com

This work is being published under the Fast Company Press imprint by
an exclusive arrangement with *Fast Company*. *Fast Company* and the
Fast Company logo are registered trademarks of Mansueto Ventures,
LLC. The Fast Company Press logo is a wholly owned trademark of
Mansueto Ventures, LLC.

Distributed by Greenleaf Book Group.

For ordering information or special discounts for bulk purchases,
please contact Greenleaf Book Group at PO Box 91869, Austin, TX
78709, 512.891.6100.

Design and composition by Greenleaf Book Group and Sheila Parr.
Cover design by Greenleaf Book Group and Sheila Parr.
Cover images used under license from ©Shutterstock/Graphyworld;
©Noun Project/Alex Burte, Kamin Ginkaew, Nawicon, Matt Wasser,
sandiindra, Vectors Point, pictohaven, and Lucia fruzza.

Publisher's Cataloging-in-Publication data is available.

Print ISBN: 978-1-63908-061-8

eBook ISBN: 978-1-63908-062-5

To offset the number of trees consumed in the printing of our books,
Greenleaf donates a portion of the proceeds from each printing to
the Arbor Day Foundation. Greenleaf Book Group has replaced over
50,000 trees since 2007.

Printed in the United States of America on acid-free paper

23 24 25 26 27 28 29 30   10 9 8 7 6 5 4 3 2 1

First Edition

For Suman, Jolie, Griffin, Ella, and Chloe.

Contents

THE CURSE OF CALIFORNIA.

About the Cover

The cover of this book is in the tradition of past portrayals of monopolies—represented as ravenous octopuses with tentacles wrapping around politicians, capitols, other industries, workers, and citizens. The images on the preceding page are how the robber barons' railroad monopoly and John D. Rockefeller's Standard Oil were depicted.[1]

In honoring this tradition, the Big Tech octopus on the cover of this book is now digital and in the cloud. Each tentacle's app represents one of the eight topics I cover in each chapter: digital surveillance, data brokers, data breaches, AI, persuasive technology, kids' online safety, extremism and disinformation, and competition.

Introduction

Although tech platforms can help keep us connected, create a vibrant marketplace of ideas, and open up new opportunities for bringing products and services to market, they can also divide us and wreak serious real-world harms.

—White House Listening Session on Tech Platform Accountability, September 2022[1]

On May 10, 1869, at Promontory Summit in the Utah Territory, railroad tycoon Leland Stanford drove a golden spike that connected the Central Pacific Railroad rails to the Union Pacific Railroad rails. Thus, the First Transcontinental Railroad across the United States was created. A technological breakthrough, the railroad enabled travel from the East Coast to California to be cut from many months—via lengthy and dangerous sea voyages or wagon trains—to less than a week by more comfortable trains.[2]

The achievement also made Stanford and the rest of the "Big Four" owners of the Central Pacific incredibly wealthy and created one of the first monopolies in the United States. Their investment of $15,800 eventually led to profits of over $200 million in their lifetimes, which equates to $6.5 billion in 2023 dollars. The Big Four's dominance over freight in California, accumulation of massive profits, association with the 1880 shoot-out in Central California over a land dispute between farmers and the railroad that left seven people dead, and political control over the state led them to be called "robber barons." Unsurprisingly, the Big Four and their railroad were depicted on a magazine cover in 1882 as a giant octopus devouring labor and other industries that relied on its rails, with the tagline "The Curse of California."[3]

Since then, the United States has had other large, powerful conglomerates and monopolies. In the late 1800s and early 1900s, John D. Rockefeller's Standard Oil monopoly was also caricatured as an octopus. American Telephone & Telegraph (AT&T) dominated the telecommunications industry for over one hundred years until its breakup in 1983. The "Big 3" in automobiles—General Motors (GM), Ford, and Chrysler— had 80 percent of the world's automobile production up until 1950.[4]

Today we have the five large "Big Tech" firms—Amazon, Apple, Google (a subsidiary of Alphabet), Meta (formerly Facebook), and Microsoft. Some are monopolies in specific large markets—for example, Google in search. And they are also duopolists and oligopolists that compete against each other in other large markets—for example, Apple and Google share the market for mobile operating systems and app stores.[5]

Big Tech has become the standard bearer for Silicon Valley innovation. For example, coming out of the dot-com bust, Google heralded the return of Silicon Valley with its IPO in 2004, and amazingly Google could give us the modern equivalent of the Library of Alexandria with just a click of the mouse. Likewise, Apple's launch of the iPhone in 2007 showed that Silicon Valley could out-innovate the world and create the next generation of smart devices, giving us a powerful computer in the palm of our hand. And Meta's IPO in 2012 shone the light back on Silicon Valley after the 2008 recession with social media as a global phenomenon that could connect us all.

Big Tech has also become the standard bearer for the American economy. This is represented by the fact that in 2022, these companies alone represented nearly one-fifth of the Standard & Poor's 500 Index, which tracks the stock performance of the five hundred largest companies in the US. In comparison, the entire oil and energy sector represented less than 5 percent, while all the financial services firms combined represented slightly over 10 percent. Moreover, if one were to map Apple's market capitalization of over $2 trillion in 2022 to gross domestic product (GDP), it would mean that Apple would be tied for eighth in the rankings of the world's largest economies by GDP.[6]

Companies like GM had a comparably large market capitalization in their heyday. For example, in 1955, with America experiencing a post–World War II economic boom, GM represented about 3 percent of the total market value of the S&P 500 Index, which implied a market capitalization of approximately $1 trillion in 2022. But, in contrast, four of the five Big Tech companies had a market capitalization of over $1 trillion in 2022, while GM in 1955 was the only company with that equivalent market capitalization.[7]

Even with that in mind, some may still say that these Big Tech firms that have emerged as the leaders in this Third Industrial Revolution— today's digital and computer age—are just the modern-day equivalents of Standard Oil and GM. Those conglomerates came from the Second Industrial Revolution, marked by mass production powered by electricity, which replaced the First Industrial Revolution, characterized by the use of steam power to mechanize production.[8]

Big Tech's broader and deeper reach

But Big Tech is not equivalent to past monopolies in prior industrial revolutions. Instead, Big Tech is more powerful and impactful than past giants, given its significantly broader and deeper reach with consumers across the globe that is unmatched in history. For example, as of 2022, Google had 4.3 billion users of its products, Meta had over 2.9 billion, and Microsoft and Apple had over one billion. And China-based TikTok, likely to be the newest member of the Big Tech club, has over one billion users as of 2022—and reached that number in just five years, three years before Meta hit that mark. Moreover, the world's population in 2022 was eight billion, so each Big Tech firm is directly interfacing with between 13 percent and 54 percent of the world's population. In contrast, it took GM over one hundred years to sell five hundred million cars.[9]

We use Big Tech's products daily to create, locate, shop, learn, entertain, work, and communicate with others. And, unlike with earlier titans, it is not just one product from each Big Tech firm that we use and rely on. For example, as of 2022, Meta's Facebook service has over two billion users, Meta's Instagram and Messenger services have 1.3 billion users each, and Meta's WhatsApp has two billion users. In comparison, Google claims it has at least nine services with over one billion users, including 3.2 billion users of the Chrome browser, 2.2 billion users of YouTube, and over 1.8 billion users of Gmail.[10]

Most of our modern daily life relies heavily on Big Tech's products that offer significant value to us. In other words, their products are not nice-to-haves but must-haves. For example, a tech reporter with the *New York Times* tried for six weeks not to use any of their products and found it "impossible." The issues included finding a computer that did not run Microsoft Windows or Apple Mac OS X or a phone that did not run Google's Android or Apple iOS. And she could not even use popular apps like Netflix or Uber because they either run on Big Tech's cloud platforms (e.g., Amazon Web Services or Microsoft Azure) or use their mapping technology (e.g., Google Maps).[11]

Furthermore, these interactions happen every day. Big Tech embeds itself in our daily lives and consumes our attention. For example, global internet users—numbering 4.96 billion in 2021—spend 2.5 hours daily on social media. And in some developing countries, Meta provides free internet access to its website and others, so Meta is the internet for millions of people. For each minute in 2021, there were 5.7 million Google searches, 240,000 shares of photos on Meta's Facebook, and twelve million Apple iMessages sent. And as of 2021, 70 percent of American adults use Meta's Facebook, and 80 percent use Google's YouTube.[12]

The threats associated with Big Tech

Not only is Big Tech's reach dramatically broader and deeper than past industry giants, and we are more reliant on their products, but Big Tech collectively represents a more significant threat to our society. The hazards include the digital surveillance business model many Big Tech firms utilize, which weakens our privacy and makes us more susceptible to identity theft. The threats also encompass Big Tech's massive investments in artificial intelligence (AI) to develop technologies that can be addictive and exploitative. And finally, the threats also involve all these firms' monopolistic power over key digital markets in our economy, resulting in suppressed competition and innovation. None of these are healthy for our society, but the threat is even more severe when two or three are combined.

Let me briefly drill down on each of these threats.

First, the mass collection and monetization of our data by companies like Google and Meta mean they know more about our behavior—our precise location, internet searches, purchases, and apps—than our friends and family. So, yes, Standard Oil was mighty. But it did not know everything about us. And we must accept the terms of use of Big Tech's products that do this intrusive data collection because their products are essential to navigating our modern life, and we have no reasonable alternatives.[13]

Historically this near-total digital surveillance has enabled those companies to profile us and utilize this deep insight to let advertisers target us. But now, this data and behavioral analysis can be weaponized against us if, for example, you facilitate or get an abortion in certain US states. Or it can be used by adversarial nation-states to attack our democracy. Furthermore, the massive amounts of data collected by these Big Tech firms and the digital advertising ecosystem they facilitate can expose millions of people to identity theft every year.

Second, Big Tech is also at the forefront of developing AI technology that simulates human intelligence by identifying patterns in data and automating decision-making. Some Big Tech firms leverage AI to build products imbued with persuasive technologies designed to suck up more and more of our attention and keep us on their platforms. This can, for example, result in us seeing more ads and, in turn, generating more revenue for them. Unfortunately, these AI systems can also increase user engagement that, if left unchecked, is addictive and can increase polarization by limiting contrary viewpoints, thereby keeping us firmly in our respective information bubbles. Or, even worse, it can push us into rabbit holes of conspiracy theories, disinformation, and extremism. Neither AT&T nor the Big 3 was addictive, nor did they weaken our democracy.

We also see that some Big Tech firms have not fully designed their user interfaces and AI-based back-end systems with children in mind. The result is that these Big Tech firms are lax in protecting children from the risks of the digital world by exposing them to addictive technologies, harmful or inappropriate content, unsolicited contact with adults, and cyberbullying. This leads to serious questions about Big Tech and its impact on children's development and mental health.

And third, all Big Tech firms have been aggressively acquiring or stifling competitors. In addition, consumers' reliance on Big Tech creates a technology toll road for its competitors, as other products must often interface with Big Tech's platforms or be sold in their app stores or marketplaces. Critics then say that Big Tech "preferences" its products in its app stores and marketplaces by treating its products more favorably in recommendations and search rankings than third-party offerings, thus limiting consumer choices and competition.

Big Tech continues to gain a competitive advantage as they get more widely used. Known as "network effects," this means as they gain more users, their platforms become more compelling and valuable— "sticky." In the case of Meta, that means consumers can keep tabs on more friends, or in the case of Google's search capabilities, it means better insight into who is clicking on what links that will drive a better ranking of search results. But network effects can be leveraged for anticompetitive behavior. For example, Big Tech has been accused of purposely not making its products interoperable with alternative solutions. This locks in consumers because if they move off of Big Tech's products, they lose the ability to communicate and socialize with friends who are still on those platforms. And critics say that Big Tech firms unfairly use their knowledge of which third-party solutions are trending with consumers in their marketplace or app stores and then will turn around and offer their knock-off versions.

So, when you combine these anticompetitive practices, one can say that Big Tech has, in effect, taken PayPal co-founder Peter Thiel's widely followed advice in Silicon Valley that "competition is for losers." In Thiel's estimation, this means that the best end state for a technology company to strive for is becoming a monopoly. That's good for the company, its investors, and its employees. But it is not healthy for society and our economy in the long run, as it concentrates power and inhibits innovation and job creation.[14]

Motivations behind this book

I have had the good fortune to have co-founded several successful Silicon Valley–based companies. My start-ups have partnered and competed with Big Tech firms. As a result, I have experienced a similar Silicon Valley journey that Big Tech companies have gone through, albeit at a smaller scale. I've navigated everything from raising money from venture capitalists, trying to get that elusive fit between product and market, taking a company public, and constantly feeling the pressure to hit your quarterly sales numbers. So, I fully understand the Silicon Valley experience and culture from which the Big Tech firms sprang. I am also an active angel investor in over a dozen technology companies that, like most technology start-ups, operate in Big Tech's shadows, including utilizing their cloud platforms.

Furthermore, much of my professional and investing career has been in cybersecurity and privacy, which is the sweet spot of many Big Tech–related issues. Businesses have deployed my companies' products and cloud offerings to help defend against cyberattacks and address privacy regulations like Europe's General Data Protection Regulation (GDPR). Consumers have also used solutions from the companies I started and invested in to protect their data, digital identities, and mobile devices. In addition, my current start-ups utilize AI to varying degrees as part of their product architecture. Finally, I started my career at database vendor Oracle, so I am familiar with large-scale data collection. Thus, I have a good sense of Big Tech's dominant market positions, its impact on consumers and other businesses, and the technologies they use to build their offerings.

Over the last few years, I have been increasingly active in policy advocacy around privacy. For example, in 2020, I was a full-time volunteer working extensively on the successful California Proposition 24 ballot initiative that significantly enhanced the California Consumer Privacy Act. And in 2022, I drafted and tried to push through a California Senate bill that upgraded California's data broker law that lobbyists for Big Tech found a way to get tabled. Finally, in 2023, I advocated for and co-drafted a proposed California Senate bill that would create an online portal for consumers to request that data brokers delete any data they have on the consumer and no longer track them.

Through these experiences, I am convinced that people need to be more aware of the threats and challenges posed by Big Tech. Interestingly, when the Pew Research Center surveyed users of Meta's Facebook social network service, it turned out that three-quarters were not aware of the type of data that Meta collected about them. But when users were directed to their Facebook ad preferences under the Settings menu and saw what was collected about them and how they were categorized to advertisers, approximately half of Facebook users became uncomfortable with the company collecting their traits and interests. So, shining a light on Big Tech's business practices makes for an informed citizenry, which is needed, given how deeply Big Tech is embedded in and directly shaping our modern lives.[15]

In addition, many significant developments have recently occurred that dramatically impact how we now need to consider Big Tech. At the top of the list is the repeal of *Roe v. Wade* in 2022. We have entered a post–abortion rights era in America, which has significantly ratcheted up how we must account for the intrusiveness and impact of Big Tech on our lives and democracy. For example, a common mindset of many Americans has been "I don't care about online privacy, as I have nothing to hide." But the repeal of *Roe* should remind us that we are in a world of near-total digital surveillance—including the ability to track our precise location and juxtapose it with our internet search history and purchases. It was, perhaps, simply about serving targeted ads in the past, but now Big Tech's hoard of data can significantly erode our rights and actively be weaponized against us.[16]

With this book, I have combined my Silicon Valley experience with my policy work to comprehensively identify and correlate all the significant issues associated with Big Tech and provide straightforward guidance on how to fix the problems. To that end, I have identified eight central and interlocking topics that will each be covered in a chapter. These topics share common themes, including the overcollection of our data, the often-problematic ways Big Tech uses AI to process and act upon our data, and the adverse side effects of Big Tech's dominant market positions.

Chapter overviews

The first three chapters focus on the mining and collecting of our data and the negative consequences that have emerged because of this. Chapter 1 looks at what Big Tech's digital surveillance–based business model means for us, including the impact of the overturn of *Roe*. Chapter 2 then covers data brokers—shadowy participants in the digital advertising ecosystem that much of Big Tech facilitates—which are an equal source of concern regarding privacy in post–abortion rights America. Finally, chapter 3 examines the impact of having so much information collected about us that it increases the chances that our data is breached and our identity is stolen.

Chapters 4 through 7 analyze how Big Tech consumes and processes this data via AI and how that has created its own unique threats. Chapter 4 will describe what AI is, why Big Tech is placing significant bets on it, how bias can seep into AI, and how it can be used for exploitative purposes. Chapter 5 discusses the harmful effects of how Big Tech's AI-based persuasive technologies attempt to change our behavior and can facilitate screen addiction. Chapter 6 examines the impact of Big Tech's use of AI on kids' online safety. Finally, chapter 7 considers how Big Tech's use of AI has enabled extremism and disinformation on their platforms, which has exacerbated polarization and weakened our democracy.

Chapter 8 examines how Big Tech's dominant market positions have harmed entrepreneurship and innovation and undermined journalism and a vibrant free press. This chapter will also show how Big Tech's monopoly positions have worsened the above issues of privacy, data protection, screen addiction, disinformation, and so on.

Each chapter will conclude with a companion road map for that topic that recommends how together we might rein in the negatives of Big Tech. My goal with each is to offer solutions and provide a clear path forward to help individuals and policymakers advocate for change. In that vein, I have included two appendices that should also be useful to consumers and lawmakers. Appendix 1 provides step-by-step instructions for individuals to protect their online privacy. Appendix 2 provides some suggested ingredients that should be part of a comprehensive US privacy law to protect against the digital surveillance we see from Big Tech.

Stopping versus containing

As I was writing each chapter of this book, I often thought of this quote from American sports commentator Dan Patrick: "You can't stop him; you can only hope to contain him." Patrick often used the expression for irony when a non-superstar athlete had a surprisingly good outing. However, its roots were in statements from athletes commenting on limiting the performance of an opposing team's superstar yet still finding a way to win.[17]

I don't want to stop Big Tech. They have built impressive and innovative products with many positive attributes and are vital contributors to our economy. And, frankly, stopping them is not even possible.

But that does not mean their momentum and impact should not be examined and curtailed. Left alone in its current trajectory, Big Tech will continue unimpeded to undermine our freedom, squash innovation, and damage our democracy. So, I want us to take the necessary steps to contain the threats and excesses of Big Tech. And, in doing so, ensure our civil rights are respected and preserved, our economy is competitive, and our democracy is protected—so we all win.

CHAPTER 1

Digital Surveillance

US Senator Hatch: "How do you sustain a business model in which users don't pay for your service?"

Mark Zuckerberg, CEO of Meta: "Senator, we run ads."[1]

Samuel Warren, the law partner of future Supreme Court Justice Louis Brandeis, was quite unhappy that numerous national newspapers' gossip columns published the intimate details of his wedding in 1883 to a senator's daughter. Warren's "deep-seated abhorrence of the invasions of social privacy" lingered, and Warren and Brandeis eventually published an essay entitled "The Right to Privacy" in 1890 in the *Harvard Law Review*. In it, they defined privacy as "the right to be let alone" while noting "recent inventions and business methods call attention to the next step which must be taken for the protection of the person," including the concern that "numerous mechanical devices threaten to make good the prediction that 'what is whispered in the closet shall be proclaimed from the housetops.'" While privacy is not mentioned in the US Constitution, this essay became the basis by the 1960s for many courts and state legislatures to recognize such a right. However, this right is now in question with the repeal of *Roe v. Wade*.[2]

But even before the *Dobbs* decision in 2022 overturned *Roe*, the reality is that Americans do not have the right to be left alone when it comes to our online activity. For example, if you think you have a medical condition and research that condition online, that condition is now linked to you—even if you misdiagnose yourself—and will be shared with advertisers who will target you with ads regarding that condition. In addition, mobile apps constantly track your location—for example, visits to mosques, cancer clinics, and Alcoholics Anonymous meeting places—and can be sold to any third party with a credit card. Or suppose you are trying to discover your sexual identity. In that case, businesses will likely know or infer your sexuality based on your online activity before your family or friends know. And suppose you research online how to get an abortion or even visit an abortion clinic. That information could be weaponized against you, as certain states will try to subpoena technology providers to determine which women have sought or gotten an abortion.

The US has no national data privacy law to protect us. As of 2022, only five states have a law that provides robust consumer data privacy rights. However, the Fourth Amendment does give citizens the right to be secure "in their persons, houses, papers, and effects" and "against unreasonable searches and seizures." But that right seemingly stops at the water's edge when digitized versions of our papers and effects are stored in the cloud services of technology companies.[3]

In this chapter, I will first discuss how Big Tech's digital surveillance capabilities emerged from a monetization strategy via advertising. Next, I will describe how the Big Tech companies collect our data. I will then examine the threats associated with this digital surveillance to our freedom and how these threats are significantly ratcheted up because we are now in a post–abortion rights America.

In response to digital surveillance, legislators have pushed for data privacy laws that give us the right to control how our personal information is collected and used. So, I will explore privacy laws and proposals in Europe and the US. Finally, I will provide a road map for how we as individuals and as a society can work toward and implement Brandeis and Warren's vision of the right to be let alone.

Big Tech as Big Advertiser

The era of online surveillance started in the early 2000s. Until then, the largest technology firms had historically generated revenue by selling computers, operating systems, databases, and applications. But if you consider two of today's most prominent tech firms—Google and Meta—the vast majority of their revenue does not come from selling products to consumers or businesses. Instead, their revenue comes from providing free online platforms that extract online behavioral data that is utilized to sell advertising.

Advertising is a massive business for both firms—for the twelve months from July 2021 to June 2022, Google did $225 billion in advertising, while Meta did over $116 billion. And it is still the core of what they do; for the first half of 2022, advertising represented 81 percent of Google's revenue and 97 percent of Meta's revenue.[4]

These two tech firms are the clear leaders in online advertising (also called "ad tech"), with over half of all online advertising revenue. Analysts have historically referred to this market as a "duopoly," but the other Big Tech firms also see abundant ad tech opportunities. For example, Amazon did $34 billion in online advertising in that same twelve-month period. Moreover, given Amazon's fast growth in advertising, analysts are now saying this duopoly is evolving into a "triopoly," as evidenced at the end of 2021, with Google, Meta, and Amazon accounting for 74 percent of all global online advertising spending and 47 percent of all money spent on advertising. The remaining two Big Tech firms are also significantly growing their online advertising revenue. For example, Microsoft did over $15 billion in advertising in that same period. At the same time, analysts project that Apple will make approximately $5 billion in 2022 in advertising revenue and will see that grow to over $20 billion by 2025.[5]

Big Tech's advertising revenue will likely continue to grow as daily internet usage continues to increase—the average daily time spent with the internet per capita rose from 75 minutes in 2011 to 192 minutes per day in 2021. This is over a 250 percent increase in just ten years. If you factor out the roughly three out of eight billion of the world's population that is not on the internet, the average internet user currently spends over six hours per day online. So, it is not surprising that the online advertising market is projected to grow from $380 billion in 2020 to $785 billion in 2025, and the percentage of digital ad spending will increase from 58 percent of all media ad spending in 2020 to 72 percent in 2025.[6]

Big Tech's game plan to grow their advertising business remains the same after twenty years—continuously surveil and collect massive amounts of information about every one of us. This collected information is in the form of "data exhaust" that we emit as we interact with the internet through websites, mobile apps, and internet-connected devices. So, just as gas-powered cars emit carbon exhaust, we emit digital exhaust in the form of data. This mining and extraction of our data exhaust enable companies like Google and Meta to offer their actual customers—advertisers—detailed information about our behavior, personal traits, interests, and so on, so advertisers can better target us with ads. This industrial-scale extraction of this human-generated data and the corresponding translation of that information into behavioral data for analysis and commerce has even been given a name—"surveillance capitalism"—by Harvard professor Shoshana Zuboff.[7]

Big Tech facilitates this surveillance by creating "walled gardens" where we are enticed to enter to take advantage of their highly valued and convenient free services. And we remain in those gardens, given their "stickiness" (i.e., a combination of our reliance on their services and the inability for us to move to alternative solutions easily) and the often-addictive nature of their services. Thus, the mining and extraction of our personal information and online behavior continue unabated, enabling more insight into our preferences, characteristics, predispositions, attitudes, intelligence, and abilities that can be used to better target us with ads.

This constant surveillance has allowed Big Tech to take a giant leap in cracking the code on the problem with advertising that was expressed over one hundred years ago by department store magnate John Wanamaker: "Half the money I spend on advertising is wasted; the trouble is, I don't know which half." Big Tech firms can appeal to advertisers with even the most niche products by serving ads to narrow audiences who meet the advertisers' targeted customer profiles.[8]

For example, say your business is manufacturing and selling diapers, and your target buyer is expecting mothers and mothers with newborns. If you placed an ad for your product on a cable news show or in a newspaper, your advertising spending would likely not be efficient, as the cable station or newspaper probably does not have exact information on how many expecting mothers or mothers with newborns are part of their demographics. But even if they did, most people seeing your ads would have no interest in diapers, as this product lacks relevance, so spending is wasted.

But in the case of online advertising, it is first possible to target your ads just to women within a specific age range who could potentially be pregnant or have young children. The platforms may also know via social media postings if a woman has revealed if she is expecting or has given birth. But in most cases, there is no explicit posting or self-identification on the internet that a woman is pregnant or has a newborn. Still, this could be inferred based on internet searches (e.g., she searched for the word "diapers") and website visits (she visited a website comparing diaper brands). It can also be inferred that a woman meets the targeted criteria based on purchases (e.g., recently purchased a crib).

The theory is that Big Tech firms can uniquely offer greater advertising efficiency when targeting an advertiser's desired audience, which would especially appeal to small businesses with limited marketing budgets. For example, Meta and Google know what consumers are searching for and clicking on, while Amazon knows what consumers are buying, how often, and from whom. And these firms have this "first party" data for billions of people.[9]

Academics and industry groups believe that a significant proportion of online advertising leverages digital surveillance. For example, one study published in 2017 estimated that behavioral targeting accounts for two-thirds of all European online advertising. So, digital surveillance is the backbone of a massive ad tech market sized at $600 billion in 2022.[10]

Finally, a crucial fact in digital surveillance is that the Big Tech players do not get paid for the ads they serve unless a user clicks on them. So, to make money on ads and maintain their high growth rates, Big Tech's digital surveillance–based advertising business model is quite simple. The formula is to (a) get as many users as possible on their "walled garden" platforms through an increasing number of high-value, convenient, and sticky free services that take advantage of a "network effect," (b) collect as much data and serve as many ads as possible even when users are off their platforms, (c) keep users on their platform as long as possible through addictive means to maximize the likelihood of clicking on ads while also maximizing the collection of data to improve their ad targeting, and (d) make it difficult to switch from their platforms.

To expand on the first two points from above, for the following five sections of this chapter, I will give an overview of each Big Tech firm, discuss their walled gardens, and describe their digital surveillance capabilities. I will discuss the latter two points—Big Tech's addictive nature and its high switching costs—in subsequent chapters.

Google

The most extensive practitioner of digital surveillance is Google.

Launched in 1998 by co-founders and Stanford classmates Sergey Brin and Larry Page, Google had set out to develop a better internet search engine that was free for any consumer to use. The company focused on building algorithms—software programs with step-by-step instructions that computers use to execute a given task—that delivered more accurate search results compared to other offerings that forced users to comb through less relevant results.

But within two years of its founding, Google had to survive the dot-com crash. In April 2000, the Nasdaq lost 34 percent of its value in one month and dropped 80 percent in October 2002 from its peak in March 2000. Of the estimated seven thousand new internet companies started in the late 1990s, approximately five thousand went out of business or were sold by mid-2003. And Silicon Valley alone lost an estimated two hundred thousand jobs from 2001 to 2004. It was a difficult time to be in Silicon Valley.[11]

Not surprisingly, after enjoying the good times of taking unprofitable internet companies public in the late 1990s, when the dot-com bubble burst in early 2000, venture capitalists (VCs) were now putting the squeeze on their portfolio companies to figure out ways to build profitable businesses. That included VC-backed Google, which had not yet cracked the code to create a "real business" that was profitable. In 1999, Google's revenue was $220,000, and it lost $6 million; in 2020, it made $19 million in revenue, but it lost close to $15 million. So even Google was feeling the heat.[12]

Switching its business model

Google's original business model was to license its search engine to other sites. The user data they collected—users' keyword searches and the results they clicked on—was utilized to improve the product: fine-tuning the most relevant search results. But based on their investors' pressure to become profitable, and despite their past reluctance to rely on an advertising business model, in 2000, Google introduced advertising targeted to consumers' search queries. This meant the data collected from consumers became dual purpose—improving their product and building a user behavior database to facilitate matching ads to keywords.[13]

Initially, the advertising model was focused on charging advertisers based on the number of times an ad was displayed, which they called the Premium Sponsorship program. In early 2002, they began offering AdWords—Google's online self-service program that let advertisers place targeted text-based ads next to search results—on a cost-per-click basis, in which advertisers would only pay Google when a consumer clicked on an ad. This became so popular with advertisers that by the end of 2003, Google abandoned the Premium Sponsorship program and solely offered advertising on a cost-per-click model. This further cemented Google's reliance on advertising and its motivation to utilize behavioral data to get consumers to click on ads, as more clicks equaled more revenue.[14]

Much like Leland Stanford connected the Transcontinental Railroad with a golden spike, Stanford University graduates Brin and Page used the surveillance-based pay-per-click model as the golden spike that linked the rail of free services with the rail of online advertising. In 2001, even during the middle of the dot-com bubble and with the significant impact of the September 11 attacks on the US economy, Google's revenue soared to $86 million, turning a profit of $7 million. Brin was quoted as saying in 2002: "Honestly, when we were still in the dot-com boom days, I felt like a schmuck. I had an internet start-up—so did everybody else. It was unprofitable, like everybody else's, and how hard is that? But when we became profitable, I felt like we had built a real business."[15]

Owning eyeballs and all the information

Google's founders had dropped their hesitation over advertising and were soon to drop another concern regarding keeping consumers on their websites for too long. Larry Page said this in 2004 in critiquing the "portal strategy": "We want you to come to Google and quickly find what you want. Then we're happy to send you to other sites. In fact, that's the point. The portal strategy tries to own all the information."[16]

But Google wanted to fulfill its vision of improving how people can connect with information, so they did pursue a portal strategy of offering more unified services that would keep users on Google-owned properties—versus quickly having consumers sent to a non-Google website. Not only did this attract more users, it also enabled more behavioral data to be mined and extracted, and more ads could now be served based on that behavior. And in doing so, they began to "own all the information."

From 2004 to 2006, Google made three acquisitions that one analyst considers three of the top ten corporate acquisitions. In 2004, they acquired Where2—which became Google Maps—for $70 million. In 2005 they acquired the mobile operating system vendor Android for $50 million. And in 2006, they acquired YouTube for $1.65 billion. That same analyst estimates that Google Maps, Android, and YouTube have created $28 billion, $112 billion, and $160 billion in market cap value as of mid-2022.[17]

Those new products created significant new sources of behavioral data—for example, your location, the places such as restaurants and stores that you visit, the apps you use, and the videos you watch. Google also organically built and released Gmail in 2004 and the internet browser Chrome in 2008. Gmail enabled targeted advertising based on the contents of your emails, and Chrome expanded Google's visibility into knowing every web page you visited. Notably, after thirteen years of consumer complaints, Google agreed in 2017 to stop scanning emails to serve targeted advertising.[18]

Extending Google's tendrils

At the same time, Google started to build and acquire more services beyond online search. Google also began to extend its behavioral-based advertising tendrils to non-Google websites and mobile apps. For example, in 2003, Google released AdSense. This online advertising network enables website publishers to let Google serve up display ads from its AdWords advertisers based on the content of the publishers' websites. This brought website publishers into the Google "network" through revenue sharing, enabling Google to collect behavioral data on non-Google properties. Google also enabled third-party websites to use its account services to let consumers log onto those websites using their Google account, giving Google additional visibility into services users are accessing and from what devices.

Its most significant move into extending its advertising reach beyond its properties was the acquisition of DoubleClick in 2007 for $3.1 billion. One analyst has called this the top corporate acquisition ever—generating a $182 billion return in terms of contribution to Google's market cap as of mid-2022—giving Google four of the top ten acquisitions of all time.[19]

The DoubleClick acquisition gave Google the industry's leading online advertising exchange that can track users going from website to website and serve up ads on those sites through a real-time advertiser bidding system. As part of Google, the DoubleClick solution now has over 85 percent market share in online advertising exchanges. So, even if a consumer is not logged into Google and is not using a Google service, Google can track users and collect behavioral data such as the third-party websites they visit, what ads they hover over, and which ads they click. Google also acquired a company that lets it serve ads in mobile apps, thus giving Google the ability to track mobile app usage. I will talk more in the next chapter about how online tracking works.[20]

The net result is that Google has built a giant walled garden through organic product development and strategic acquisitions. This garden has nine services with over a billion users each; can collect information about consumers from devices, websites, and mobile apps; and has a massive network of tendrils that reaches beyond its garden's walls.

Google loves your data

To give you a sense of how much data Google collects in a day, I went to myactivity.google.com and looked at what activity Google logged on me for just one day. On that day, Google captured 237 unique activities, which means, on average, every six minutes, something is being logged regarding my online behavior. For example, Google captured every app I opened on my Android phone, every notification I got on my phone, every website I visited via my Chrome browser, and every internet search I did. It also captured that I was served up Double-Click-powered ads on various websites I visited. And because my TV is a Sony that runs Android, it also knows that I used Netflix on my TV that day. The myactivity website also provides a YouTube history showing all the videos I watched.

Google also has deep insight into my offline behavior, as I have an Android phone that, in the background, collects my location even when I am not using it. To see this, I went to Location history on the myactivity website and viewed my Location history for that same day. Google drew a map with all the places I visited, the routes I took, and how much time I spent in the car. Google also knew I went for a thirty-minute walk that morning. And Google knew I spent forty-five minutes at a tennis court, exactly how long I spent at a restaurant for dinner, and the name of the restaurant I ate at.

To give you a feel for the volume of data being collected on each of us, various journalists have used the Google Takeout tool (takeout.google .com) to request an export of all the data that Google has collected on them. The export files they received from Google for their accounts were typically above 5 gigabytes, equivalent to three million Word documents of information that Google collected on them. I did a similar export of my data, minus my email, and the file size was approximately 6 giga-bytes. Seeing the level of tracking of my daily life and the volume of data collected on me was unsettling. As I will detail later, Google's expansive digital surveillance practices are under scrutiny by regulators and law-makers in multiple countries.[21]

Meta

Meta is likely the second-largest practitioner of digital surveillance.

Meta was formed in 2004 and is the world's largest social network. Meta's stated mission at its initial public offering (IPO) in 2012 was to "make the world more open and connected." Meta's business model from its early days enabled advertisers to engage with Meta's users. Like Google, Meta does not sell or share the identity of users with advertisers but provides access to users who may find the advertisers' products of interest.

The core of Meta's social network is that users provide their "authentic identity"—their real name, connections to their real friends, and genuine interests—to the platform. From there, a "social graph" can be created that maps the affiliations between people and interests. Not surprisingly, this is of great appeal to advertisers to target real people, as "authentic identity" addresses the adage and meme of internet anonymity in which "on the internet, nobody knows you're a dog."[22]

Besides knowing that ads are being served to real people, Meta also offers advertisers vast reach with its 2.9 billion monthly average users and high degrees of relevance in that users can be targeted based on demographic factors and interests that have been shared directly with or inferred by Meta. Shared information includes the schools you attended, your relationship status, birth date, gender, political and religious affili-ations, and more—the information you entered in your profile in Meta's Facebook social networking service. In addition, inferences about users are generated based on your friend network, the groups you join on Facebook, your location via being tagged in photos or if you "check in" via Facebook to a business, and your interactions with content (e.g., you

Like or Share certain types of videos or articles). Meta utilizes this shared and inferred information to create a profile of you that is available to advertisers. It also uses this data to segment you into "interest" categories that advertisers can target.

Buying the competition

Like Google, Meta has expanded its walled garden beyond its flagship Facebook service by acquiring and organically building additional apps and services. For example, Meta acquired Instagram in 2012 for $1 billion. This acquisition is considered by one analyst to be the second-best one in history by adding an estimated $175 billion in market cap value to Meta as of mid-2022. Meta also acquired WhatsApp in 2014 for $19 billion. Instagram has 1.3 billion users, WhatsApp has two billion users, and the organically developed Messenger has 1.3 billion users as of 2022. These new services in their walled garden significantly contributed to Meta's monthly active users, growing by two billion in ten years.[23]

This product expansion attracts additional users and facilitates further data collection, enhancing Meta's appeal to advertisers. The motivation for Meta is quite simple: in 2013, the average American's data was worth approximately $19 per year in advertising sales to Meta, while in 2020, the data per user was worth $164 per year. More services, users, and data mean more revenue.[24]

Extending Meta's tendrils

And, also like Google, Meta has embraced a strategy of extending its tendrils outside its garden to non-Meta apps and websites to gather more information about users and further extend its advertising reach. The Facebook login lets users log into other sites and apps using their Facebook account, which provides users the convenience of having one less username and password to remember. And it also gives Meta additional visibility into what non-Facebook services you are using and from what types of devices. The Facebook social plugin you see on web pages that encourages you to Like or Share the content is not passive—Meta receives information regarding your visit even if you don't Like or Share that web page. And comparable to what Google has with its AdSense offering, the Meta Audience Network lets websites and mobile apps show ads from Meta advertisers. In doing so, information about the user's visit to the website or the use of the mobile app is also sent to Meta.

Not content with collecting high-level user information regarding "Off-Facebook Activity" from the above services, Meta introduced in 2015 the "Meta Pixel" that collects detailed user behavior data. It added this capability so advertisers could better "retarget" users. An example of retargeting is when you browse for red shoes on website A and see an ad for the same shoes on website B later that day.

When embedded on a publisher's website, the Meta Pixel sends data to Meta about user activity, including what you are viewing, your searches on websites, purchases you have made, items added to a shopping cart, and even information you filled out in online forms. Meta calls this activity "interactions." It sends this information back to Meta even if you don't have a Facebook account. The website publishers can then use this information to retarget you by advertising their products when you are on a Meta property or through the Meta Audience Network for non-Meta websites and mobile apps. As of 2018, over two million websites had the Meta Pixel installed, and a researcher found that Pixel was installed on 30 percent of the top one hundred thousand websites. In addition, this technology is available for mobile apps, and it is estimated that it is embedded in sixty-one of the one hundred most popular mobile apps.[25]

Meta loves your data too

To give you a feel for how Meta follows you around the internet and captures your activity and interactions with websites and mobile apps, I looked at Meta's "Off-Facebook Activity" tool for my Facebook account. Note I probably use the Facebook service about once a year and launch the Instagram app maybe once every few weeks, so I am not a power user of Meta's services. Meta captured my interactions with 793 different websites and mobile apps. It knew every time I launched the HBO Max app on my TV. It captured hundreds of interactions I had on LinkedIn. It knew I had purchased socks. It knew I made two visits to the website of the UK newspaper *The Times*, once in October 2020 and another in February 2022. And it knew I searched for an appointment and scheduled a test from a COVID testing center.

Like my reaction to Google's tracking of me, uncovering this data was unsettling from both a breadth (e.g., number of sites and apps) and depth (my interactions on those websites and apps) of surveillance, especially in light that I am rarely, if ever, on any Meta service. To paraphrase one reporter's observations about Meta's tracking: it was as if I was on a reality TV show and the cameras were always on. As with Google, I will detail how regulators are also looking at Meta's data collection practices.[26]

Amazon

Amazon is aggressively ramping up its digital surveillance capabilities through acquisitions and investments in its fast-growing advertising business.

Amazon was founded in 1994 with the initial focus on providing an online book marketplace. However, through the years, Amazon has expanded to become the online "everything store" with nearly 40 percent market share of the US e-commerce market and $486 billion in revenue for the twelve months ending June 30, 2022.[27]

Amazon is obsessed with collecting your data

From its early days, Amazon has been obsessed with capturing customer data. Its chief technology officer was quoted in 2005 as saying that Amazon tries to "collect as much information as possible" so it can provide consumers with recommendations to buy more goods on Amazon. So, unlike Google and Meta, which collect massive amounts of data to facilitate advertising, Amazon's main goal regarding its data collection is to sell you more things.[28]

Amazon collects your data from three primary sources: data you give directly to Amazon and its various services, data that those services collect "behind the scenes" as part of your usage of the services, and third-party data.[29]

The data Amazon has on you includes all your purchases on Amazon .com, anything you searched for or put in your cart on its website, your credit card details, and the contact information of anyone you sent a package to. This data collection also applies to Amazon-owned web properties, including Diapers.com and Zappos. Amazon also knows any books you purchased with Kindle, what passages you highlighted, and how much time you spent reading. With Prime Video, Amazon knows the movies you have watched, searched for, and purchased for rental, plus the time spent watching. Through its ownership of Whole Foods, it knows your grocery purchases. In addition, Amazon's Ring doorbell service will create recordings of motion or doorbell rings. And Amazon has other services such as Fire TV sticks and tablets (personal internet devices), IMDB (a movie and TV database), Audible (audiobooks), and Goodreads (a community of book lovers) that collect the data you provide the service.[30]

Special mention should be given to Alexa, Amazon's voice-controlled virtual assistant technology. Alexa can answer questions or look up information (e.g., find a recipe), play music, and control your smart home, among other features. The audio recording of your Alexa interaction—triggered by the "wake" words such as "Alexa"—and the transcription of the recording are kept by Amazon as data associated with a given user. For example, one reporter who requested access to his data from Amazon found that Amazon had collected over ninety thousand recordings in three and a half years—about seventy per day— including the names of his children and their favorite songs.[31]

Combining all this data from these sources allows Amazon to make inferences about what you will likely purchase next. The more Amazon services you use means more data for them to determine what type of person you are and what you can be enticed to buy from them.[32]

Amazon is now an ad tech company, too

But Amazon has also realized that this data can serve another purpose, which is to allow advertisers to target consumers based on demographics, previous purchases, and interests. Now one of its fastest-growing businesses, Amazon claims it creates "audience segments" for advertisers who can "serve interest-based ads based on a variety of anonymized shopping activities such as browse and purchase behaviors." In a few short years, Amazon's advertising business is now one-quarter the size of Meta's advertising revenue. This means its obsession with collecting our data will only increase.[33]

Microsoft

While online advertising is less than 10 percent of its total revenue, Microsoft still generates billions of dollars in digital surveillance–based revenue.

The oldest of the Big Tech firms, Microsoft was founded in 1975 by Bill Gates and Paul Allen. Now a $200 billion-per-year revenue company as of mid-2022, Microsoft's main business segments include "More Personal Computing," which includes Microsoft Windows, Xbox, and Bing; "Productivity and Business Processes," which includes Microsoft Office and LinkedIn; and "Intelligent Cloud," which includes its server products and its Azure cloud service.[34]

Microsoft competes against other Big Tech firms in various markets. Microsoft Windows runs on 1.4 billion active devices, giving Microsoft a dominant market share of 75 percent of desktop and laptop operating systems as of mid-2022, with its next competitor, Apple Mac OS X, at 16 percent. When broadened to include mobile devices, Microsoft Windows' share of the operating system market was 30 percent, with Google Android the leader at 42 percent, followed by Apple iOS at 18 percent and Mac OS X at 6 percent. Microsoft Office had a slight market share lead against Google in the office productivity market as of early 2022. Microsoft had a 21 percent market share in cloud computing compared to Amazon's 34 percent and Google's 11 percent at the end of 2022. And

Microsoft Edge has a 5 percent share in the browser market compared to Google Chrome having over 65 percent.[35]

Specific to markets that have a digital surveillance business model, Microsoft's product offerings include online search (Bing), digital advertising (Microsoft Ads), and social networking (LinkedIn). As of 2022, Bing is at a 3 percent market share in search compared to Google's 92 percent and, like Google, captures user searches. Microsoft Advertising is the product that provides pay-per-click advertising on the Bing, Yahoo!, and DuckDuckGo search engines, as well as Microsoft's consumer properties such as Xbox, MSN, and Outlook.com, where behavioral data is also captured. Like Google, Microsoft Advertising serves targeted "personalized ads" based on demographic and user behavior data. It generated over $10 billion in advertising revenue in 2021. Finally, over 875 million professionals have entered their data on the LinkedIn platform. LinkedIn sells access to that data to facilitate targeting by salespeople or recruiters or even have targeted ads served within LinkedIn.[36]

So, while not the ad tech heavyweight that Google or Facebook is, Microsoft still collects personal and behavioral data on hundreds of millions of users every month and, through Microsoft Advertising and LinkedIn, does over $15 billion in digital advertising annually. And its digital surveillance practices have come into question with regulators, as evidenced by France's data protection agency fining Microsoft over €60 million in December 2022 because it placed advertising cookies on website visitors' computers to track user behavior across websites and did so without users' consent.[37]

Apple

Apple prides itself on designing its products to minimize the amount of data Apple or any third party can access. It is the sole Big Tech firm that does not utilize a digital surveillance business model for its product offerings.

Founded in 1976 by Steve Jobs and Steve Wozniak, Apple, as of 2022, had the biggest market capitalization of any company in the world and the largest annual revenue of any technology company. In 2022 Apple had the second largest market share of mobile operating systems behind Google and evenly split the tablet market. Most of Apple's revenue comes from selling consumer devices such as Macs, iPhones, or iPads.[38]

Apple advertises privacy as a key product differentiator. It tells consumers, "What happens on your iPhone, stays on your iPhone," and has taglines like "Privacy. That's iPhone." Apple's messaging system uses end-to-end encryption by default, and most user data is processed on the user's device. For example, its Siri voice assistant technology does language processing on the mobile device rather than sending data back to Apple's cloud servers. Apple CEO Tim Cook has called protecting consumer privacy "the most essential battle of our time."[39]

Where there has been criticism of Apple's data privacy practices, it has involved the backup of consumers' user-generated content on their devices that consumers have elected to store in Apple's iCloud cloud service. Per Apple, consumers can store "photos, documents, contacts, calendars, bookmarks, Safari browsing history, maps search history, messages, and iOS device backups." But iCloud backups have historically not supported end-to-end encryption, so there has been concern that law enforcement could subpoena consumers' data stored on iCloud, or a hacker could access this data with a stolen iCloud account. To address this concern, Apple announced in December 2022 an end-to-end encryption technology called Advanced Data Protection (ADP) that supports iCloud, Notes, and photos. ADP was rolled out to US-based consumers in December 2022, with availability to other parts of the world in early 2023.[40]

Privacy advocates will also look to see if Apple's growing incursion into advertising on its App Store and News and Stock apps results in Apple gathering more consumer data. For example, French privacy regulators fined Apple €8 million in January 2023 for not getting sufficient consumer consent before Apple's App Store gathered information from consumers' iPhones to serve targeted ads. However, the French regulator said that version 15 of iOS—the iPhone operating system released in late 2021—does ask for the appropriate consent.[41]

But most significantly, Apple is using its market position in mobile to put a dent into other companies' digital surveillance–based business models. In 2021, Apple added a feature called App Tracking Transparency (ATT) that requires mobile apps to prompt users of Apple iOS devices (e.g., iPhones and iPads) to give permissions before companies can begin to track user activity. It is estimated that as of mid-2022, approximately 75 percent of Apple iOS users opted out of tracking. Meta subsequently claimed that this loss of tracking data from Apple devices would cause a $10 billion revenue shortfall in 2022, as less behavioral and "interaction" data is being collected, thereby diminishing their ability to target ads. Apple also implemented "intelligent tracking prevention" in its Safari browser to block cross-website user tracking and "mail privacy protection" to block email marketers from tracking if you have opened and read emails.[42]

The threats of digital surveillance

We have seen that the surveillance by Big Tech firms such as Google, Meta, and Amazon is simply staggering. I have put instructions in appendix 1 that can help you reduce or delete some of the data that Big Tech collects on you. But even if you go through this manual exercise of limiting what can be collected about you, we still face many threats from this surveillance-based business model.

The downside of living in an online world with the cameras always on

To start with, to be constantly observed is to lose the sanctuary of exploring and incubating our "authentic self." We should not have to reveal our "authentic identity" as we figure out who we are and what we want to be. Part of that process in our modern world requires internet searches, private chats and messages, visits to different places, purchases, and connecting with people. We should have the right to be forgotten, especially with any ideas or thoughts we discard along our path to finding ourselves. And I don't think anyone would want everything they have done, including our online research, to be on our "permanent record" that is available for a real-time auction to anyone with a credit card. So, I think constant surveillance inhibits our ability to develop as humans and can even lead to the loss of human dignity by feeding into the belief, which a European Commission working group aptly summarized, that we are merely treated as "objects sifted, sorted, scored, herded, conditioned, or manipulated."[43]

Weaponization and discrimination

This surveillance can also be weaponized against us in today's post–abortion rights America. As an experiment, I did internet searches involving the keywords "abortion," "abortion pill," and "nearest abortion clinic." I visited websites and clicked on ads for those keywords. I used Google Maps to find the nearest abortion clinic and drove to it and back from my home. I created a calendar event with the clinic's address and the title "Abortion Appointment." And I searched my email and calendar using those keywords. In myactivity.google.com, Google captured all the abortion-related searches (including searches I did inside my email and calendar), websites I visited, and clicked ads. Google also showed the route I took from my house to the clinic, and it even captured the calendar notification on my phone that I had an appointment at a clinic. Google had a complete dossier on my abortion-related research and travel. If I had a pregnancy tracking app on my phone, Google would know when I started and stopped using it.

The Meta Pixel also collects sensitive personal information that should not be collected. For example, *The Markup* found in 2022 that one-third of the top 100 US hospitals sent sensitive healthcare data to Meta via the Meta Pixel, including "patients' medical condition and prescriptions from the hospitals' patient-facing electronic health record systems." This appears to violate the Health Insurance Portability and Accountability Act (HIPAA), which protects the personal privacy of patient healthcare. *The Markup* also discovered in 2022 that the US Department of Education sent sensitive data from their financial assistance website to Meta. And in addition, *The Markup* found that various tax preparation firms were sending sensitive taxpayer data such as "income, filing status refund amounts, and dependents' college scholar-ship amounts," which may have violated IRS regulations governing tax preparers. In all these examples, this happened even if the consumers entering data on these websites did not have a Facebook account.[44]

Meta claims it discards this type of sensitive information sent by websites using the Meta Pixel. But in my "Off-Facebook Activity," I saw that Meta had captured me searching and scheduling a Covid test on a healthcare provider site, so my health-related information was making its way to Meta's database.

This sensitive data collected by Big Tech is now being subpoenaed. A real-world example involves a seventeen-year-old from Nebraska and her mother being charged in June 2022 with several felonies and misde-meanors for performing an illegal medicated abortion. The key evidence was the police obtaining the pair's private chat and message history from Meta. Meta had that data because, at the time, it did not offer support by default for end-to-end encryption of chats and messages on Messenger. This is likely because Meta has historically wanted to target you with ads on Messenger based on the unencrypted content of your conversations.[45]

Big Tech's surveillance collection of our sensitive personal data can also be used to facilitate advertising that discriminates against us. For exam-ple, it was discovered that landlords and real estate brokers could take advantage of Meta's advertising platform to prevent women or families with children from seeing ads for housing rentals. In addition, landlords using Google AdWords were also found not advertising to nonbinary or transgender people by taking advantage of the ability to exclude people of "unknown gender"—people who have identified themselves as neither male nor female—from seeing their ads.[46]

Weakening our national security and democracy

Big Tech's surveillance of us also potentially adds a national security threat. For example, in June 2022, Google reportedly shared user data through its ad network with a sanctioned Russian ad company. Per *ProPublica*, this allowed the Russian company to harvest users browsing Ukrainian-based websites and access "unique mobile phone IDs, IP addresses, location information, and details about users' interests and online activity." Russian intelligence could use this data to track people or locations of interest. So, behavioral-based advertising can easily be used for nefarious purposes. And in the case of the popular app TikTok, it was reported in July 2021 that some TikTok employees based in China could access US user data, thus raising concerns that the Chinese government may have backdoor access to detailed online tracking of US citizens.[47]

Digital surveillance by Big Tech is also being used to attack our democracy. The most well-known example is the Cambridge Analytica scandal of 2016, which highlighted how Big Tech's amassing of personal data could be misused for political manipulation. Cambridge Analytica was able to improperly obtain troves of personal data from Meta and then construct psychological profiles that targeted voters based on their concerns and fears. I will cover Cambridge Analytica in more detail in chapter 3 on data breaches. Another example is how Russia's Internet Research Agency targeted Black communities in 2016 to dampen voter participation. Suffice it to say, behavioral-based advertising to sell us diapers can easily be steered toward political manipulation.[48]

Legislation to combat digital surveillance

In each chapter, I will discuss legislation we can pass that can better regulate Big Tech to contain its harmful business practices. Typically, I will first discuss what Europe is doing—as they have been taking the lead and setting the standard for consumer protection in our digital age—and then consider laws and regulatory activity in the US. This chapter will examine current and proposed legislation concerning data privacy and digital surveillance.

European legislation

Europe considers privacy to be a fundamental right. In 1948 the Council of Europe adopted the European Convention of Human Rights, which stated: "Everyone has the right to respect for his private and family life, his home and his correspondence." Furthermore, in 2009 the European Union (EU) enacted into law the EU Charter of Fundamental Rights, which updated for the modern age the above definition of privacy to replace "correspondence" with "communications" and add that "everyone has the right to the protection of personal data concerning him or her."[49]

This European movement to consider privacy and personal data protection to be fundamental human rights eventually led to the passing of the General Data Protection Regulation (GDPR), which went into effect in 2018. The GDPR provides a legal framework that protects the fundamental rights and freedoms of natural persons (i.e., individuals), including the right to the "protection of personal data." Furthermore, it sets guidelines for collecting and processing personal information and imposes obligations onto businesses everywhere if they collect data related to individuals in the EU.[50]

The GDPR has become the "gold standard" of online privacy. But Europe is not stopping with the GDPR and is looking to put a more significant dent in using personal data for targeted advertising. In 2022, the EU passed the Digital Services Act (DSA), which regulates online content and the selling of goods over the internet in Europe, and the Digital Markets Act (DMA), which introduces competition rules for the large platform "gatekeepers" to operate in Europe. Both will be fully enforced by 2024. The DSA explicitly bans online behavioral advertising that targets children or utilizes sensitive personal data such as religious beliefs, sexual orientation, and ethnicity. The DMA bans tracking end users outside the gatekeepers' platforms for targeted advertising without consent. The GDPR, DSA, and DMA are great examples of Europe's "Brussels effect," the name associated with the administrative center of the European Union that increasingly sets global regulatory standards for technology.[51]

US legislation

The United States has neither a constitutional right to privacy nor an overarching federal privacy law. The result is that proposed rules moving privacy forward have been happening at the state level, especially in California. This is part of California's lead in other aspects of consumer protection (e.g., auto emission standards), and the "California effect" often drives the rest of the US.

For example, California voters amended its state constitution in the early 1970s to include the right of privacy among the "inalienable" rights of all people. It was the first to enact a comprehensive data breach notification law in 2002. Finally, the most significant privacy legislation in the US was passed in California with the California Consumer Privacy Act (CCPA) in 2018. It was enhanced with Proposition 24 in 2020 with the passage of the California Privacy Rights Act (CPRA).[52]

At the federal level, sector-specific laws protect our personal data associated with a given industry or type of data. These federal privacy laws have been enacted based on a variety of factors, including the following:[53]

- *Who's Got the Data?* This started in the late 1960s when the federal government and credit bureaus were the only ones that had personal data on millions of people. Two laws in this category that Congress passed were the Privacy Act in 1974 (which regulates personal data held by the federal government) and the Fair Credit Reporting Act in 1970 (which governs data held by credit bureaus).

- *Lawmaking by Anecdote.* These laws have come up when a specific incident has made headlines. A good example is the Video Privacy Protection Act of 1988, which was triggered due to a reporter finding out what Supreme Court nominee Robert Bork's video renting tastes were.

- *Privacy Laws as Part of Some Other Data Sharing Initiatives.* The best examples are the Health Insurance Portability and Accountability Act (HIPAA) in 1996 for healthcare and the Gramm–Leach–Bliley Act (GLBA) in 1999 for the financial services industry. HIPAA has strict definitions of what entities are covered under the law, namely those that conduct certain electronic transactions, such as sending a claim to a health insurance company to request payment for medical services. So, for example, your hospital is covered under HIPAA but not your health app on your phone, even though the app may process and store your sensitive health data.

- *Special Harm, Special Concern.* These laws have been introduced to address privacy concerns in particular areas. Examples include the Children's Online Privacy Protection Act (COPPA) of 1998 and the Genetic Information Nondiscrimination Act (GINA) in 2008.

You may notice that the last major federal privacy-related laws passed were HIPAA and GLBA in the 1990s, well before the IPOs of Google and Meta, and pre-iPhone. So clearly, federal law needs to keep up with the technology, and online surveillance by Big Tech has mainly gone unregulated in the US. So, for example, we now find ourselves in a situation where we can have our personal health information weaponized against us because HIPAA or any other federal privacy law does not cover sensitive healthcare data collected by website searches, messenger apps, or mobile apps.

Various congressional legislators, for decades, have attempted to introduce an updated and comprehensive federal privacy law, the most recent being the American Data Privacy and Protection Act (ADPPA). Introduced in June 2022, it is a bipartisan federal omnibus privacy bill that provides a comprehensive privacy framework on par with Europe's GDPR and California's CPRA. It does include a ban on targeted advertising to minors. The ADPPA passed the House Committee on Energy and Commerce by an impressive 53–2 vote in July 2022. But to get bipartisan support (namely Republicans on board), the ADPPA preempts state laws and therefore neuters the ability of states like California to pass any privacy legislation that builds upon it. In other words, it sets a ceiling for privacy versus a floor, unlike most privacy-related bills mentioned above.[54]

The ADPPA could not make it to a full House vote in the 2022 legislative session. This was because the California delegation, including Speaker Nancy Pelosi, wanted to maintain California's ability to pass future privacy legislation to address new threats from Big Tech. There was also opposition from Senator Maria Cantwell of Washington State, the chairperson of the Senate Commerce Committee, who felt the ADPPA lacked powerful enough enforcement. In addition, other, more narrow legislation introduced in 2022, such as the Banning Surveillance Advertising Act, did not progress in the 2022 legislative session.

Road map to contain digital surveillance

We need to be vocal in our concerns about digital surveillance. For example, after years of consumer complaints, Google agreed in 2017 to stop scanning emails to serve targeted advertising. A more recent example is after the overturn of *Roe*, public concern and employee pressure led Google to announce in early July 2022 that it would delete location data when users visit abortion clinics. But in my experimentation, I did not see that occur.[55]

Apple's ATT feature can significantly reduce the amount of data collected about us on our Apple devices. Therefore, similar pressure should be put on Google to let consumers turn off tracking for Android devices to match what Apple does. And pressure should also be placed on Google and Microsoft to have their browsers turn tracking off by blocking third-party cookies by default. I doubt they will do that, as both rely on targeted advertising using our behavioral data, but it can't hurt to remind them that we prefer to have privacy options turned on by default. I will talk more about online and mobile tracking and third-party cookies in the next chapter.

We also need to push politicians for federal and state privacy legislation. The good news is that following the "California effect," four other states now have privacy laws, and we have gotten a bit further than we ever have on federal privacy. But we need more state laws. And we must finally pass a comprehensive federal privacy law that sets the "floor" for privacy rights. In appendix 2, I have compiled the essential ingredients for a comprehensive US privacy law. But any federal privacy bill that passes must refrain from preempting the ability of the states to innovate in this area.

Some legislators have proposed an outright ban on online behavioral advertising. As mentioned, behavioral ads could benefit small businesses by enabling more efficient and targeted advertising spending. But the problem is that in most cases, consumers are not consenting to this data collection, and people should be given a clear and unambiguous choice to be tracked or not (e.g., have the right to say no). Furthermore, there should be significant limitations on what types of sensitive data (e.g., health, location, etc.) can be used for behavioral advertising, and children should not be surveilled and served targeted ads.

Interestingly, recent studies have shown that behavioral advertising may be less effective than contextual advertising (i.e., serving ads based on the context and content of the web page versus behavioral data). So, there needs to be more research on the efficacy of contextual versus behavioral advertising and if the latter is worth the significant societal downsides.[56]

In summary, the data collection practices of Big Tech firms that in the past facilitated online advertising are increasingly being weaponized against us and our democracy. For example, law enforcement is now using this data in a post–abortion rights America to go after women having abortions. Furthermore, Big Tech firms like Google and Meta have created and fostered an advertising ecosystem where shadowy third-party companies known as data brokers thrive by also deeply surveilling us. The next chapter will dig into those companies as I seek to complete the story of how our behavioral data is mined and extracted.

CHAPTER 2

Data Brokers

If we accept as normal and unavoidable that everything in our lives can be aggregated and sold, then we lose so much more than data. We lose the freedom to be human.

—Tim Cook, CEO of Apple[1]

In 2021, a Catholic news outlet obtained location data correlated to the mobile device of Monsignor Jeffrey Burrill, an executive officer of the United States Conference of Catholic Bishops. The location data showed that the priest had visited gay bars while using the location-based hookup Grindr in numerous cities from 2018 to 2020, even when traveling on assignment. The priest resigned before the investigation was published. And in 2022, just after *Roe* was repealed, a reporter purchased a week's worth of information on where people came and went from a Planned Parenthood. It cost the reporter only $160 to get that information.[2]

It's not just the Big Tech firms' collection of our data exhaust that can be used against us. For example, the entities that collected and sold the Burrill and Planned Parenthood location data are known as data brokers. Data brokers are companies we don't have a direct relationship with—and likely have never even heard of—that, like Big Tech firms, collect massive amounts of personal information about us. For example, one data broker claims it collects over eleven thousand personal attributes—such as our religion, estimated income, and family members' cell phone numbers—for over 2.5 billion people. And it is a big and growing industry, with an estimated four thousand data brokers globally. The market is projected to grow from $233 billion in 2019 to $345 billion in 2026.[3]

So, while Big Tech firms were not directly responsible for collecting the data in these two examples, Big Tech has created and nourished an ad tech ecosystem in which data brokers flourish. Advertisers will complement the "first-party" data that Big Tech collects directly from us with the "third-party" data indirectly collected by data brokers to target us with ads further or even make predictive "scores" on us. Even more alarming, sometimes Big Tech firms act as data brokers themselves, as in the case of Meta Pixel collecting data on users who don't have a Facebook account. So as much as Big Tech may distance itself from the seedier side of data brokers, like those that sell our location data, the reality is that Big Tech firms and data brokers are the sharks and remoras in the surveillance ocean, sharing a mutually profitable and symbiotic relationship.

The last chapter covered how Big Tech plays a starring role in the story of digital surveillance, but to complete the story, this chapter will be about the supporting cast members—data brokers—that are enabled by Big Tech. And unlike Big Tech, which primarily collects our online activity, data brokers collect information about us both from online and offline sources, thus surveilling us just as significantly. Their data sources include property records, purchase history, social media profiles, and online web and mobile app activity tracking. So, for example, data brokers know the websites you have visited (e.g., a website on depression), your credit card purchases (e.g., you purchased adult diapers), and the apps you have installed (e.g., a gay dating app or a Muslim prayer app). And their hooks in your mobile apps can even track all your locations (e.g., you visited a Planned Parenthood).[4]

This chapter will explain how we got to where anyone with a credit card can track our movements and precise geolocation. I will first look at how data brokers have evolved and their online and offline data sources, including how they leverage Big Tech's online tracking ecosystem. From there, I will analyze how they profile, segment, and score us. I will then examine the threats associated with data brokers to our online and physical safety, civil rights, national security, and democracy. Finally, I will close the chapter with suggestions on how we can better protect our privacy from data brokers and discuss legislative solutions that can better regulate data brokers. But to be clear, Big Tech could put a severe dent into data brokers if they wanted to.

From whence they came

Data brokers did not just magically pop up in the internet era. We have had "people directories"—phone books—since the late 1800s. The use of computers by businesses in the 1950s and 1960s ushered in the birth of consumer data and direct marketing firms that collected data from government and commercial records, surveys, and sweepstake entries. Then, these firms digitized that data for marketers and advertisers to do targeted mailings and phone calls. Acxiom, one of today's largest data brokers, started in 1969 by creating mailing lists based on data from phone books. And historically, there have been firms that perform background checks utilizing public records like court filings, property records, marriage licenses, divorce records, birth certificates, and bankruptcy records.[5]

We have also had credit reporting agencies and bureaus for over one hundred years. Those entities—plus banks, insurers, and retailers—would scour through public records and even hire private investigators to research consumer personalities, habits, and health details to determine their creditworthiness. Today, credit reporting and scoring are primarily handled by the "big three" financial information data brokers (Experian, Equifax, and TransUnion). They also provide risk mitigation brokerage services that businesses use to detect fraud or verify their customers' identities.[6]

With these roots of the data broker industry in mind, some significant trends have led to today's data broker industry and the larger digital surveillance market. First, in the 1990s, we saw the growth of loyalty programs and database marketing. This meant that in exchange for discounts on goods and services, we traded our demographics and let businesses more granularly track our purchases. Then, in the 2000s, we saw the internet and e-commerce explosion with Google and Amazon. So, for decades, all our website visits and online purchases have been tracked in some capacity and for some gain. What's more, the growth of social networks in the late 2000s, led by Meta, enabled our user-generated content and profile information to be collected. And finally, the simultaneous advent of smartphones, led by Apple and Google, allowed for better insight into our daily activity, including what apps we installed and the locations we visited (and when we visited them).[7]

Today, in the 2020s, we are experiencing an explosion of the Internet of Things (IoT) devices led by Big Tech. For example, consumers have numerous "smart" or internet-connected cars, refrigerators, virtual assistants like Amazon's Alexa, thermostats like Google's Nest, fitness watches like Google's Fitbit, doorbells like Amazon's Ring, smart locks, televisions, video game consoles like Microsoft's Xbox, and so on. These devices can provide insight into where we are, what we are watching on our television or phone, how fast we are driving or running, the temperature inside our house or refrigerator, if someone is at our front door, the online games we are playing, and so on. In 2021, over ten billion IoT devices were used—more smart devices than people in the world—and that number is expected to grow to over twenty-five billion by 2030.[8]

It doesn't end there. Another current-day trend is that we are increasingly providing our biometric data to establish individual identity with businesses and the government, including imagery of the iris, retina, fingerprint, face, hand, palm, vein patterns, and voice recordings. For example, our biometric data provides the identity verification needed to board airplanes via our face or to initiate stock transactions via our voice. We even offer our DNA to "ancestry" apps—over twenty-six million people have done that as of 2019.[9]

As we become an increasingly cashless society, the increased use of credit cards, debit cards, and mobile payments means more transactions are stored and accessible in structured digital formats. For example, in

2016 in the United States, over 31 percent of transactions were cash; in 2021, that number dropped to 20 percent. The result is that these transactions are more easily collected and processed by data brokers.[10]

Not surprisingly, Covid-19 accelerated our spending more time online, which means we are tracked more often. For example, in 2021, the average American occupied eleven hours per day viewing media and spent roughly 40 percent of that time on mobile devices. And Americans spent 67 percent more time online in 2022 than in 2015.[11]

The result is that the traditional consumer data, people directory, background check, and credit reporting industries have now converged with database marketing, loyalty programs, and online trackers to create today's data broker industry. Combining this with mobile, IoT, and biometrics means almost all human activity generates digital exhaust that data brokers can eventually hoover up. And the scale of data brokers' ability to collect, aggregate, store, and analyze this data has also grown exponentially—so they are keeping pace with our growing digital footprint.[12]

Where does the data come from?

The entire data broker industry is built on a lack of transparency. It starts with the fact that users of websites, mobile apps, and internet-connected devices and services are mainly unaware of how our data is collected, how it is used, and if it is subsequently sold or shared with data brokers.[13]

Furthermore, even though data brokers collect information about consumers from government, commercial, publicly available sources, and web and mobile tracking, they also use other data brokers as significant sources of data. Per the Federal Trade Commission (FTC), the result is that it is "virtually impossible" to trace how a data broker obtained your data.[14]

And finally, as the FTC has further noted, this lack of transparency extends to the fact that consumers are fairly oblivious to the existence of data brokers, as they don't directly interact with them. Even if you identify a data broker who may have your data, they are generally reluctant to reveal their data sources. But let's crack open the window a little and examine their data sources.[15]

Government sources

Data brokers collect a lot of government-generated data. For instance, at the federal level, the US Census provides demographics at the city block level, including age, ethnicity, income, education level, and occupations. The Social Security Administration provides its Death Master File, which includes names and dates of deaths. The US Postal Service produces data regarding address changes. And there is also data from federal bankruptcy proceedings. All of which are consumed by data brokers.[16]

There is also much data available from state and local governments, including property records, court filings, criminal convictions, professional (e.g., hairdresser) and recreational (e.g., fishing) licenses, marriage licenses, divorce records, birth certificates, bankruptcy records, voter registration information, and vehicle registration records. And some of this is directly purchased from government agencies. For example, *Vice* reported in 2019 that various state departments of motor vehicles were selling names, addresses, and car registration information to credit reporting agencies and firms engaged in background checks.[17]

To give you a feel for the vast amount of data collected from government sources, LexisNexis claims data from 1.5 billion bankruptcy records, 6.5 billion personal property records, and 6.6 billion motor vehicle registrations. It says it has data from over 37 billion public records involving criminal investigations. And another data broker, CoreLogic, says it has data on "more than 99.99 percent of all properties in the United States," including over one billion property records.[18]

Commercial sources

Data brokers' commercial data sources include purchase history, warranty registration, credit information, and loyalty card data. For example, one data broker, Nielsen, claims it collects 80 percent of all credit card transactions, 30 percent of all debit card transactions, purchase history across over ninety million households, and purchase data from eighteen thousand retailers. Equifax advertises it has paystub data on more than half the US workforce. In 2016, Spotify announced a deal with advertising and marketing service company WPP that gave WPP access to the "unique listening preferences and behaviors" of Spotify users, thereby letting advertisers get a better sense of consumers' moods and activities. Datalogix, a data broker firm that Oracle acquired, claimed that it collected data representing over $1 trillion in consumer spending.[19]

Publicly available sources

Data brokers collect from publicly available social media profiles, forum posts, media reports, business listings, and telephone books. Some of this data is only available in hard-copy format, and data brokers will scan these records into a digital format for uploading. But in most cases, data brokers utilize "web crawlers" or "scraper bots" that parse through web pages to extract data. Think of them as a search engine's web crawler but solely focused on the hunt for your personal information, with a significant focus on public profiles and postings from social media sites. For example, it was reported in 2017 that data broker Oracle aggregated three billion profiles from fifteen million websites while collecting over seven hundred million messages from social media networks, blogs, and consumer review sites daily.[20]

Web tracking

The most significant source of personal data that data brokers collect is online tracking. Nearly all websites, mobile apps, and IoT device providers actively share behavioral data with other companies. According to the Electronic Frontier Foundation (EFF), the average web page shares data with "dozens" of third parties, as does the average mobile app—including location data when the app is not even in use—and is "largely invisible" to the average consumer.[21]

On websites, tracking is facilitated through cookies. A cookie is a small file that stores user data that identifies a specific visitor to a domain (i.e., website) when you visit a website from a browser. "First-party" cookies are tied to a particular domain and will remember your past activity on that site. For example, it may recognize you had an item in a shopping cart, if you had previously logged in (so you don't have to log in again), and other settings that personalize the experience on the website. In effect, first-party cookies can help improve your direct relationship with the business's website.[22]

But in many cases, businesses also configure their websites to have "third-party" cookies. Third-party cookies are used by online ad networks that act as aggregators of ad inventory from website publishers. Ad networks facilitate the sale of this inventory to advertisers. To enable this, ad networks provide software code that publishers embed into their websites to facilitate ad campaign delivery and tracking. So, each time a user visits a website with this code, a cookie is downloaded that tracks the user's online activity and behavior across other websites that also have this code. That is why, for example, you can be browsing for red shoes on website A, and then later that day, you start seeing an ad for the same shoes on website B—an online advertising tactic known as "retargeting."[23]

In addition, a website publisher typically works with multiple ad networks, so multiple third-party cookies are downloaded when a user visits a given website. For example, if you visit the Huffington Post website, it will install over twenty tracking cookies, including those from Google, Meta, Amazon, and so on.

So over time, enough data is collected from online activity (e.g., entering addresses and phone numbers in online forms, what is purchased, etc.) that the cookies often can be linked to real people. Moreover, this online activity can be sold to or shared with data brokers.

Ad networks also participate in ad exchanges—such as Google's DoubleClick, the dominant player in this market—that further promulgate access to third-party cookies and corresponding user activity. An ad exchange is a cloud service that facilitates the buying and selling of online advertising inventory from multiple ad networks. Pricing is set based on the real-time bidding of serving an ad to a given user, and the determination of the user is based on the user's cookie. The ad exchanges will share the third-party cookies with advertisers as part of the bidding process. The advertisers, in turn, leverage data management platforms— that tie in data from data brokers to better link a cookie to an actual user—to then let the advertiser make a more well-informed bid.[24]

Mobile tracking

Unsurprisingly, tracking also occurs with mobile apps. Instead of cookies, a mobile advertising ID (MAID) is created by Apple or Google (depending on if you have an iPhone or Android phone) that gets assigned to each phone that acts as the identifier. And the library of code provided by third parties, such as ad networks, is in the form of software developer kits (SDKs) embedded into the mobile app. So, whenever a user opens and uses an app that uses the SDK, the mobile app makes requests to the third party's servers. Unlike on the web, where browsers can distinguish between first-party and third-party cookies (and you can configure a browser to block third-party cookies), in the case of mobile apps, if you grant permissions to the app—to access your camera or location—then any third-party code embedded in the app gets those same permissions. And because the request back to the third party's servers contains the advertising ID, the user can now be profiled across multiple apps.[25]

Mobile apps can transmit sensitive personal information such as health status. For example, researchers discovered that healthcare apps such as the Drugs.com Medication Guide sent data to over one hundred outside entities, including device identifiers and queried terms such as "herpes," "HIV," "Adderall," "diabetes," and "pregnancy." Unfortunately, consumers have little recourse, as HIPAA does not apply to mobile apps unaffiliated with your doctor, hospital, or insurance carrier.[26]

In addition, mobile apps often send their location data to back-end servers on the internet. This data can be used to pinpoint people's precise movements. Not surprisingly, location data is of great interest to advertisers. For example, according to *The Markup*, Burger King ran "a promotion in which, if a customer's phone was within 600 feet of a McDonalds, the Burger King app would let the user buy a Whopper for one cent." Another use case of location data is measuring and analyzing foot traffic to specific stores or buildings. Some developers of mobile apps add these SDKs, not to advertise inside their apps but to send users' location data to data brokers in exchange for payments for the data.[27]

In summary, Big Tech's advertising ecosystem enables data brokers to collect online activity—for both web and mobile—and to be used as a data source to facilitate online advertising. But one significant ray of sunshine is that Apple's App Tracking Transparency (ATT) has put a monkey wrench into this data collection on the iPhone, with 75 percent of Apple iOS users opting out of third-party tracking. This has not only impacted the amount of data that data brokers collect but also blocks trackers from Big Tech firms such as Meta. To work around ATT, data brokers are increasingly collecting location data directly from mobile app developers to avoid the "digital footprint" of relying on an SDK that Apple would detect when reviewing an app submission.[28]

What data brokers do with our data

Once data brokers have all this data, besides selling and sharing the raw information directly, they use technologies such as artificial intelligence (AI) to aggregate the data and draw inferences from it. I will discuss AI in more detail in chapter 4. This data processing is often facilitated using Big Tech's cloud computing platforms to crunch the data. The following are examples of what data brokers will do with our collected data.

Profiling

Even though a given data source may only provide relatively few data elements, as data brokers correlate and aggregate more data elements from disparate data sources, they can form a more detailed composite "profile" of a consumer and their life. Or, as EFF puts it, "these humble parts can be combined into an exceptionally revealing whole."[29]

Data brokers not only collect "actual data elements" associated with a consumer but also create inferred or "derived data elements" that are predictive and become part of a consumer's profile. For example, researchers at Cambridge have shown that "sensitive personal attributes such as ethnicity, religious and political views, relationship status, sexual orientation, and alcohol, cigarette, and drug use can be quite accurately inferred from someone's Facebook likes." Another example is a data broker might infer that a consumer is likely to default on a loan based on their past financial behavior.[30]

Segmenting

Data brokers will then group and further profile consumers into "segments" or "categories" based on actual or derived data elements or a combination of the two. Some of the segments are populated based on "look-alike models" that predict a consumer's behavior based on the past behavior of similar people.[31]

Say a credit card company wants to buy data on households segmented by demographic characteristics, including age, income, home ownership, presence of children, and spending patterns. One data broker, Epsilon, has broken down US households into twenty-six segments (e.g., "Big Spender Parents" that are "dominated by middle-aged, traditional family households with children" with an average income of $207,000). Another data broker, Experian, classifies people into categories like "Credit Hungry Card Switcher" and "Insecure Debt Dependent." And during the Covid-19 pandemic, Experian created different "At-Risk Audience" segments based on their access to data about consumers defaulting on mortgages and filing for unemployment.[32]

Or perhaps a pharmaceutical company may want to target new clients. So, for example, they could work with a data broker that has created segments for people with health matters such as "Expectant Parent," "Diabetes Interest," and "Cholesterol Focus." Or they could engage with another data broker that has created categories of consumers with the following medical conditions: bedwetting, bowel irregularity, trouble sleeping due to breathing, diet concerns, using adult diapers, cold sores, and depression.[33]

Scoring

Data brokers also score us. Scores are predictions about consumer behavior based on actual and inferred data elements that software algorithms make to facilitate automated decision-making. And per a US Senate report on data brokers, scoring provides insight into consumers by "assigning a number or range that signifies the likelihood that a consumer . . . [will] exhibit certain characteristics or perform certain actions."[34]

Most of us are familiar with the concept of credit scores that predict our likelihood of defaulting on a loan. Organizations use credit scores to decide whether to offer a consumer a credit card or a mortgage. They also determine your credit limit or the interest rate you receive on a credit card or loan.[35]

But scoring has gone beyond its roots of analyzing creditworthiness or detecting fraudulent financial transactions. It now applies to all aspects of our lives. For example, certain data brokers can create scores that predict if a potential tenant will break a lease, absorb rent increases, or pay the rent on time. Per the *Washington Post*, another data broker can manufacture a score regarding whether a potential employee should be hired based on "analyzing 'tens of thousands of factors' including a person's facial expressions and voice intonations." Marketing data brokers can "lead score" your likelihood of buying a specific product. Your hold time for customer support can depend on your score as a profitable customer. Even your health is scored—based on your purchases, your ethnicity, and the amount of online shopping you do—which can influence your health insurance coverage.[36]

Threats associated with data brokers

Let's now look at the threats data brokers pose to us as individuals, our national security, and even our democracy.

Threat to our online safety

Identity theft is a big issue with consumers. The Federal Trade Commission recorded over 1.4 million identity theft cases in 2021, compared to 650,000 in 2019—a doubling in two years. According to the Identity Theft Resource Center (ITRC), identity theft can "destroy a person's credit, make it difficult to get housing, and, in some cases, drive people to contemplate suicide." A recent survey by ITRC found that 67 percent of respondents said they could not pay their bills because of identity theft.[37]

Hackers could use the vast amount of information available through data brokers to guess your account login security questions (e.g., "what high school did you attend?"). But, even more significant, getting your email address and data—such as who your relatives are—can be all hackers need to send impersonation emails from those trusted parties to "phish" (i.e., trick) you into revealing your passwords or credit card information.

If hackers don't want to buy this information from data brokers, they can always steal it. Data brokers are highly sought-after targets, given the massive amounts of highly sensitive data they store. Equifax was hacked, affecting 145 million people. Acxiom was breached in 2003, with 1.6 billion records stolen. Epsilon was hacked in 2011. LexisNexis has been breached. And in 2015, Experian's servers were hacked, with over fifteen million records accessed. They were then breached again in 2020. And these are large corporations with substantial security budgets, so smaller data brokers have likely been targets too.[38]

Threats to our physical safety

We increasingly see heated disagreements with local public officials and employees—such as county health commissioners, school board members, police officers, and judges—resulting in disgruntled citizens "doxxing" these officials. Per the *Atlantic*, doxxing refers to the "uncovering and deliberate weaponization of private, personal information." Doxxing takes its name from hacker culture, in which the online posting of private data "documents" was used as a means of revenge. This personal data includes photos, home addresses, cell phone numbers, email addresses, and details about family members, including kids' schools. For example, in 2020, the personal information of a San Jose police officer and his family was posted online with the note to "do with this information what you will." Therefore, the leaking of personal data gathered and sold by data brokers can lead to the threat of bodily harm to public officials and law enforcement.[39]

The same applies to victims of stalkers. According to the letter sent to the FTC in 2021 by Senators Amy Klobuchar and Lisa Murkowski, "One in four women and one in nine men experience intimate partner violence and often are forced to relocate to a relative's house to find safety." However, considering that people-search data brokers make it easy to see names and addresses of relatives, it becomes "difficult or impossible for victims to safely relocate with relatives."[40]

Threat of exploitation

When such sensitive personal data is collected, sold, and shared, it can lead to exploitation through scams and even blackmail. A third party could, for example, buy a list of segmented consumers with a specific medical condition and then target those consumers with a fraudulent quack cure. Or say a person is gay but has not informed their friends, fellow employees, or family members of that fact. But the online tracking of the person in terms of web searches or website visits could identify that person as gay. So now, data brokers and whomever they sold that information to have intimate knowledge of something a person has elected to keep secret and that could be used as leverage against that person.

This threat of exploitation is not theoretical. For example, the data broker Data Axle USA sold a list of nineteen thousand elderly sweepstakes players to a group of experienced scam artists. The scam artists then stole over $100 million by calling the victims and impersonating government officials who needed the victims' bank account information. Another example is the FTC fining the data broker firm Epsilon $150 million for helping to facilitate elder fraud scams. In the deferred prosecution agreement (DPA) signed with the FTC, Epsilon acknowledged it sold consumer lists to many mass-mailing fraud schemes. The fraudsters had sent false "sweepstakes" and "astrology" solicitations that "disproportionately affected the elderly and other vulnerable individuals."[41]

Threat to our civil rights

The profiling, segmentation, and scoring of consumers by data brokers can lead to discrimination. Examples include *The Markup* finding dozens of cases where consumers were denied housing because screening services used incorrect data from data brokers. *Fast Company* also documented instances where consumers could not get jobs because of inaccurate data. In fact, reporting has shown that a significant portion of data brokers' data on us is incorrect. For example, NATO did a comprehensive analysis and found that "quantity overshadows quality in the data broker industry" and that "on average only 50–60 percent of data can be considered precise." This means essential life decisions (getting a job, a loan, etc.) for consumers can be influenced or made by businesses based on scores and profiles that leverage inaccurate data.[42]

The sensitive nature of the collected and inferred data provides many opportunities for intentional discrimination. For example, potential employers may be influenced by political interests or affiliations (e.g., one data broker advertises to consumers interested in the NAACP, National LGBTQ Task Force, and Planned Parenthood) or medical conditions such as pregnancy in their hiring decisions. Your inferred medical conditions, such as cancer, could also affect your insurance premiums. Or your financial score could be used by a college to turn you down, as you may only be considered likely to pay for part of the four years.[43]

The use of our location data raises further civil rights concerns. For example, four members of Congress wrote a letter in 2020 to the data broker firm Mobilewalla expressing their concerns that the firm had "identified characteristics of American protestors at Black Lives Matter demonstrations using location data, including data on where protesters resided." Another example is that various LGBTQ dating apps sold users' location data to a broker. And multiple data brokers were found to have been selling the personal data—including location data—of users of Muslim prayer apps to US military contractors.[44]

A big issue emerging in post–abortion rights America is to what extent citizens or governments will use data from data brokers to track people coming and going from abortion clinics. They could also buy data on who is doing internet searches for words such as "abortion" and who is using period tracking apps. For example, two firms offering location data made headlines in the spring of 2022 when reporters could purchase data from them that could track phones going to and from Planned Parenthood—one firm had sold the data for $160. And in May of 2022, it was reported that another data broker was selling personal data regarding who had installed period tracking apps. The reporter had bought a sample of that data for $100.[45]

In all these cases, the data brokers have said they only provide MAIDs associated with the data, ensuring anonymity. But researchers have found it is easy to correlate MAIDs with actual consumers when combining that data with other data sources. Or by simply tracing patterns of movement with the location data, it is possible to deduce who the individual is being tracked (e.g., a mobile device is traced returning to a single-family residence every evening). For example, data broker Fog Data Science, which claims it has billions of data points on 250 million devices, says it can provide a person's "pattern of life," which lets its customers track individuals to their "bed downs" (i.e., places where people sleep) and commonly visited "locations of interest."[46]

Finally, data brokers directly help the government procure sensitive data about Americans' behavior and activities for which the government would typically need a warrant. For example, the Supreme Court held in 2018 that the government must obtain a warrant before getting cell phone location data from telecommunications carriers under the Fourth Amendment. But according to a congressional probe, buying data from data brokers lets the government "buy its way around the Fourth Amendment," as restrictions do not apply to "commercially obtained data," even for US citizens.[47]

Government purchase of sensitive personal data from data brokers for use in warrantless searches is, in fact, common. For example, *Ars Technica* reported in 2020 that the US Secret Service bought location history data from a data broker firm. The article further noted that "agencies under the Department of Homeland Security—including Immigration and Customs Enforcement (ICE) and Customs and Border Protection (CBP)—have purchased access to cellphone location activity for investigations." Specific to ICE, it was also reported by *CNet* in 2022 that the agency skirted around state sanctuary laws that restricted its ability to get data from state and local enforcement. Instead, it utilized data brokers like LexisNexis to "provide real-time access to immigrants' personal data and whereabouts."[48]

Threat to our national security and democracy

Three major data brokers—Acxiom, LexisNexis, and Nielsen—advertise their ability to provide data on former, current, and active-duty US military personnel. This can be used to determine where soldiers both live and are deployed. There is no law restricting to whom data brokers can sell personal data regarding military personnel. Hence it is conceivable that foreign entities or even front groups for terrorist groups could acquire this data for nefarious purposes.[49]

Another example of the threat data brokers can pose to our national security is that it is possible to surveil personnel associated with the Central Intelligence Agency (CIA) and National Security Agency (NSA). In April 2022, *The Intercept* reported that a company called Anomaly Six claimed it had purchased "reams" of location data from various data brokers and could now track roughly three billion devices in real time. The company was also able to demonstrate how it could track one individual "around the United States and abroad to a training center and airfield roughly an hour's drive northwest of Muwaffaq Salti Air Base in Zarqa, Jordan, where the US reportedly maintains a fleet of drones." Not surprisingly, Anomaly Six pointed out this capability was enabled "by general ignorance of the ubiquity and invasiveness of smartphone software development kits, known as SDKs."[50]

And as will be discussed in the next chapter, the Cambridge Analytica scandal of 2016 showed how reams of personal data taken from Facebook could be misused for political manipulation. Similarly, Russia's Internet Research Agency targeted Black communities in 2016 to dampen voter participation. So, foreign entities could use data brokers' treasure trove of personal data such as email addresses, phone numbers, and demographic data to attempt to sway public opinion. For example, emails or texts could be sent to voters urging support for or opposition to particular candidates. Or emails and texts could be sent impersonating candidates or purposely communicating false information regarding how and when to vote.[51]

Legislative fixes

Data brokers are less prevalent in Europe, given that Europe's privacy law requires consent for data collection. There has been activity in the US to regulate data brokers, but the results are mixed.

US state legislation

Vermont passed the first "data broker registry" law in 2018, and California passed its version in 2019. However, attempts to pass similar laws have failed in other states, such as New York and Maine, and, most recently, have failed in 2022 in Oregon and Washington.

Vermont's and California's data broker registry laws are relatively similar. First, they provide a similar definition of a data broker, emphasizing that data brokers are "businesses that collect and sell to third parties the personal information of a consumer with whom the company does not have a direct relationship." Second, both require the registration of data brokers with state agencies. Third, they both require the data broker to specify how a consumer can opt out and, in the case of California, how the consumer can request deletion. And finally, both levy a small fine for failure to register on time—$50 per day for Vermont and $100 per day for California. At the end of 2021, over three hundred data brokers registered in Vermont and over four hundred in California. In total, 540 unique data brokers were registered between the two states in 2021—well below the estimated four thousand data brokers worldwide.[52]

Even with these two states' registries, the onus is still up to the consumer to contact every data broker to request opt out and deletion. Assuming it takes thirty minutes per broker and there are five hundred brokers registered across the two states, opting out from all of them would require 250 hours of work. While, in theory, you could pay an opt-out service that removes you from data brokers' databases, the most I could find that an opt-out service would cover was approximately two hundred data brokers. So, even if you are willing to pay for this service, it would cover only 40 percent of the data brokers registered across the two states. And there is no requirement for data brokers to fulfill those requests if you use an opt-out service, except for California residents, given that California has a privacy law.

Finally, in Spring 2023, California state Senator Josh Becker proposed a bill to create an online portal for consumers to request that registered data brokers delete any data they have on the consumer and no longer track them. This California bill is based partly on a federal proposal called the DELETE Act (which I discuss below) while building upon the existing California data broker registry law. State Senator Becker is my local representative, and I proposed this bill to him and helped draft it.

US federal legislation

At the federal level, there have been various calls for the Federal Trade Commission (FTC) to create a data broker registry and further allow consumers to make global deletion requests of data brokers in the registry. For example, Apple CEO Tim Cook proposed in a 2019 *TIME* magazine opinion piece that the FTC should establish a "data-broker clearinghouse." This would facilitate consumers being able to track the data brokers "that have bundled and sold their data from place to place." And the clearinghouse would also give consumers "the power to delete their data on demand, freely, easily and online, once and for all."[53]

A bipartisan federal proposal came out in February of 2022 to provide such a data-broker clearinghouse. Introduced by US Senators Bill Cassidy and Jon Ossoff and Representative Lori Trahan, the bill is the Data Elimination and Limiting Extensive Tracking and Exchange

(DELETE) Act. The bill would "direct the Federal Trade Commission (FTC) to create an online dashboard for Americans to submit a one-time data deletion request that would be sent to all data brokers registered." In addition, it would also create a "do-not-track list" to protect registrants from future data collection. Underpinning this proposal is the creation of a federal data broker registry.[54]

In April 2021, several US senators introduced the bipartisan Fourth Amendment Is Not For Sale Act. This bill "closes the legal loophole that allows data brokers to sell Americans' personal information to law enforcement and intelligence agencies without any court oversight—in contrast to the strict rules for phone companies, social media sites, and other businesses that have direct relationships with consumers."[55]

In May 2022, US Senators Bill Cassidy, Elizabeth Warren, and Marco Rubio introduced the Protecting Military Servicemembers' Data Act of 2022. This bill protects the data of US service members by preventing data brokers from selling lists of military personnel to adversarial nations, including China, Russia, Iran, and North Korea. In addition, this bill acknowledges that the personal data of military personnel can be sold to adversaries without any restrictions and thus is a threat to our national security.[56]

The Daniel Anderl Judicial Security and Privacy Act, named after the son of a New Jersey judge whom an angry litigant murdered, was introduced in 2021. It would protect judges' personal information from being sold by data brokers.[57]

In anticipation of the overturning of *Roe v. Wade*, Senator Elizabeth Warren introduced in June 2022 the Health and Location Data Protection Act, which bans the selling and transferring of sensitive health and location data by data brokers. In addition, it would require the Federal Trade Commission (FTC) to create regulations and make exceptions for HIPAA-compliant activities.[58]

Finally, a bipartisan federal omnibus privacy bill called the American Data Privacy and Protection Act (ADPPA) was proposed in June 2022, incorporating the DELETE Act's substance.

Despite strong support from consumer protection and civil society groups, none of these bipartisan proposals moved forward at the end of the 2022 legislative session, except for the Daniel Anderl Judicial Security and Privacy Act, which, among other provisions, gives data broker deletion rights to judges.

Road map to contain data brokers

The first step in containing data brokers is shining a light in the shadows and understanding who they are and the threats they pose. Hopefully, this chapter clarified how we got to a place where data brokers can sell to any third party the ability to track our movements and precise geolocation, which is highly relevant in a post-*Roe* world.

There are actions we can individually take to limit data brokers from collecting and selling our data, such as blocking third-party cookies to stop online tracking and requesting to get your data deleted from the largest data brokers. I provide more details on these options in appendix 1.

But we must get legislation passed to regulate data brokers. At the very minimum, we need the following:

- We need the DELETE Act that creates a federal data broker registry with global deletion capabilities. This would be the equivalent of the FTC's Do Not Call registry to give us a single place to go to where we can request that our data be deleted from hundreds of data brokers.

- We should ban the selling and sharing of sensitive personal information such as health and location data unless there is explicit consent. For example, we have that protection for our health data that applies to "covered entities" under HIPAA, but it should be extended to all businesses who sell and share our sensitive health data.

- We need a law that bans the selling of our data to high-risk foreign countries.

- We need a comprehensive federal privacy law in line with what I spell out in appendix 2. At the very minimum, this should give us the right to know and access what data is being collected on us, the right to say no to the selling and sharing of our data, and the right to correct incorrect data. And that privacy law should obligate businesses to get our permission to collect this personal data, only collect the bare minimum data needed, and use best practices to protect that data. These rights and obligations should apply to all businesses, irrespective of whether we have a direct or indirect relationship.

Next, given that Big Tech owns the mobile operating systems Apple iOS and Google Android, and the browsers Google Chrome, Microsoft Edge, and Apple Safari, they could shut down online tracking by third parties by default if they wanted to. Apple has primarily done so on its platforms, but others have yet to follow suit. Now, Google did announce in 2020 that it would deprecate support of third-party cookies in its Chrome browser within two years, but since then, it has pushed back its deadline multiple times. It should be noted that an estimated 80 percent of advertisers rely on third-party cookies to track users online. So, if Google were to live up to its words, it would put a dent in data brokers. Therefore, we need to make our voices heard to stop the collecting, selling, and sharing of our data and have the other Big Tech players join Apple in prioritizing privacy.[59]

As you can see from this chapter and the last, we experience digital surveillance from both a "first party" perspective (Big Tech firms with whom we have a direct relationship that continuously extract our personal and behavioral data) and from a "third party" perspective (data brokers we don't even know that collect both online and offline data about us and are enabled by Big Tech's ad tech ecosystem). In the next chapter, I will examine the cybersecurity risks of having so much of our data collected because of digital surveillance and how it opens us up to identity theft.

CHAPTER 3

Data Breaches

We do not have an adequate level of control and explainability over how our systems use data, and thus we can't confidently make controlled policy changes or external commitments such as "we will not use X data for Y purpose."

—Meta privacy engineers, 2021 internal leaked memo[1]

Over 4,100 data breaches were reported in 2021, exposing billions of user records. The US government defines a data breach as an incident "in which sensitive, protected or confidential data is copied, transmitted, viewed, stolen or used by an individual unauthorized to do so." At an estimated average cost to a business of $4.35 million per data breach, the total economic cost of data breaches to businesses in 2021 was well over $18 billion.[2]

But this calculation does not include the cost to consumers whose data was stolen. Unfortunately, hackers often use stolen personal data from these breaches to impersonate consumers and steal their identities for financial gain. One survey estimated that in 2021 over forty-two million Americans were the victims of identity fraud, costing them over $52 billion in total losses.[3]

As discussed in the last chapter, all the largest data brokers have been breached. But, as the largest technology companies in the world, one would surmise that Big Tech firms would have enough budget and technical wherewithal to avoid being hacked or have it be an infrequent occurrence. However, except for Apple, with whom there have been no public reports of an incident involving stolen end-user data, numerous data breaches have been associated with Big Tech firms.

For example, Meta has had data leaked or stolen at least nine times since 2013. In 2019 alone, four significant breaches were reported. One was reported in March 2019 with at least 600 million user passwords affected, another in April 2019 with 540 million users' records, and another in September 2019 with 419 million user IDs, phone numbers, and locations. Finally, in December 2019, there was a breach of 309 million users with phone numbers and names. And the most significant known breach of Meta occurred in April 2021, of 533 million users with phone numbers, dates of birth, user locations, and email addresses.[4]

Amazon, Google, and Microsoft have also been involved in numerous incidents. In 2018 and before Black Friday, Amazon announced a breach of customer names and email addresses. Amazon also experienced several instances where internal employees were caught selling customer data in exchange for bribes. Google's failed Google+ social networking service had numerous bugs that exposed the data of over fifty million users. And Microsoft had over five hundred million LinkedIn users' data scraped and sold. These are just a few examples.[5]

Generally, the more personal data a firm collects and stores, the more likely hackers or malicious insiders will target it. There are also increased chances that this data will leak out via vulnerabilities in internal software systems. Putting it another way, you can't have a breach or leak of information you don't have. As a result, more and more companies are now viewing personal data as "radioactive material," as there is increased risk and liability associated with having that data.[6]

So why do Big Tech firms have so much radioactive material in the form of personal and behavioral information when, in theory, it puts them at a more severe risk of being hacked or having their data leak out? Unsurprisingly, the answer goes back—again—to the fact that most Big Tech firms (Google, Meta, and Amazon) have a digital surveillance business model that motivates them to "overcollect" and "over-retain" our data. This is because they fundamentally believe that if they gather and store more data over long periods, they eventually gain more insight into us, thus enabling them to facilitate better-targeted advertising or sell more products. In other words, they can't say no to data and always want more.[7]

Furthermore, for Big Tech firms, the penalty for being breached is relatively small, so there is less of a stick to change their data collection and retention practices. For example, Amazon was fined $885 million in 2021 by the European Union (EU) for unspecified data processing violations of the GDPR privacy law. And Meta was fined $5 billion in 2019 by the Federal Trade Commission (FTC) for violations of a 2012 FTC order. Meta's fine emanated from the investigation of Cambridge Analytica, which harvested data from its platform. Yet the penalties to Amazon and Meta were drops in the bucket compared to both companies' profits and cash balance—the Amazon fine represented approximately 2.5 percent of Amazon's 2021 profits, and the Meta fine in 2019 represented less than 10 percent of its cash at the time. Even worse, when the FTC settlement was announced, Meta's stock rose because investors thought the fine could have been greater.[8]

In addition, Big Tech's dominant market position makes them less likely to stop their aggressive data collection and retention practices and, in turn, lessen their data breach risk. For example, Big Tech knows that users are locked into their walled gardens and have not moved away despite past breaches. Their monopoly positions translate into them not being pushed by competitors to do more in privacy and data protection. I will talk more about competition in chapter 8. Unfortunately, because of what critics say is Big Tech's "too big to care" attitude, we should expect the data breaches to continue and get bigger and bigger, with more dangerous consequences.

In this chapter, I will continue examining Big Tech and its advertising ecosystem's data collection practices by looking at the threats and concerns regarding the protection and security of this collected data. However, I will not discuss incidents where external hackers broke into

Big Tech firms, as bad people will do bad things, and Big Tech firms, like any other company, are not to blame for actions by criminals.

Instead, I will explore the problems associated with Big Tech firms' practice of oversharing consumer data with their partners and how that can introduce data breaches. I will use the Cambridge Analytica scandal as a case study of this, which, when it came to light in 2018, was a seminal event in raising the consciousness of the threats of Big Tech. I will then discuss Big Tech's problems with oversharing sensitive data with employees and contractors and the issues that have arisen. Next, I will look at data breach legislation. Finally, I will conclude with recommendations on containing the risks associated with data breaches and Big Tech.

The Facebook—Cambridge Analytica data breach scandal

The poster child of Big Tech's often careless handling of our data is Cambridge Analytica.

Precursors to Cambridge Analytica

In 2010, Meta decided to open the Facebook platform to third-party developers. By building apps on top of Facebook, Meta hoped it would direct more users and data to its platform. As part of that initiative, Meta released the Graph application programming interface (API) at its annual developer conference in April 2010 to facilitate access to its data. But critics expressed concern that this API could introduce privacy issues, such as third parties accessing users' data without proper consent. Based on this and other concerns, Meta CEO Mark Zuckerberg apologized in May 2010 and promised users simpler privacy controls and a more straightforward way to turn off third-party services.[9]

As criticism mounted of Meta's privacy practices, the Federal Trade Commission (FTC) began an investigation of Meta. This led to a settlement between the two parties in August 2012. One of the FTC's

charges against Meta was that it "made deceptive claims about consumers' ability to control the privacy of their personal data." Another
charge alleged that Meta let users choose a setting that limited access
to their information to just "friends" without disclosing that another
setting allowed their data to be shared with developers of Facebook
apps that their friends used. To settle the case, Meta agreed to an order
that prohibited it from making misrepresentations "about the privacy
or security of consumers' personal information, and the extent to which
it shares personal information, such as names and dates of birth, with
third parties." The order further required Meta to maintain a privacy
program that protected user data.[10]

That same year, Zuckerberg looked to open the Facebook platform further to third parties. Zuckerberg wrote in an email in late
2012 that his goal was "to enable people to share everything they
want, and to do it on Facebook. Sometimes the best way to enable
people to share something is to have a developer build a special purpose app . . . and to make that app social by having Facebook plug into
it." And to build an app ecosystem to generate more shared data for
Facebook, Zuckerberg allowed developers even greater access to the
voluminous amounts of data that Meta had collected from users via
the "side door" of applications.[11]

Cambridge Analytica harvesting of consumer data through a Facebook app

In 2018, whistleblower Christopher Wylie revealed that a London-based
election consulting firm called Cambridge Analytica had exfiltrated
the data of over eighty-seven million Facebook users, including over
seventy million users in the US. The data trove included, per a 2022
lawsuit filed by the attorney general of the District of Columbia (DC)
against Mark Zuckerberg regarding the Cambridge Analytica scandal, "Facebook users' ages, interests, pages they've liked, groups they
belong to, physical locations, political affiliation, religious affiliation,
relationships, and photos, as well as their full names, phone numbers,
and email addresses."[12]

The data had been collected through a third-party app on the Facebook platform called "thisisyourdigitallife." The app was written by Aleksandr Kogan, a researcher affiliated with Cambridge University. Available in late 2013, the app offered a personality survey and generated a personality profile for consumers. During the installation process, the app portrayed to Facebook users that its access and use of their data was purely for academic research. Meta did not review the app before it was allowed on the Facebook platform, nor did it verify the purpose of the app, even though it was given access to consumers' data.[13]

Over 290,000 consumers eventually installed the app, and not only did the app harvest the survey respondents' data from Facebook, but it also harvested all of their Facebook friends' data, resulting in approximately eighty-seven million users having their data collected. However, as noted in the DC lawsuit against Mark Zuckerberg, "The vast majority of these Facebook friends never installed the App, never affirmatively consented to supplying the App with their data, and never knew the App had collected their data."[14]

In 2014, Kogan sold the personal data of eighty-seven million users to Cambridge Analytica for $800,000. Cambridge Analytica then used the data as part of its consulting contracts to target political ads for the 2016 presidential campaign, initially for Ted Cruz and then for Donald Trump. Cambridge Analytica also used the data to create psychographic profiles that helped the campaigns determine which ads would be most effective in influencing opinion.[15]

Meta became aware by December 2015 that Kogan had sold Facebook user data to Cambridge Analytica. Still, after terminating the app's access to the Facebook platform, Meta continued to allow Kogan and Cambridge Analytica to access the Facebook platform. Furthermore, it is alleged in the DC lawsuit that Meta did not audit Kogan or Cambridge Analytica nor take any action to "determine whether the Facebook consumer data that was harvested by the App had been accounted for, deleted, and protected from further use and sharing." According to regulators, Meta kept the harvesting of millions of its users' data secret for several years until the whistleblower went public in 2018.[16]

FTC fine and restrictions

A year after the Cambridge Analytica news broke and the resulting uproar had Meta apologizing and Zuckerberg testifying in front of Congress, the FTC in July 2019 fined Meta $5 billion for violations of the 2012 FTC order, making this penalty the "largest ever imposed on any company for violating consumers' privacy." In its settlement order with Meta, the FTC alleged that Meta deceived "its users when the company shared the data of users' Facebook friends with third-party app developers, even when those friends had set more restrictive privacy settings." The FTC also alleged that Meta waited four years to stop sharing user information relating to Facebook friends with third-party apps, even though it had announced in 2014 that it would stop this data collection practice. Other allegations include not properly policing app developers on its platform and not consistently enforcing privacy policies. The complaint also alleged that Meta told users it would only collect phone numbers for security purposes (e.g., two-factor authentication, in which a text is sent with a code that the user enters alongside their password) but, in fact, used those phone numbers to serve ads.[17]

The settlement ordered Meta to meet new privacy requirements, including tighter control over Meta's ability to share data with app developers, the need to encrypt passwords, and the prohibition of using phone numbers obtained to enable security features for advertising.[18]

The settlement drew a strongly adverse reaction from politicians in both parties, saying it did not go far enough to rein in Meta's intrusive data collection practices. Critics also said the fine was a "drop in the bucket" for Meta and that the settlement's shielding of Meta for violations before 2019 gave the company and its executives a free pass from paying the consequences of past actions.[19]

Data breach or not?

Meta insisted at the time that equating the Cambridge Analytica incident to a data breach was a "completely false" argument. Meta defiantly stated in a blog post in March 2018 that "Aleksandr Kogan requested and gained access to information from users who chose to sign up to his app, and everyone involved gave their consent. People knowingly provided their information, no systems were infiltrated, and no passwords or sensitive pieces of information were stolen or hacked."[20]

But as later came to light, the victims were not to blame, as most of the Facebook friends whose data was caught up in this breach never installed the app and never consented to supplying it with their data. Furthermore, while this was not a security incident in the form of a hacker infiltrating the Meta systems, the definition of a breach includes the transmission or use of sensitive data by an unauthorized user, and Kogan was clearly not authorized to transmit and sell this data.

So, Cambridge Analytica does represent a significant data breach. This breach was made possible by Meta's willingness to share user data with third parties to facilitate getting even more user data, by not putting the proper auditing controls in place, and by misleading consumers about their ability to control who has access to their data. However, it should be noted that the same Meta spokesperson did acknowledge in a subsequent blog post posted in August 2019 that "Cambridge Analytica was a clear lapse for us, which we have worked hard to address."[21]

There is no doubt that Facebook users would not have wanted their Facebook postings and personal data taken and used without their permission, given to a political campaign, and then utilized to manipulate or shape their opinion. Given this happened in relation to the 2016 US presidential campaign in which Russian intelligence also used Facebook to spread disinformation, which Meta also initially downplayed, this data breach and the subsequent hefty fine by the FTC justifiably led to significant consumer and lawmaker distrust of Meta. In later chapters, I will discuss the release in 2021 of internal Meta documents—dubbed the "Facebook Files"—by whistleblower Frances Haugen that showed Meta was fully aware of its products' harmful societal effects, thereby taking distrust of Meta to an even higher level.

Meta is still facing the impact of the Cambridge Analytica breach years after it came to light. In December 2022, Meta agreed to pay $725 million to settle a class-action lawsuit involving Cambridge Analytica. The lawsuit alleged that Meta gave third parties access to consumers' Facebook data without their consent and that Meta had "failed to adequately monitor the third parties' access to, and use of, that information." Besides this $725 million settlement and the $5 billion fine levied by the FTC, Meta also paid $100 million to settle a case filed by the US Securities and Exchange Commission (SEC) that it had allegedly made misleading statements and disclosures about risks involving the misuse of consumer data.[22]

Oversharing our data with internal employees

This culture of not putting proper auditing and controls in place with their partners is equally applicable to the fast and loose restrictions that Big Tech firms have often had for their employees. This lack of governance has led to unauthorized access being impactful from a national security, personal safety, and fraud perspective.

TikTok

China-based TikTok, likely to be the newest member of Big Tech, represents a recent example of how a data breach can occur due to internal users having unauthorized access. It was reported in mid-2022 that tech personnel at ByteDance's corporate headquarters—the parent company of TikTok, based in China—had full privileges to access TikTok's user data. Given that the Chinese government has the authority to access the data of Chinese-based companies, it raises national security concerns that an adversarial nation-state may have access to behavioral data associated with US citizens, which could be utilized for blackmail or espionage. Furthermore, there is a concern that the Chinese government could influence TikTok's algorithms by censoring objectional content or promoting content to benefit its foreign policy goals. As a result, by the end of 2022, over fourteen states and the US federal government passed bans on using TikTok on government-issued devices. In addition, politicians such as Senator Marco Rubio introduced bills at the end of 2022 that outright ban TikTok in the US.[23]

When the story broke, TikTok said it would never "target" or "monitor" any US users "in the way the article suggested." Yet a few months after the article came out, ByteDance announced in December 2022 the results of an internal investigation that revealed that ByteDance employees had, in fact, inappropriately targeted and obtained the personal user data of the reporters who disclosed the story mentioned above. Apparently, ByteDance personnel responsible for monitoring employee conduct had tried to find the internal sources of the leaks that led to this story. In doing this research, this team improperly gained access to the reporters' TikTok user data, including location data, to determine if the reporters had been in similar locations as ByteDance employees. ByteDance admitted that employees had "misused their authority to obtain access to TikTok user data" and fired the four employees involved in this data breach. This episode acknowledges the concerns the original article laid out and has made TikTok's position with the US government even more tenuous.[24]

Meta

Another example involves Meta. Critics have claimed that Meta has had a culture with few guardrails protecting access to user data. For instance, it was reported that Zuckerberg rationalized this lack of control as a way to "cut away the red tape that slowed down engineers and prevented them from producing fast, independent work." Yet in the 2014–15 time frame, this lack of guardrails allowed fifty-two male Meta engineers to view photos, locations, and private messages of women they had dated or were interested in. In one instance, an engineer tracked a woman's location by accessing her Facebook user data and saw that she frequented a park in San Francisco. He would then head to the park, hoping to run into her.[25]

Ironically, Meta's culture of unrestricted access to sensitive material enabled Frances Haugen to gather internal documents in early 2021 to bolster her claims that Meta "chooses profits over safety." Coupled with the fact that Meta has so much data, it is no surprise that an internal Meta document leaked in 2022 revealed that Meta has little idea where user data goes internally or what it does with all this data.[26]

Amazon

Wired reported in November 2021 allegations that Amazon had not adequately protected consumer data. The report described how "Amazon's vast empire of customer data" had become "so sprawling, fragmented, and promiscuously shared within the company" that Amazon's security division for its retail platform could not map all of the data, let alone secure it. It was alleged that this broad access to customer data came from the culture of Amazon that was so focused on satisfying the customer that "broad swathes of its global workforce" were given "extraordinary latitude to tap into customer data at will." The report quoted a former chief information security officer (CISO) at Amazon who said it was a "free-for-all" of "internal access to information" that left the company open to "internal threat actors."[27]

The *Wired* report gave several examples to back up its reporting. For instance, Amazon employees had snooped on the purchases of celebrities. Others had taken bribes from sellers to scrub negative reviews by customers or sabotage competitors' listings. The report also documented how millions of credit cards were found in an insecure location in the company's network, and the Amazon security team could not determine if this data had been accessed. Another example was via an internal discovery that "a Chinese data firm had been harvesting millions of customers' information." Finally, one former Amazon lawyer noted that internally, "user personal data flowed like water."[28]

It should be noted that an Amazon spokesperson told the *Wired* reporter that its reporting was based on "old documents" that "do not reflect Amazon's current security posture."[29]

Legislation

Europe has again taken the lead, this time in data breach notification and data protection. Europe's privacy law, the General Data Protection Regulation (GDPR), requires that an organization report a breach within seventy-two hours of becoming aware of it. Furthermore, it requires businesses to implement the "appropriate technical and organizational measures to ensure a level of security appropriate to the risk" associated with personal data being collected and retained. This could include requiring data to be encrypted.[30]

The US does not have a national data breach notification law. However, some federal laws require notice in certain circumstances; for example, the Health Insurance Portability and Accountability Act (HIPAA) requires notification if a covered entity (e.g., a hospital) is breached. But regulation in this area is primarily through a patchwork of state laws—with California again leading the way with the first-ever data breach notification law. These state data breach notification laws aim to notify consumers that their data has been caught up in a breach, thereby giving consumers a chance to take defensive measures (e.g., change passwords or monitor for credit card fraud). Data breach notification laws also motivate businesses to strengthen their security and data protection posture. Further examples include California's privacy law requiring businesses to "implement reasonable security procedures" appropriate to the nature of the personal information collected to "protect the personal information from unauthorized or illegal access."[31]

Road map to contain Big Tech's data breaches

If you have the impression that the security and protection of your data are collateral damage as Big Tech looks to sell more ads and products, you are probably not alone. Unfortunately, much like consumers' concerns regarding Big Tech's lackadaisical protection of our privacy, the combination of Big Tech's digital surveillance business model, their monopoly positions, and addictive technology increasingly open us to being impacted by data breaches.

Passing a comprehensive national data privacy law would force companies to get our consent to collect our data. A privacy law would also require those same companies to minimize data collection solely to the purposes that were consented to, thus reducing the amount of data sloshing around in Big Tech's systems. And a privacy law would give us the right to access and delete the personal and behavioral data that Big Tech has collected on us. Furthermore, banning digital surveillance of children and banning the use of sensitive personal information such as sexuality, religion, and ethnicity for targeted advertising would also make us more secure. As author and tech critic Cory Doctorow noted, "You can't leak data you never collected, and once you delete all copies of that data, you can no longer leak it."[32]

As discussed in later chapters, by introducing more competition, Big Tech would be forced to strengthen its privacy and data protection features to be competitive in a normal market. In addition, by requiring design changes that reduce the addictive nature of their products, less time would be spent on their platforms, thereby reducing data that could be stolen.

Concerning US federal legislation, as previously mentioned, besides not having a national privacy law, the US also does not have a national data breach notification law. Ironically, the US government tracks the number of pigs, hurricanes, plane crashes, and shark attacks, but it does not centrally track hacks and their financial impact. But we need a strong central authority that can track breaches, aid hacked companies and consumers, and dole out fines when companies have been lax in their cybersecurity practices. Much like the Federal Aviation Administration (FAA) is the go-to agency for plane crashes, we need the federal equivalent for cybersecurity. And higher duties of care should be placed on gatekeepers with more "radioactive material" in the form of personal data, just like we have higher safety requirements for nuclear plants.

In the first two chapters, I revealed who is surveilling us—Big Tech and data brokers that thrive in Big Tech's ad tech ecosystem—and what their digital surveillance–based business model means for us. In this chapter, I examined the cybersecurity implications of these companies mining, collecting, and storing so much of our personal and behavioral data that it makes it more likely our data gets breached. In the next chapter, I will discuss the underlying technology—artificial intelligence (AI)—that Big Tech utilizes to process this collected data to make better predictions, find patterns, and automate decision-making. In using AI so extensively, they aim to take their behavioral advertising business to new levels, among other strategic uses. But doing so introduces new threats.

CHAPTER 4

Artificial Intelligence

I view [artificial intelligence] as the most profound technology that humanity will ever develop and work on . . . if you think about fire or electricity or the internet, it's like that. But I think even more profound.

—Sundar Pichai, CEO of Google[1]

In June 2022, the Department of Justice (DoJ) announced that it had settled a complaint with Meta regarding allegations that Meta had engaged in discriminatory practices violating the Fair Housing Act (FHA). What triggered this investigation was that it had been discovered that landlords and real estate brokers could take advantage of Meta's housing advertising system to prevent women or families with children from seeing ads for housing rentals. Because Meta developed its AI-based advertising system to determine which users receive which housing ads, and this system factored in FHA-protected characteristics such as race, color, familial status, and sex, it was a straightforward case of discriminatory advertising under the FHA. As part of the settlement, Meta agreed to stop using its existing advertising system for housing ads and build a new system. Meta also paid a penalty of slightly over $100,000. This case represented one of the DoJ's first-ever involving AI bias.[2]

This case study of how AI can be biased is just a tiny speed bump in Big Tech's rush to use and deploy AI. Big Tech sees immense promise in AI as a competitive differentiator, given its ability to simulate human intelligence to solve problems and automate decision-making. Thus, Big Tech firms are in an arms race around AI. For example, Big Tech and a few other large technology companies are responsible for $2 of every $3 spent on AI. These same firms are also among the largest recipients of US patents for AI and are responsible for the vast majority of acquisitions of successful AI start-ups. Meta CEO Mark Zuckerberg best summed up Big Tech's focus on AI, stating in 2022 that "AI is the major technology wave we're riding today."[3]

AI technology is commonplace in Big Tech's services and can deliver significant value to consumers and Big Tech's customers. For example, e-commerce sites like Amazon.com use AI to provide personalized recommendations to shoppers based on online behavior, past purchases, or searches. In addition, AI allows Big Tech's virtual assistants like Apple's Siri and Amazon's Alexa to interpret questions, provide recommendations, or even perform tasks such as playing music, making a phone call, or sending a calendar invite. Furthermore, AI is used by Big Tech firms to determine which of their customers' ads would best resonate with consumers. And AI can optimize search results for a given individual based on past searches and recommend the most relevant web pages on a given topic based on crawling billions of websites.[4]

But despite these positives, AI can introduce bias or be misused by Big Tech. I gave an example previously with housing ads. Another example is Meta utilizing AI to maximize user engagement on their platforms. But in doing so, critics claim that their AI-based recommendation systems can promote content that favors controversy, disinformation, and extremism. Critics say this has led to users becoming measurably more polarized.[5]

Taken to extremes, AI can be used to implement "Big Brother" monitoring that goes beyond the digital surveillance we now experience. For example, the *New York Times* reported in 2019 that China's government was using AI-based facial recognition to "track and control" the Uighurs—a Muslim minority population within China. According to the *Times*, the AI system "looks exclusively for Uighurs based on their appearance and keeps records of their comings and goings for search and review." *Business Insider* further reported that China has also implemented an AI-based "social scoring" system for monitoring its citizens. China scores citizens based on "bad driving, smoking in non-smoking zones, buying too many video games, and posting fake news online" and other factors. Low "social credits" punishment includes banning citizens from taking flights or throttling their internet speed. People with high "social credits" get rewarded in various ways. Companies in China are also encouraged to check potential employees' scores before hiring.[6]

Through the first three chapters of this book, I have been examining the collection of our online behavioral data and personal data by Big Tech and its ad tech ecosystem. AI is increasingly the technology used by Big Tech that processes this data to find patterns, facilitate problem-solving, and automate decision-making. AI is fueled by data and requires vast amounts of computing power—which Big Tech uniquely has in abundance. And AI can learn, which makes it more powerful but also fraught with risks.

I will use this chapter to give an overview of AI and explain why Big Tech is placing significant bets on it. In light of Big Tech's growing use of AI, I will also examine the threats associated with AI. Specifically, how bias seeps into AI that can introduce unfair outcomes for certain groups of people. I will also analyze how Big Tech and others can utilize AI for exploitative purposes. This will set up future chapters on how Big Tech's use of AI enables screen addiction, puts kids' online safety at risk, and spreads disinformation and extremism. Finally, I will discuss proposed legislation to regulate AI, and provide recommendations on accentuating AI's positives while containing its risks.

Algorithms and artificial intelligence

Algorithms are the building blocks of AI. An algorithm solves a problem or completes a task via mathematical instructions. The word "algorithm" gets its name from the Latinized pronunciation of the name of a ninth-century Persian mathematician. Arithmetic algorithms have been used throughout history, even as long ago as the Babylonians, circa 2500 BC, the Egyptians in 1500 BC, the Greeks in 240 BC, and so on. Today, algorithms are built by human experts using software programming languages that represent preset coded recipes with step-by-step instructions that computers use to execute a given task.[7]

But today's software programmers are not stopping at algorithms that follow step-by-step instructions. Humans for centuries have envisioned machines that could become intelligent and make human-like decisions. There have been myths about robots, automatons, and artificial beings since ancient Greece (e.g., the myth of Pandora, who unleashed ills upon the world). Likewise, literature throughout history has dreamt of creating human-like creatures and thinking machines (e.g., Mary Shelley's *Frankenstein*). In 1950, British mathematician Alan Turing asked whether machines could think and reason like humans and then developed the Turing test to measure a machine's intelligence and whether the machines can think autonomously. A few years later, MIT professor John McCarthy coined "artificial intelligence," replacing the previously used expression "automata studies." Since then, artificial intelligence has become the study and practice of "making intelligent machines" that are programmed to think like humans—endowed by their creators with reasoning and learning.[8]

Fast-forward nearly seventy years, and AI is no longer a theoretical exercise for academics but is taking over the computing world. The European Parliament in 2020 called AI "probably the defining technology" of the last decade and perhaps the next. The creation of new algorithms coupled with massive increases in computing power and storage—facilitated using cloud computing—and the availability of voluminous amounts of data for analysis has led to major AI breakthroughs.[9]

One way to think of AI vis-a-vis algorithms is that AI represents a collection of algorithms that can dynamically modify itself and even create new algorithms based on its learning from the data it continuously collects and processes. AI's "learning" algorithms are known as "machine learning," or ML. ML dynamically learns and evolves without software engineers explicitly programming them and can adapt and change based on the vast amounts of information fed to them. As a result, ML is used in most applications that utilize AI.[10]

ML can make predictions and find patterns, and with more data being ingested and analyzed over time, ML can improve its capabilities. One technology CEO even noted that "AI is fueled by data. The more the machine learns about you, the better it can predict your needs and act on your behalf." And the amount of available fuel is rapidly expanding each year, with the world's data projected to grow from 33 zettabytes in 2010 to 175 zettabytes in 2025.[11]

Another popular AI technology is "deep learning" (DL). DL is modeled after the neural network of the human brain. DL stacks algorithms in a hierarchy, with each level created with knowledge obtained from the preceding level of the hierarchy. DL mimics a human's ability to learn by example. For instance, say a child knows the word "dog." The child points to a photo of an animal, and an adult says "yes" or "no" if that object is a dog, and the process repeats itself. Over time the child figures out the features that dogs possess, resulting in the child developing a hierarchy of knowledge of what constitutes a dog. DL learns like this at scale, is highly accurate, and can even outperform humans in complex decision-making.[12]

DL is very good at processing unstructured data, such as audio, video, and images. As a result, DL is heavily used in AI products such as facial recognition, digital assistants, medicine, and self-driving cars. For example, in self-driving vehicles, DL can recognize a traffic sign and distinguish a bike from a motorcycle and a pedestrian from a lamppost. In medicine, DL can be used to detect cancer cells by analyzing test results.[13]

Another subset of AI is natural language processing (NLP) technology. NLP understands and translates human language. An AI-based virtual assistant product such as Apple's Siri needs both NLP and ML. NLP interprets what users say, but ML learns the context of what is said and refines more accurate and better ways to respond to a user over time.[14]

AI deployments and benefits

The deployment of AI is now widespread. Besides usage in online shopping, virtual assistants, and internet search, other uses include the following:[15]

- Cybersecurity—AI can detect attacks and provide remediation. For example, AI helps block viruses and phishing attempts that target users of Big Tech's email systems like Google's Gmail and Microsoft's Hotmail.

- Self-driving automobiles—AI provides navigation and can determine unsafe driving conditions.

- Finance—AI can detect credit card fraud and automate trading. For instance, it is estimated that AI-based systems execute 60 percent of trades on Wall Street with little to no real-time oversight from humans.[16]

- Medicine—AI can interpret medical tests and spot diseases.

- Smart homes—smart thermostats powered by AI can learn from occupants' behavior to save energy. An example of this is Google's Nest thermostats.

- Text-to-image generators—AI that receives text as input (e.g., "panda in a spacesuit in outer space in the style of Monet") and then generates realistic art and images as output. Examples include DALL-E from OpenAI (which has received a $13 billion investment from Microsoft), Imagen from Google, and Stable Diffusion from Stability AI.

- Chatbots—AI that lets you have human-like conversations with it, such as getting answers to questions ("What songs from Bob Dylan mention Woody Guthrie?") or recommendations ("What are the best Greek islands to visit with teenage children?"). An example is ChatGPT from OpenAI. In a move to better compete with Google's search engine, Microsoft announced in February 2023 that it would enhance its Bing search engine with the AI technology behind ChatGPT to provide straightforward text answers to search queries instead of returning a list of links. Google countered that same month with its announcement of its ChatGPT rival solution called Bard, which would also be integrated into its search offering.[17]

Not surprisingly, the resulting benefits to both businesses and consumers are significant, including the following:

- AI can help businesses become more efficient. It can automate business processes and, in doing so, reduce costs. It can also detect inefficiencies such as excessive energy usage or improve machine maintenance. For example, the European Parliament believes that AI can improve manufacturing efficiency by 6–8 percent per year. Decision-making is also improved via enhanced pattern matching and deeper analysis.[18]

- AI can also help businesses compete better and provide improved services. For example, with AI, products can become "smart" and "intelligent" and better appeal to customers, given their ability to evolve as they learn how customers use their products. AI can also provide better customer service via chatbots to diagnose complex customer support problems without the consumer calling customer support and waiting for a technician to get on the phone line.[19]

- AI can empower employees, improve their productivity, and make them safer in the workplace. It can automate routine tasks to free employees to focus on higher-value tasks. For example, the European Parliament projected that labor productivity could increase by 11–37 percent by 2035 with the increased use of AI. In addition, workplace safety can be improved via robots taking over more dangerous parts of a job, and analysis of past workplace safety issues can lead to improved working conditions.[20]

- AI can make consumers safer and healthier. For example, wearable personal devices use AI to monitor our health.

In light of the widespread deployments and numerous benefits, it is not surprising that the consulting firm PwC says that AI "represents the largest economic opportunity of our lifetime." They also projected that AI would contribute nearly $16 trillion to the global economy by 2030. In addition, IBM in 2020 estimated that business adoption of AI would grow by 90 percent by 2022. And interestingly, a survey in 2019 of senior business executives revealed that 75 percent of executives felt that if their companies did not scale up their AI efforts over the next few years, their companies risked going out of business. So, it is full steam ahead with AI.[21]

AI bias

Humans build AI systems, and human beings have biases—more than 180 biases, according to psychologists. Moreover, human bias exists in even subconscious ways. For example, judges have made decisions that their background and personal characteristics have unconsciously influenced. And decisions by employers regarding whom they will bring in for interviews have been influenced by last names reflecting different races— even though identical resumes had been submitted. So, it is not surprising that our human-created "thinking machines" can also be impacted and influenced by human bias—even if that was not the intent of the people involved. And given its widespread deployment, AI can even significantly amplify human bias on a massive scale.[22]

Definition and risks

AI bias is the unjustified differential treatment of or outcomes for different subgroups of people. It results in systemically unfair decisions for specific groups of people based on the inappropriate use of certain traits and characteristics such as disabilities, race, gender, and sexual orientation. Note these characteristics and sensitive attributes are also typically protected from a legal perspective, so a discussion of AI bias cannot be divorced from the concept of bias in discrimination laws and regulations in areas such as housing, employment, and finance. So, when advocacy groups bring up the idea of "digital redlining"—creating and perpetuating inequities through technology with already marginalized subgroups—it calls for a hard look at the impact of AI bias.[23]

Bias in AI can harm humans. With AI increasingly embedded in much of the technology we use, it influences who is admitted into a school, gets a job, is authorized for a bank loan, or gets accepted or rejected as a rental applicant. It can even determine what kind of medical treatment one receives. So, AI bias can have a far-reaching impact on individuals but also impacts everybody by reducing people's ability to participate in our society and economy fully and fairly. Bias builds mistrust in AI that may discourage future use, which could benefit humanity.[24]

AI bias is introduced in the design of the underlying AI-based systems and the data that humans feed them. And humans can also make mistakes when interpreting the results of AI. This is not surprising to many in the technology community—the analyst firm Gartner predicts that "85 percent of AI projects will deliver erroneous outcomes due to bias in data, algorithms, or the teams responsible for managing them." So, let's drill down on bias that emanates from AI design and data.[25]

Bias in design

It is easy to blame the data fed into AI systems as the source of bias— "garbage in" will result in "garbage out"—but bias starts with flaws in the design of the AI-based systems. For example, say the goal for a bank is to build an AI system that predicts which bank loans are least likely to default. The system can't factor in sensitive attributes such as race for legal reasons. But the reality is that the AI system could still be prejudiced, as it could base its decision-making on related factors such as zip codes that represent a stand-in for race. This is known as "proxy discrimination," in which AI yields, per the Brookings Institution, a "bias against a group without making decisions based on a person's membership in that group." For gender, the proxies could be weight or height. So, it is possible to design an AI system that doesn't directly utilize a protected characteristic but, in the end, produces the same outcome.[26]

So, getting the design "right" is key to AI. And some of the bias introduced in the design of AI systems is likely because the teams building these systems are relatively homogenous and may not have a broad worldview and diversity of background. For example, despite being half the population, only 18 percent of computer science graduates are women, and less than one-fifth of AI researchers or professors are women. In the technology industry, Whites are overrepresented, and Black and Latinx are underrepresented. As a result, the people building them may not fully understand how AI impacts end users who are different from them.[27]

Bias in data

AI bias can also be introduced by having low-quality data to train the AI systems. This data can reflect historical or social inequities. For instance, if AI is trained on social media posts or news reports, the resulting output will likely reinforce societal prejudices. Another example of this was Amazon's development of an AI project designed to automate the recruiting process by analyzing job applicant resumes and scoring them. The project aimed to save recruiters time and effort in manually screening candidates. Amazon trained the AI system with the prior ten years of resume submissions and hiring decisions. But because the tech industry is historically male-dominated, and at the time, Amazon's workforce was 60 percent male and men held 74 percent of the company's management positions, the data being fed in was statistically biased. Unsurprisingly, the system taught itself that male candidates were better suited for the open positions, including penalizing resumes with the word "women's" in the text. As a result, Amazon subsequently abandoned the project.[28]

A further illustration of this concept is the historical prejudicial treatment of people of color concerning law enforcement. For example, *ProPublica* in 2016 claimed that an AI-based system called COMPAS—Correctional Offender Management Profiling for Alternative Sanctions—to predict recidivism was biased against African Americans. Specifically, their analysis of COMPAS's recommendations from Broward County, Florida, showed African American defendants scoring as "high-risk" at twice the level for White defendants. Equivant, the vendor of COMPAS, pushed back on these claims and argued *ProPublica* used the wrong metrics to assess the system's fairness.[29]

Another source of AI data bias is flawed data sampling. The under-representation of training data is one such cause. For example, the US Department of Commerce found that many facial recognition technologies misidentify people of color more than Whites. And mistaken matches by these systems have led to wrongful arrests. MIT researcher Joy Buolamwini discovered that three facial recognition systems—including one offered by Microsoft—failed to recognize people with darker complexions. For example, across the three systems, she found that they misidentified females with darker skins 35 percent of the time, while they only had an error rate of 1 percent with White males. In 2018, the American Civil Liberties Union (ACLU) claimed that Amazon's Rekognition facial recognition software exhibited racial bias. Amazon then announced a one-year moratorium on the sale of Rekognition to police departments and has subsequently extended the moratorium until further notice.[30]

Or you could have an over-representation in the training data that may skew decisions to a particular result. For example, say law enforcement has historically over-patrolled a specific location. This would likely result in the AI system predicting that crimes were most likely to occur in that area.[31]

AI can also introduce bias by being given inaccurate data. As discussed in the chapter on data brokers, data from data brokers feeds into systems that score consumers and make decisions impacting their ability to obtain credit, whether they receive an interview or job offer, which products are advertised to them, and so on. Many of these systems are increasingly powered by AI. But it has been documented that data from data brokers is highly inaccurate—for example, NATO found that "quantity overshadows quality in the data broker industry" and that "on average only 50–60 percent of data can be considered precise." So "garbage in" will result in "garbage out," but unfortunately, this has real-world implications for people not getting loans, interviews, or apartments.[32]

Finally, the COMPAS example demonstrates the difficulty in determining to what extent an algorithm is truly biased, so transparency is needed. But many companies consider their AI systems proprietary trade secrets, so it is hard for outsiders to access and open these complex black boxes. In fact, given the inherent complexity of these systems, even the programmers with access to the code of the AI systems may not understand how an AI system reached its conclusion. It also gets to a question of "fairness" in AI systems' scoring and predictions, even when factoring out sensitive attributes such as race. However, defining fairness is tricky when applying AI to social problems—for example, decisions regarding sentencing and bail—as fairness is more a human or political decision than a technological or mathematical determination.[33]

Exploiting AI

AI can also be designed for intentional damage or to change behavior. Following are some examples.

Deepfakes

A powerful example of the exploitative use of AI is a technology called "deepfakes"—with that expression coming from the combination of "deep learning" (DL) and "fakes." Deepfakes are created when DL is programmed to replace a person's likeness with another. Deepfakes rely on DL to map out the individual's facial features from various angles from multiple "source" video clips and then insert those features onto a "target" video. For example, the video clips can be of an actor or actress in various movie roles, and the target video could be a home video of a birthday party. This technology has been rapidly improving, making it more challenging to determine whether a video is a deepfake.[34]

While it might be interesting to see deepfakes of an actor like Nicolas Cage magically appearing as Indiana Jones in classic movies like *Raiders of the Lost Ark*, deepfakes can have severe implications and lasting consequences. For example, deepfakes have been created with actresses' faces transposed into pornographic movies—without their consent—thus demeaning the actresses by causing humiliation, distress, and potential impact on their brand. In addition, deepfakes have been used as a variation of revenge porn—defined by WebMD as "digital abuse in which nude or sexually explicit photos or videos are shared without the consent of those pictured." Finally, deepfake pornography can also be used for blackmail.[35]

Deepfakes are also used for political disinformation and misrepresentation. For example, after Russia invaded Ukraine in 2022, a deepfake was created of Ukrainian President Volodymyr Zelenskyy telling his soldiers "to lay down their arms and surrender the fight against Russia." While it is unclear who made this video, the Ukrainian government had previously warned about Russian information warfare that could include the spreading of manipulated videos. Because of the widespread use of social media, deepfakes can go viral and reach millions of users long before the video is determined to be fake.[36]

Dark patterns

A "dark pattern" is software that intentionally misleads and tricks us into doing things we did not intend to do—changing our behavior or acting against our best interest. For example, dark patterns have been built to hide the option to let us block third-party cookie tracking on websites. Or they make it difficult to unsubscribe from services we signed up for by providing confusing language or forcing us through many convoluted steps—a "roach motel" where it is easy to enter but difficult to exit. For example, in Europe, Amazon has been accused of creating a dark pattern that makes it difficult for consumers to cancel their Amazon Prime membership.[37]

AI is increasingly powering dark patterns. Take YouTube's autoplay capability, for example. It automatically plays another video after the video you chose to watch is done. The AI system's learning algorithm selects the next video to keep you engaged. Each autoplayed new video will be even more provocative and attention-getting to keep you watching. This is to the benefit of the platform provider, as the more videos you watch, the more ads they display, resulting in increased monetization. Of course, you might not have started off intending to watch five or six videos. Still, the system led you down that path by changing your behavior, motivating you to keep watching videos. While adults may not be as affected by this example of a dark pattern, these techniques are a concern when they involve vulnerable groups such as children. I will cover this in more detail in chapter 6, on kids' online safety.[38]

AI legislation

Over sixty countries have put forth some form of AI public policies since 2017, thus indicating the growing concerns regarding the potential misuse of AI. Let's review what's happening in Europe and the US.[39]

European legislation

Europe has been the leader in regulating privacy and other technology areas over the last decade, so it is not surprising that they are taking the lead in regulating AI. For example, Europe implemented the General Data Protection Regulation (GDPR) in 2018, representing the gold standard for privacy and data protection laws. Section 22 of GDPR does give Europeans the right not to be solely subject to an automated decision-making process that significantly affects them. This also applies to profiling, which in the context of the GDPR means using personal data to evaluate and score a data subject, as in using an AI-based system to predict their performance at work, health, personal preferences, and so on.[40]

But Europe realizes that more is needed than simply giving its citizens the "right to object" to decision-making and profiling being done by AI. There is a growing concern regarding AI and its potential impact on the fundamental rights protected under the EU Charter of Fundamental Rights. In April 2021, the European Commission proposed the Artificial Intelligence Act (AI Act). The final compromise text of the AI Act was adopted in December 2022, but it will be a few years before it gets approved and implemented. It would ban specific AI (such as the social scoring system that China has implemented) and requires other AI systems to be assessed and audited (for example, AI involving employment or housing). In the fall of 2022, the EU introduced the AI Liability Directive, which gives companies and people the right to sue if harmed by an AI system.

The AI Act and AI Liability Directive would complement the recent passage of the Digital Services Act (DSA), which by 2024 will allow inspections by the European Commission of businesses' AI systems that moderate content and facilitate targeted advertising. So, much as it did with GDPR, the EU clearly wants to continue to "export its values across the world" and extend the "Brussels effect" of setting global tech standards to include the regulation of AI.[41]

US city and state legislation

AI regulation is starting to catch on in a few states and New York City. However, these regulations have been narrowly focused, centering around automated employment decision-making (e.g., recruiting, hiring, promotion, and work scheduling). In addition, these regulations ensure that AI does not present a barrier to equal employment opportunities or prevent diversity in the workforce. This is partly a reaction to the increased use during the Covid-19 pandemic of AI-based employee assessments and algorithmically analyzed video interviews.

An example of state legislation is the Illinois Artificial Intelligence Video Interview Act in 2019, which went into effect in January 2020. The law regulates the use of AI in video interviews for employment decision-making purposes. Another example is New York City local law 1894-A, which passed at the end of 2021, requiring a "bias audit" to be conducted on automated employment decision-making tools, with enforcement starting in April 2023.[42]

US federal legislation

Existing US law can regulate AI systems to some degree when proven to discriminate. For example, under Section 5 of the Federal Trade Commission (FTC) Act, unfair or deceptive practices are prohibited, including the sale or use of racially biased AI systems. The FTC is also responsible for the enforcement of the Fair Credit Reporting Act (FCRA)—along with state attorney generals and the Consumer Financial Protection Bureau (CFPB)—and in specific scenarios, these entities could bring enforcement actions if a business's AI system was found to discriminate in employment, housing, credit, or insurance. In addition, the CFPB is the enforcement agency for the Equal Credit Opportunity Act (ECOA). For example, the ECOA would make it illegal if a business utilized an AI system that discriminated based on "race, color, religion, national origin, sex, marital status, age, or because a person receives public assistance."[43]

That said, US lawmakers realize that more can be done to regulate AI better. Based on the belief that Americans need protection from businesses' use of AI systems that can "exponentially amplify safety risks, unintentional errors, harmful bias, and dangerous design choices," Senator Ron Wyden proposed in February 2022 the Algorithmic Accountability Act (AAA) of 2022. The AAA requires companies to assess the impact of their AI systems for bias and effectiveness when those systems make critical decisions, and then to submit those algorithm impact assessments to the FTC.[44]

Regulating AI also appears in various proposed antitrust bills. For example, the American Innovation and Choice Online Act (AICOA) was introduced in 2022 to tackle anticompetitive actions by giant digital "gatekeepers," as in Big Tech firms. It has a specific section that does not allow these companies to design AI systems that favor their products, as in Google's or Apple's app stores or on Amazon's e-commerce website.[45]

Finally, a comprehensive federal privacy bill—the American Data Privacy and Protection Act (ADPPA)—was proposed in June 2022 and incorporated many elements of the Algorithmic Accountability Act.

Despite solid support by consumer protection advocates, neither the AAA, AICOA, nor ADPPA has moved forward in the 2022 legislative season.

Road map to contain AI

Pandora in the Greek myth brought powerful gifts but also unleashed mighty plagues and evils. So likewise with AI, we need to harness its benefits but keep the potential harms that AI can cause to humans inside the proverbial Pandora's box.

When Dr. Timnit Gebru, founder of the Distributed Artificial Intelligence Research Institute (DAIR), was asked by the *New York Times* about how to confront AI bias, she answered in part with this: "We need to have principles and standards, and governing bodies, and people voting on things and algorithms being checked, something similar to the FDA [Food and Drug Administration]. So, for me, it's not as simple as creating a more diverse data set, and things are fixed."[46]

She's right. First and foremost, we need regulation. AI is a new game, and it needs rules and referees. She suggested we need an FDA equivalent for AI. In effect, both the AAA and ADPPA call for the FTC to act in that role, but instead of drug submissions and approval being handled by the FDA, Big Tech and others should send their AI impact assessments to the FTC for AI systems. These assessments would be for AI systems in high-impact areas such as housing, employment, and credit, helping us better address digital redlining. Thus, these bills foster needed accountability and transparency for consumers.[47]

In the fall of 2022, the Biden administration's Office of Science and Technology Policy (OSTP) even proposed a "Blueprint for an AI Bill of Rights." Protections include the right to "know that an automated system is being used and understand how and why it contributes to outcomes that impact you." This is a great idea and could be incorporated into the rulemaking responsibilities that the FTC would have if the AAA or ADPPA passed. The point is that AI should not be a complete black box to consumers, and consumers should have rights to know and object—much like they should have with collecting and processing their personal data. Furthermore, consumers should have a right of private action if AI-based systems harm them. And websites with a significant amount of AI-generated text and images should have the equivalent of a food nutrition label to let us know what AI-generated content is versus human generated.[48]

We also need AI certifications. For instance, the finance industry has accredited certified public accountants (CPAs) and certified financial audits and statements, so we should have the equivalent for AI. And we need codes of conduct in the use of AI as well as industry standards. For example, the International Organization for Standardization (ISO) publishes quality management standards that organizations can adhere to for cybersecurity, food safety, and so on. Fortunately, a working group with ISO has begun developing a new standard for AI risk management. And in another positive development, the National Institute of Standards and Technology (NIST) released its initial framework for AI risk management in January 2023.[49]

We must remind companies to have more diverse and inclusive design teams building AI. As Olga Russakovsky, assistant professor in the Department of Computer Science at Princeton University, said: "There are a lot of opportunities to diversify this pool [of people building AI systems], and as diversity grows, the AI systems themselves will become less biased."[50]

As regulators and lawmakers delve into antitrust issues concerning Big Tech firms, AI should not be overlooked. To paraphrase Wayne Gretzky, regulators need to skate where the puck is going, not where it has been. AI is where the puck is going in technology. Therefore, acquisitions of AI companies by Big Tech companies should be more closely scrutinized. In addition, the government should consider mandating open intellectual property for AI. For example, this could be modeled on the 1956 federal consent decree with Bell that required Bell to license all its patents royalty-free to other businesses. This led to incredible innovations such as the transistor, the solar cell, and the laser. It is not healthy for our economy to have the future of technology concentrated in a few firms' hands.[51]

Finally, our society and economy need to better prepare themselves for the impact of AI on displacing workers through automation. Yes, we need to prepare our citizens with better education and training for new jobs in an AI world. But we need to be smart about this, as we can't say, "Let's retrain everyone to be software developers," because only some have that skill or interest. Note also that AI is increasingly being built to automate the development of software programs, so even knowing what software skills should be taught in an AI world is critical. As economist Joseph E. Stiglitz pointed out, we have had problems managing smaller-scale changes in tech and globalization that have led to polarization and a weakening of our democracy, and AI's changes are more profound. Thus, we must prepare ourselves for that and ensure that AI is a net positive for society.[52]

Given that Big Tech is leading the charge on AI, ensuring its effects are positive should start with them. AI is incredibly powerful, and Big

Tech is "all-in" with AI, but AI is fraught with risks if bias is introduced or if it's built to exploit. And as I documented, Big Tech has had issues with its use of AI. This means that not only are the depth and breadth of the collection of our sensitive data a threat, but how Big Tech uses AI to process this data and to make automated decisions is also threatening.

Thus, in the same way we need to contain digital surveillance, we must also ensure Big Tech is not opening Pandora's box with AI. I will explore this topic in more depth in three areas over the following three chapters. In chapter 6 on kids' online safety, I will discuss how Big Tech's AI systems can put children at risk. And in chapter 7 on extremism and disinformation, I will discuss how Big Tech's AI-based recommendation systems have been accused of steering users to more controversial and divisive content, thereby increasing societal polarization. But first, I will discuss in the next chapter how Big Tech leverages AI to make its services addictive—an essential element of its strategy to monetize via surveillance-based advertising—through persuasive technology, and the negative consequences of that.

CHAPTER 5

Persuasive Technology

My morning-time ritual became an afternoon ritual to a night ritual, to an all-day ritual where I would habitually check my phone every hour, eagerly waiting for the next notification to come in.

—Social media experience shared by Sam, age eighteen, as part of #MySocialTruth project[1]

In 2011, venture capitalist and former Netscape co-founder Marc Andreessen proclaimed in a *Wall Street Journal* editorial that "software is eating the world." This was his shorthand for his belief that software would eventually take over "large swathes" of the economy, given that more and more industries would eventually be run on software and delivered as online services. And new, "world-beating" Silicon Valley companies would be doing this "creative destruction," enabled by the lower cost and massive scalability of cloud computing and the growth of broadband internet. To Andreessen, the result would be "a global economy that for the first time will be fully digitally wired."[2]

If software is eating the world, data is the fuel that powers software. In the case of Big Tech firms whose primary business model is digital surveillance–based advertising, that fuel is in the form of digital exhaust that each of us emits as we interact with websites, apps, and other internet-based services. This collection and analysis of personal and behavioral data are also indispensable to the significant future bets that Big Tech is making in machine learning (ML), a key component of AI. But like the overuse of natural resources like oil, this pervasive and never-ending data extraction harms our freedoms, society, and democracy.[3]

So, data may be the new oil, but in the global economy that is digitally wired, it turns out that attention is the scarcer resource. In other words, for firms like Meta and Google to be successful in their surveillance-intensive business model, they need to persuade us to spend significant amounts of time on their platforms to generate the necessary data they need to facilitate targeted advertising. Furthermore, they need to incent and motivate us to post photos, videos, likes, shares, comments, and messages on their platforms—in other words, have us generate organic content—to get us to attract and encourage others to also enter their walled gardens. This has the advantage of more users generating even more data to be consumed for Big Tech platforms. It also gives these platforms the economic benefits of a network effect in that their platforms become a sticky and indispensable means of communication and socialization between people, and adoption grows.[4]

But we only have so many waking hours in the day and can generate only so much data and content in that limited time. Economics is defined as the study of how scarce resources are allocated. So, in the case of our attention, the allocation and competition for it are referred to as the "attention economy."[5]

We always have had competition for our attention. Over the last fifty-plus years, traditional media, such as television, radio, newspapers, records, and magazines, have jockeyed for our eyeballs and wallets. But given that we are spending more time on mobile and computer screens—the average American spends eleven hours per day consuming media, with 40 percent of that time spent on a mobile device—and traditional media is now accessed on those same screens due to the digitalization of its content, the competition for that medium is intense. In light of this arms race for our attention, some technology companies even see sleep as a competitor.[6]

So, per Professor Scott Galloway of the New York University Stern School of Business, the formula is quite simple in today's attention economy: "The more attention, the more data, the more money, the more relevant offering(s), the more attention . . . and so on and so on." Galloway calls the most successful players in the attention economy—Meta and Google—"weapons of mass distraction" or "WMDs." It has also led to the rise of adult and teenage "influencers" who use Big Tech's social media platforms to monetize attention through "viral" content designed to increase the number of people following them. But with this constant pressure to grab attention and "go viral" by being provocative to garner likes and shares, we are now in a world where technology is influencing people—especially kids—to create less authentic versions of themselves.[7]

Unfortunately, we are facing several other issues in the same vein. For example, the progressively addictive nature of Big Tech's services—which are increasingly built using AI that analyzes our behavior to discover how to best influence us—has created societal problems such as reduced attention, impaired emotional and social intelligence, social isolation, lack of sleep, and more. So, much like digital surveillance-based advertising has its distinct harms, the persuasive technologies that Big Tech employs to keep us on our screens create their own set of adverse effects. Moreover, screen addiction significantly impacts the most vulnerable in society, our children, which I will cover in the next chapter.[8]

I will use this chapter to describe the techniques by which Big Tech goes about "hijacking our minds" by leveraging persuasive technology, including "dark patterns." I will provide two case studies of this. The first is how Meta's "growth division" worked to maximize "user engagement." The second is the rapid growth of TikTok and how it has quickly become what Galloway calls the "apex predator" in the attention economy.[9]

I will then go into more detail on persuasive technology's threats and negative consequences. I will also review legislative and regulatory proposals to rein in the widespread use of it. Finally, I will provide some recommendations on how to contain and reduce its impact.

Overview of persuasive technology

Persuasive technology is interactive computing systems designed to change people's behavior, opinions, and attitudes. Computers were not initially intended to persuade but instead focused on the collecting and processing of data. However, in the late 1990s, persuasive technology started taking off with the advent of the internet. For example, even in its early days, upon checkout Amazon would recommend other books based on the same topic, past visits, and what had been bought or recommended by what Amazon considered "like" people. Amazon's goal, of course, was and is to get you to buy more products, which may be separate from your initial goal of just buying one book.[10]

The study of persuasive technology was formalized by Stanford Professor BJ Fogg, who wrote a book on the topic in 2002 appropriately titled *Persuasive Technology: Using Computers to Change What We Think and Do.* The book and the course he taught at Stanford influenced many software engineers who eventually joined Silicon Valley tech companies, including Big Tech firms. As early Facebook investor and venture capitalist Roger McNamee noted in his book *Zucked*, an exposé of Meta's damage to society, Fogg's insight was that it was possible to combine both psychology and persuasive technologies into software programs, like those found in slot machines, in ways that were hard for humans to resist.[11]

To be clear, we have had traditional media like print advertising, television commercials, and radio spots for a long time, all of which have been trying to influence and change our behavior. But as Fogg notes, persuasion is most effective when it is interactive, when the influence tactics change as the situation evolves. In the same way a good sales representative will change the sales pitch based on the feedback and reaction from a sales prospect, the ability to adjust based on user-specific data gives the persuasion more power.[12]

Big Tech's use of AI and its machine learning is ideally suited to enable interactive and personalized scoring and predictions on what would best persuade you. This is continuously enhanced using the thousands of engineers that Big Tech has at its disposal, the massive amounts of behavioral data it has collected to create a "digital voodoo doll" of you, and the vast arsenal of computing power that it can leverage to predict what would make you click on an ad or purchase a product. It is hard for us not to be persuaded and manipulated when facing this formidable lineup of deep insight into us, technology that simulates human intelligence, and significant engineering resources backed by companies with trillion-dollar market caps.

Furthermore, today's persuasion technology has other significant advantages over past methods of influencing you via traditional media. For example, unlike a TV ad, these interactive systems are persistent, ubiquitous, and adaptable, with the ability to follow you around online and nag you until you finally click accept or watch a video ad. They can also deliver different modalities to influence you with a combination of text, videos, and messages across multiple devices versus just hearing a radio spot on one radio station.[13]

Tricks of the trade to hijack our minds

So, how does our mind get "hijacked" using persuasive technology? Former Google data ethicist Tristan Harris, who created the Center for Humane Technology to encourage companies to deliver more humane technology that respects users' time, has documented many examples (i.e., tricks). I have summarized some of the top examples in the following paragraphs. Most involve "intermittent variable rewards," which, like slot machines, deliver random rewards at irregular intervals to encourage the user to continue, leading to addictive behavior. While most of these persuasive technologies apply to their social media offerings, all the Big Tech vendors use some of these tricks to have users return to their platforms.[14]

The first example is the "fear of missing something important." Because of their network effects, Big Tech's platforms have become a critical channel for socialization and communication with people you care about. Therefore, they play on your fears that you might miss something vital with the essential people in your life, so you are sucked into constantly using their products.[15]

Big Tech's use of push notifications is a compelling case study of the fear of missing something important. Notifications in the form of vibrations, red dots, and buzzing mimic signs of danger or importance, so you are explicitly drawn to check the notification and access the app in case you are missing something important. As the Center for Humane Technology states: "A designer intentionally made the decision to put those dots there, put a number in it, and make it red instead of, say, green, because we instinctively respond with urgency to red." And if the notifications build up and are not attended to, we feel compelled to check the app. Note that many Big Tech firms turn notifications on by default, no matter how trivial the notification is, which is a further brain hack to make what might be trivial seem urgent.[16]

Another example is "social approval," which is often tied to "social reciprocity." Or, in layperson's terms: we want to belong and to be approved of. According to Harris, getting tagged in photos on Meta's Facebook or Instagram plays to our need for social approval. Social media platforms feed on this desire by encouraging and assisting you in finding followers and inviting your friends to their platform, with the subliminal correlation that having more followers and friends on their platforms will equal more chances for social approval. And when you get an invitation to connect, for example, on Microsoft's LinkedIn, you feel a bit guilty for not accepting, so odds are you accept as an act of social reciprocity. But the platform suggested the connection request in many cases, so they are trying to nudge you to create a social graph on their behalf, not yours.[17]

"Infinite feeds," a bottomless soup bowl that never stops refilling itself, is another persuasive technology designed to keep you on Big Tech's platforms. For example, consider the Facebook News Feed—the service's central feature that provides a personalized and constantly updated running tab of posts and photos from friends as well as news stories—which is purposely designed to auto-refill as you scroll down. The result is there is never a reason to stop scrolling, as it continues to provide new content, encouraging people to keep consuming the soup even if they are no longer hungry.[18]

One final example of persuasive technology is dark patterns. As previously discussed, a dark pattern intentionally misleads you into doing things you did not intend to do or that are against your best interest. For example, if you refuse to accept cookies on a given website, the website will take you to a menu of settings where you must manually disable the different types of third-party cookies. This means the websites purposely make it time-consuming to opt out of tracking, so most people will throw up their hands and accept tracking. Or, in the case of Meta's Instagram, it will show users a pop-up window asking if they want Instagram to "use your app and website activity" to "provide a better ads experience." Users are given two choices: a dark button where one can choose to "make ads less personalized" or a bright blue button that will "make ads more personalized." What they don't tell users is that "activity" is "online tracking," and "personalized" is "targeted advertising."[19]

So, as you can see, persuasive technology favors designs that leverage human vulnerability—all in the name of changing your behavior to meet their goals, not yours.

Case study: Meta and persuasive technology

Meta has historically deployed all the above design tricks to "maximize engagement." For example, they experimented with the colors of buttons and the frequency of notifications, all aiming to get users to return to their platform. But once Meta saw the power of AI and machine learning, they quickly figured out that they could use it to predict who would click on an ad and determine who would Like or Share a given post. This "feedback loop" would let Meta give more prominence to specific posts and personalize who sees what posts on Facebook based on a user's evolving preferences. So, AI has become their latest weapon to keep users returning and spending more time on the platform.[20]

The design decisions on how Meta uses AI to increase "user engagement" became evident in late 2021 when the "Facebook whistleblower" leaked internal Meta documents—dubbed the "Facebook Files"—to the *Wall Street Journal*. Frances Haugen, a former Meta product manager, emerged as the whistleblower. Through these documents and her congressional testimony, she alleged that Meta had "willfully chosen not to fix the problems on its platforms." Chief among the issues she identified was Meta's platform design decisions primarily focused on the "growth" of users and time spent on its platform to the exclusion of the health and safety of its users.[21]

The documents revealed that the Facebook service's comments, likes, and reshares declined throughout 2017. As a result, there was a fear inside Meta that users would stop using the Facebook service altogether. Based on this concern, as well as the desire to improve "meaningful social interactions" between family and friends, Meta in 2018 changed the algorithms behind its News Feeds to "encourage people to interact more with friends and family," with the belief that this would strengthen the bonds between people and improve well-being. And, of course, by doing so, the decline in engagement would stop. Part of that change to the algorithm was to provide a heavier weight to reshared material so that content would bubble up higher in the News Feed.[22]

The algorithm change did improve user engagement, but as internal staffers noted, instead of improving well-being, the weighting of reshared material "made the angry voices louder." For example, one Meta researcher pointed out in an internal memo: "Misinformation, toxicity, and violent content are inordinately prevalent among reshares." This is because this type of content got users riled up, and then the algorithms would see this type of content was getting engagement and amplify it in the News Feed, leading to even more engagement.[23]

Haugen points out that Meta's primary focus for its updated Facebook News Feed algorithm was not to evaluate what was being engaged with but to measure and analyze the engagement metrics. Haugen also revealed that Meta is dismal in determining "good" versus "bad" content in the English language and that the AI systems it created to evaluate content were even worse in other languages.[24]

The Facebook Files also revealed that because website publishers and political parties get a lot of web traffic from their Facebook postings, they noticed this shift in Meta's Facebook algorithms in 2018. Therefore, they began to reorient their content on the Facebook service to sensationalism and outrage, which produced high levels of engagement in the forms of comments and reshares, which elevated their content higher in the Facebook News Feed. So, it became an arms race on who could provide the most attention-getting and provocative posts. Internal documents even showed that some political parties reported back to Meta that they were shifting policy positions so it would resonate better on Facebook. They even expressed concern about the long-term effect on democracy in this race to the bottom.[25]

Reporting further revealed that numerous internal Meta studies confirmed that the changes to the News Feed algorithms did maximize engagement but increased polarization. These studies also found a correlation in that reducing the promotion of polarizing content would impact engagement. So Meta was aware of the downside of the changes it had made.[26]

Haugen claimed in her congressional testimony that in the end, Meta "focused on scale over safety" and purposely "chooses profits over safety." That argument has some validity in that the incentives Meta offered its product team were primarily tied to the number of "meaningful social interactions" their products generated versus other metrics such as user safety or well-being. The leaked documents also revealed that Meta CEO Mark Zuckerberg resisted some of the proposed fixes to curb the tendency for its AI system to reward outrage and lies. He purportedly was concerned that those changes would reduce user engagement and the company's growth.[27]

Case study: TikTok and persuasive technology

The newest member of the Big Tech club will likely be TikTok. TikTok is a video-based social media and entertainment platform owned by ByteDance, a China-based company that, as of mid-2022, was the most valuable start-up in the world with a valuation of $360 billion. This valuation was larger than the combined values of Netflix, Snap, Twitter, PayPal, and Uber. TikTok is projected to grow revenue from $4 billion in 2021 to $12 billion in 2022. It has 1.6 billion monthly active users—more than Twitter, Snapchat, and Microsoft's LinkedIn combined. TikTok reached one billion users three years earlier than it took Meta to hit that same number.[28]

TikTok's formula to capture attention is short and addictive videos. As Galloway noted, TikTok has more user engagement than Meta's Facebook and Instagram services combined, making it "one of the most powerful WMDs in the world." So, it is unsurprising that TikTok is the world's most visited website and most downloaded app as of 2022. Furthermore, the average user utilizes TikTok eight times per day, and children with TikTok accounts spend an estimated seventy-five minutes per day on it, thus making it the world's most popular social media platform for that demographic. The app has done so by fusing persuasive technology and AI to new levels.[29]

TikTok plays its videos in autoplay, an endless scroll. TikTok serves you the next video it picks, forcing you to either watch or skip ahead. In addition, TikTok is in complete control of what you see, including not displaying the progress or duration of a video you are watching, thus further hooking you with its bottomless bowl of soup.[30]

The average TikTok session lasts eleven minutes, and the average video length is approximately twenty-five seconds, meaning that an average session will have about twenty-six videos. Within that session, TikTok captures dozens of "microsignals" from you per video, including, per Galloway, "whether you scrolled past a video, paused it, re-watched it, liked it, commented on it, shared it, and followed the creator, plus how long you watched before moving on." So, for each session, hundreds of different data points are mined and extracted from you, all of which are immediately fed into TikTok's AI systems, helping them optimize and personalize future videos for you, ultimately resulting in captivating you as long as possible.[31]

Over 50 percent of users create their own videos on TikTok. That's over eight hundred million people creating content, which, per Galloway, is over one thousand times the number of people employed by the entire film and television industry. However, TikTok only pays $200 million to all its top creators combined, a minimal amount compared to the $17 billion that Netflix spends for original content. Top

TikTok creators or "influencers" make most of their income via product or brand endorsements.[32]

When guided on how to create and post videos, content creators are told they have three seconds to capture viewers' attention before viewers move on to the following video. If a video is skipped over, then TikTok's AI system will not promote or amplify the video. Therefore, the focus becomes on creating content that, per one privacy expert who spent thirty days analyzing TikTok, is "irreverent, socially awkward, scary, performing admirable abilities, showing exposed bodies, and so on." In addition, TikTok provides filters, music, and other effects to further liven up videos. Thus, the pressure on content providers becomes about attention-getting and being provocative, feeding TikTok's monetization and engagement wheel.[33]

Finally, and as mentioned in chapter 3 on data breaches, politicians in multiple countries are concerned that the Chinese government may subtly influence TikTok's AI systems to influence opinions or even directly access the behavioral data of over one billion people. The Chinese government does have the authority to access the data of Chinese-based companies, and it was reported in mid-2022 that tech personnel at ByteDance's corporate headquarters do have full privileges to access TikTok's user data. US politicians in both political parties have referred to TikTok as a trojan horse, given its potential for both nation-state influence and espionage, and at least fourteen states in 2022 banned the use of the application on state-owned devices. Furthermore, at the end of the 2022 legislative session, Congress passed a ban on using TikTok on devices owned by the federal government, and legislators have proposed bills that would outright ban TikTok in the US.[34]

Threats and consequences of persuasive technology

Unfortunately, Big Tech's use of AI systems designed to maximize engagement can lead to our news feeds filling up with what the Center for Humane Technology refers to as "metaphorical car crashes." These same systems can also keep us in a bubble, telling us what we want to hear, leading to confirmation bias. This can weaken our democracy as we become angrier and more polarized in our bubbles.[35]

Persuasive techniques such as constant notifications also impact our ability to prioritize what is essential and contribute to us having to multitask all the time. It also appears that constant notifications and prolonged use of technology shorten our attention spans. A study published by Microsoft in 2015 showed people in 2000 could focus on a task for twelve seconds, but that figure had dropped to eight seconds by 2013. That reduction was attributed to the increased use of devices and more content and apps that fight for our attention.[36]

When our attention span becomes degraded, we lose our ability to empathize. So, when we hear disheartening news that requires reflection, we have been conditioned to swipe or scroll to move on to something else.

The persuasive technology unleashed in the attention economy encourages seeking without fulfillment as well as constant social comparison. It undermines relationships by having us focus on short communications and "likes" versus having meaningful dialogue. And it motivates us to seek attention in this world versus seeking our authentic selves.[37]

Scientists have studied the effects of extensive screen time and found additional potentially harmful results, including disrupted sleep, social isolation, impaired emotional and social intelligence, and impaired brain development. Given that most of these effects impact children and teens more acutely, I will cover them in more detail in the next chapter.[38]

Persuasive technology legislation

European legislation

Europe continues to set the standards for the regulation of Big Tech. As is the case with AI and privacy, the area of persuasive technology is no different. In 2022, the EU passed the Digital Services Act (DSA) and the

Digital Market Act (DMA), with enforcement happening by 2024. The DSA provides consumer protections related to online platforms, while the DMA focuses primarily on ensuring fair competition involving the giant "gatekeepers" of the internet (e.g., the Big Tech firms).[39]

One of the regulations in the DSA requires the European Commission to issue guidelines regarding three specific use cases of dark patterns. The first is "asymmetric choice," which is a trick that gives prominence to a specific choice when asking for a decision (e.g., the Instagram example where the choice to enable tracking was in a brighter color button and had more positive language). The second is "nagging," where a user is repeatedly asked to make a choice even after a choice was made (e.g., being nudged to consent to accept cookies that will do online tracking). And the third is "hard to unsubscribe," where the process of terminating an online service is significantly more difficult than subscribing to it (e.g., in the case of Amazon being sued in Norway due to the difficulty users have in terminating their Amazon Prime subscription).[40]

In addressing the broader issue of persuasive technology, the DSA reflects the knowledge that many persuasive technologies are more subtle than showing up as a deceptive pop-up choice in a user interface. Instead, increasingly persuasive technology is embedded in AI systems that are fed behavioral data. So, the DSA also requires online platforms to perform risk assessments of AI systems that may result in behavioral harm—such as screen addiction—and allows the European Commission to conduct inspections of these AI systems.[41]

The DMA also seeks to address dark patterns by defining them as a form of decisional interference. Thus, large online "gatekeepers" must present choices to users in a neutral way and must not "subvert or impair user autonomy, decision-making, or choice." The eventual interpretation of this could be pretty interesting, as persuasive techniques such as infinite feed (i.e., the "bottomless soup bowl" you get with the Facebook News Feed or autoplay of videos that you get with TikTok or YouTube) may be considered impairing user autonomy. The DMA also explicitly bars "gatekeepers" from utilizing the "hard to unsubscribe" dark pattern.[42]

US legislation

In US state laws, the California Privacy Rights Act (CPRA) and the Colorado Privacy Act (CPA) prohibit using dark patterns when collecting consumer consent to collect and process personal information.

At the US federal level, the Federal Trade Commission (FTC) issued a new enforcement policy in October 2021 stating that the FTC would start cracking down on companies that utilize dark patterns that trap consumers into subscription services. For example, it was reported in 2022 that the FTC was continuing its investigation into Amazon's allegedly deceptive dark patterns that make it difficult for consumers to cancel their Prime membership services. And in December 2022, Epic Games, the developer of the Fortnite video game, reached a settlement with the FTC whereby Epic would pay out $245 million in consumer refunds to address its alleged use of dark patterns that tricked consumers into making unintended purchases.[43]

In terms of federal legislation, in 2019 Senators Mark Warren and Deb Fischer introduced the Deceptive Experiences To Online Users Reduction (DETOUR) Act. The goal of the proposed bill is to prohibit large online platforms with over one hundred million monthly active users from using dark patterns to trick users into handing over personal data. It refers to dark patterns as user interfaces that "intentionally impair user autonomy, decision-making, or choice." The DETOUR Act would also prohibit user design intended "to create compulsive usage among children under the age of 13 years old." Also in 2019, Senator Josh Hawley introduced the Social Media Addiction Reduction Technology (SMART) Act that would ban "addictive" persuasive technology such as autoplay and infinite feeds. In addition, the bill would require that products "be designed with natural stopping points."[44]

Finally, the proposed American Data Privacy and Protection Act (ADPPA) introduced in 2022 would prohibit obtaining consent for collecting and processing personal data by deploying user interfaces that are misleading or manipulative. Unfortunately, the DETOUR Act, SMART Act, and ADPPA have yet to get more consideration.

Road map to contain persuasive technology

We must prohibit dark patterns via legislation or enhanced FTC enforcement. That includes dark patterns acting as "roach motels" to make canceling subscriptions difficult or that subvert you from not wanting to be tracked across mobile apps and websites. Legislation could also prohibit online services from behavioral or psychological experiments without users' informed consent.

Going even further through the checklist of persuasive technologies that cause screen addiction, we need to address tricks such as infinite feeds and autoplay. For children, that would include designing less addictive technology with natural stopping points and requiring online services to have tools that monitor and cap the time spent on the service.

Furthermore, the addictive capabilities of online services also need to be addressed; the underlying AI systems that are being fed behavioral data serve us up content that keeps us on our phones and computers. For example, we can reduce the personal data that Big Tech collects, making it less likely for their AI systems to find our vulnerabilities to maximize our engagement with their services. In other words, the less data they have on us, the less likely these companies can build a digital voodoo doll of every one of us that they can use to poke us to change our opinion and behavior, including spending more time on their platforms. So having a comprehensive privacy law that provides more regulation over the collection and processing of our data by both Big Tech and data brokers would significantly help fight against screen addiction.

Much like the EU's Digital Services Act will require online platforms to perform risk assessments of AI systems that may result in behavioral harm, such as screen addiction, we need an "FDA" for AI in the US. This entity would allow for auditing high-risk AI systems that cause harm, which, for example, would likely include AI systems that are highly addictive or amplify content that fosters extremism and polarization.

Finally, while many Big Tech players utilize persuasive technology to hook us on their platforms, the fact that their platforms are critical channels of communication with people we care about also manipulates us into using their services for long periods each day for their gain. Big Tech knows that, and they have made it difficult for us to switch to other products because once you leave their platform, you can't use different products to socialize and communicate with your friends and families who are still inside their walled gardens. This lack of interoperability and high cost to switch, as well as recommendations to address this, will be explored in chapter 8 on competition. But suffice it to say that laws requiring gatekeepers to be interoperable with other services would also help address us being forced to be in their walled gardens for extended periods.[45]

In summary, Big Tech purposely hijacks our minds by leveraging AI-powered persuasive technologies, including dark patterns, so their "growth teams" can get users to "maximize engagement" with their platforms as they compete for our attention. But there are significant costs associated with this attention economy, including wasted time, reduced attention spans, and the creation of less authentic versions of ourselves as we are motivated by the platforms to seek attention for ourselves. In the next chapter, I will discuss how Big Tech's use of AI impacts kids and their online safety.

CHAPTER 6

Kids' Online Safety

The thought process that went into building these applications,
Facebook being the first of them . . . was all about: "How do we
consume as much of your time and conscious attention as possible?"
God only knows what it's doing to our children's brains.

—Sean Parker, co-founder of Facebook[1]

In the fall of 2021, reporters with the *Wall Street Journal* decided to experiment and see what it would be like to experience TikTok as children aged thirteen to fifteen. To do this, they created a few dozen automated accounts that simulated teen users and programmed them to browse TikTok's For You feed, which is TikTok's feed of never-ending short videos. Unfortunately, the reporters soon discovered that TikTok's underlying AI systems drove the minors' accounts into "rabbit holes" of "endless spools of adult content." For example, one account registered as a thirteen-year-old saw 569 videos about drug use. Collectively the accounts saw over one hundred videos recommending pornography sites, plus other videos encouraging drinking and eating disorders.[2]

Social media should not create rabbit holes for us to fall in, let alone ones as explicitly dangerous as these. While adults may be able to navigate around or climb out of these rabbit holes, it is much harder for kids, primarily because our brains typically don't fully mature until we are in our mid-twenties. Moreover, kids find it even more challenging to resist staying online because they lack critical cognitive capabilities. This is especially the case when kids face a nonstop selection of extreme and inappropriate videos that are continuously being algorithmically selected to maximize engagement.[3]

Studies have also shown that children have difficulty determining what's an ad and what's not. They also don't fully understand what they should and should not share online. The teen years are when kids undergo neurological changes that promote the heightened desire for social attention and feedback, which we already know are vulnerabilities that online businesses can and do exploit.[4]

This exploitation of kids' developmental vulnerabilities is an increasing concern, especially given kids' growing use of online services and mobile devices as we come out of the Covid-19 pandemic. An estimated one in three internet users is a child. Researchers have also estimated that children under the age of eight now consume two and a half hours of digital media per day, while teens spend, on average, over seven hours per day of screen time that is non–school related. In addition, over two-thirds of kids aged five to eight have their own tablet, and 94 percent of households with children between eight and eighteen have access to a smartphone. And social media usage by kids is also extensive. For example, with US teens aged thirteen to seventeen, as of mid-2022, over 95 percent use Google's YouTube, 67 percent use TikTok, 62 percent use Meta's Instagram, and 59 percent use Snapchat.[5]

Kids' unique vulnerabilities, combined with their widespread use of technology and social media, must be considered as we look at the increasing mental health issues associated with kids. For example, studies have shown that depression rates among teenagers have doubled between 2009 and 2019, and suicide is now the second leading cause of death among US youth. Tragically, the suicide rate among young people aged ten to twenty-four in the US has increased by 57 percent between 2007 and 2018. In addition, emergency room visits for teen girls aged twelve to seventeen years old that involve eating disorders have doubled from 2019 to 2022.[6]

Researchers have pointed out that the increase in youth mental health issues is attributable to many factors. Still, the growing use of social media and its corresponding exposure to harmful content, unhealthy social comparisons, and cyberbullying have exacerbated the above trends. For example, as revealed in the Facebook Files, Meta's internal research shows how toxic Instagram could be for teen girls. Internal Meta presentations documented how "aspects of Instagram exacerbate each other to create a perfect storm" that sends struggling kids into a "downward spiral" in which "mental health outcomes . . . can be severe." And even the American Psychological Association noted that while "Instagram, YouTube, TikTok, and Snapchat have provided crucial opportunities for interaction . . . they've also been increasingly linked to mental health problems, including anxiety, depressive symptoms, and body image concerns."[7]

In this chapter, I will explore in more detail the impact of Big Tech on children. First, I will discuss the unique online safety issues that kids face, such as the effect of behavioral advertising on kids, the exposure to harmful or age-inappropriate content, and the promotion of unhealthy social comparisons. I will also cover the toll addictive technologies have on kids, the enablement of unsolicited contact from adults, and cyberbullying. I will then delve into what is happening regarding regulations and laws on these issues and provide recommendations.

Behavioral advertising and kids

As previously discussed, we are constantly surveilled when we are online. This mining and extraction of our data exhaust enable companies like Google and Meta to offer their customers—advertisers—detailed information about our actual or inferred behavior, personal traits, demographics, and interests. This lets advertisers deliver "highly relevant" ads that are "personalized." The targeting and placement of those ads are optimized using Big Tech's AI-based advertising platforms. This form of advertising is referred to as either behavioral or surveillance advertising.

There are many problems associated with behavioral advertising and kids. The first is whether personal and behavioral data—which can be traced back to an individual by correlating multiple data points—should be mined and extracted from children. Third parties would be arrested as stalkers if that happened in the physical world. One researcher claims that global advertising firms hold the equivalent of seventy-two million pieces of data on the average child by the time the minor is thirteen years old, showing the depth and breadth of surveillance occurring with children.[8]

To give you a deeper feel for the pervasiveness of online spying on children, in 2022, the *Washington Post* reported on a study that showed that more than two-thirds of the one thousand most popular Apple iPhone apps that are likely to be used by kids would collect and send behavioral data to third parties. On Google Android, that number was 79 percent. Other studies have shown that 90 percent of educational apps sent data back to ad tech firms, and two-thirds of the apps played by a sample group of 124 preschool-aged kids also collected and shared behavioral data. A 1998 US federal law—the Children's Online Privacy Protection Act (COPPA)—bans collecting data from children under thirteen without parental consent. But the law calls for "actual knowledge" that users are children. The *Washington Post* noted that Big Tech and app vendors use this as a loophole despite marketing features targeting children.[9]

Second, targeted and personalized advertising is also very concerning because kids have fewer developmental tools to resist the marketing messages and are likely to accept ads as being truthful, unbiased, and accurate. For example, research estimates that 75 percent of eight- to eleven-year-olds cannot distinguish and tell the difference between ads and other online content. Only 25 percent of eight- to fifteen-year-olds can identify the top results from a Google search as paid advertisements, despite the ads being clearly labeled as such. And given that kids have always been vulnerable to the power of advertising and don't fully understand the purposes behind advertising, this "super-charged" form of advertising that targets them personally increases the risks associated with this vulnerability, including making them more susceptible to manipulation.[10]

Third, the volume of online advertising is staggering compared to what they have traditionally seen on other mediums such as TV. For example, one analysis claims that one out of every three posts seen by children on Meta's Instagram is an advertisement. Another study claims that teenagers will see an ad every ten seconds in their social media feeds, which is the equivalent of 420 advertisements per hour. Considering that teens, on average, are online for over seven hours per day, that equates to over two thousand ads per day, which is twenty times the volume of ads they see on TV. In the US, the Children's Television Act limits the amount of advertising broadcast during television programs aimed at children. Still, there is no equivalent for the online world; thus, children can face a firehose of ads.[11]

Studies have shown the negative impact of the volume of online advertising children see. For example, there has been a correlation between seeing more ads and kids wanting more products and services and thus becoming more materialistic. Other studies have shown that more materialistic kids can have "lower well-being, perform worse academically, be less generous toward others, and care less about the environment."[12]

Fourth, just like content shown to kids while online, there is little to no regulation on the ads displayed in kid-centric mobile apps and websites. The United Nations issued a report in 2020 that children are "being bombarded" with ads promoting harmful products ranging from fast food to alcohol to tobacco. The report noted that this exposure to advertising promoting sugary beverages and junk food could lead to purchasing unhealthy foods, being overweight, and obesity.[13]

Finally, widespread behavioral advertising can also open kids to abuse and exploitation. For example, in 2017, the *Australian* reported that Meta told advertisers in Australia it could identify teenagers feeling "insecure" and "worthless." The company told advertisers that it could infer this by real-time monitoring of posts by young people. It could also further infer when someone is "stressed," "defeated," "overwhelmed," "anxious," "nervous," "stupid," "silly," "useless," and a "failure." After the report was published, Meta subsequently apologized for this research. Still, it shows that behavioral data gathered on young people can be utilized in ways that may not have their well-being in mind.[14]

Algorithmic amplification of harmful content

I previously discussed how TikTok could push children to age-inappropriate content. Because it is difficult for kids to critically assess what they are seeing and experiencing, this can influence and even normalize how they perceive drugs, pornography, and alcohol. But as with other social media platforms like Meta's Instagram or Google's YouTube, children are also pushed to posts that emphasize unrealistic body images or highlight eating disorders.[15]

For example, the Facebook Files revealed that Meta was aware that its content-ranking algorithm on its Instagram platform—designed to maximize engagement—was worsening teenage girls' mental health. One internal Meta research presentation said that "thirty-two percent of teen girls said that when they felt bad about their bodies, Instagram made them feel worse." Another presentation stated, "We make body image issues worse for one in three teen girls." And Frances Haugen, the Facebook whistleblower, testified to the US Senate that Meta's engagement-based AI systems were causing "teenagers to be exposed to more anorexia content."[16]

This linkage between exposure to harmful or age-inappropriate content and mental health is not confined to teenage girls. For example, Meta's internal research found that 14 percent of teen boys in the US said Meta's Instagram made them feel worse about themselves. Unfortunately, it was difficult for some Instagram researchers to get fellow Meta colleagues to hear the significance of their findings, as they were "standing directly between people and their bonuses." This was because employees' bonuses were focused on maximizing engagement over other factors such as safety and well-being.[17]

Promotion of unhealthy social comparisons

Social media platforms run by Big Tech firms and others can also lead to what is known as "social comparison." This is when, per the Facebook Files exposé published by the *Wall Street Journal*, "people assess their own value in relation to the attractiveness, wealth, and success of others." For children, this can have a significant negative impact on their mental health. The Facebook Files revealed that Meta was aware that "social comparison is worse on Instagram" because it focuses on the body and lifestyle, while other social platforms like Snapchat "focus on the face" and TikTok is more about making viral videos.[18]

Meta's internal research documented examples of social comparison, including "the tendency to share only the best moments" and the "pressure to look perfect." When combined with algorithmic amplification of harmful content and addictive technology, it was found that Instagram could "send teens spiraling toward eating disorders" and cause them to have an "unhealthy sense of their own bodies." The research concluded that these "aspects of Instagram exacerbate each other to create a perfect storm," leading to depression and mental health challenges. As noted by Stanford Professor Clifford Nass, considering that services such as Instagram present an "unrealistic world view" comprised of "happy curated postings," it is not surprising kids may come to the erroneous conclusion that "everyone is happy, except me."[19]

Other features of social media platforms that lead to social comparison among children include the platforms promoting follower counts or like or share buttons that can quantify popularity, further exacerbating the potential damage to mental health.

Screen addiction and kids

I previously covered many persuasive technologies Big Tech uses to keep users on its platforms. But given children lack key cognitive capabilities, they are more easily manipulated by these tricks to keep their attention and engagement. For example, autoplay keeps kids using the services, while nudges and notifications motivate children to check the platforms by leveraging their fear of missing out (FOMO). In addition, some online services don't offer "save buttons," so kids are forced to stay online to complete a task. Technology companies will also use another persuasive technology— dark patterns—to get kids to stay on the platform longer or provide additional data. For example, they will sneakily prompt kids to give the contact information of their friends as the "app is more fun if you connect with friends." Or they will have a "No" button labeled "No, I hate fun."[20]

Some platforms play on kids' vulnerability to social obligations by encouraging "streaks." This is when two users send messages, photos, or videos to each other daily, and the number of consecutive days this occurs is tracked and displayed by the platform. Thus "streak management" becomes a means to pressure kids to return to the platforms daily to maintain the streaks. Breaking a streak can be viewed as an "indictment" of a friendship and can lead to social awkwardness with peers. And, of course, countless hours are burned to keep streaks alive.[21]

Independent researchers have shown that there is an addiction problem among young people. For example, Common Sense Media found that one in three US kids between twelve and eighteen struggled to cut down on their use of mobile devices, and half said they believed they were "addicted to their mobile devices." In the UK, the nonprofit Internet Matters documented that over one-third of school-aged children felt "worried that they are addicted to the internet."[22]

The kids know they are addicted. The Facebook Files revealed that teens told Instagram researchers that they "don't like the amount of time they spend on the app but feel like they have to be present." Meta researchers also documented how teens "often feel 'addicted' and know that what they're seeing is bad for their mental health but feel unable to stop themselves."[23]

This addiction leads to stress and arguments with parents. Common Sense Media found that 70 percent of US teens fight with their parents about mobile devices, and 32 percent do it daily. In the UK, 40 percent of parents with kids between the age of twelve and fifteen "struggle to control their child's 'screen time.'"[24]

Excessive use of social media has also been linked to mental health issues. For example, one study found that teens who use social media over five hours a day are twice as likely to be depressed as teens who do not.[25]

Lack of sleep is one of the effects of screen addiction and can lead to mental health issues. In the UK, a study showed that the nighttime use of mobile devices doubles the risk of poor sleep among children. A study in the US has shown that teens who use a lot of social media get one hour less sleep a night, which is concerning in light that sleep deprivation is correlated to depression among teens. Between 2011 and 2016, sleep deprivation increased by 17 percent among US teenagers—just as social media usage and depression significantly grew among teens.[26]

Parents in the US are taking matters into their own hands and have filed over seventy lawsuits claiming that Meta, Google, TikTok, and Snap are "hooking" their kids. According to *Bloomberg*, these lawsuits involve claims from children and young adults "who say they've suffered anxiety, depression, eating disorders, and sleeplessness as a result of their addiction to social media." And in seven of the cases, the lawsuits are from parents of children who died by suicide.[27]

Even a US school district is suing Big Tech firms over the mental health crisis among youth. The public school district of Seattle sued TikTok, Meta, Google, and Snap in January 2023, alleging that these companies have "successfully exploited the vulnerable brains of youth, hooking tens of millions of students across the country into positive feed-back loops of excessive use and abuse" of their platforms. This school district claims that this has resulted in the school district having to hire additional mental health professionals.[28]

The tech firms are defending themselves in these lawsuits by citing Section 230 of the Communications Decency Act (CDA), arguing this statute gives them immunity from claims regarding harmful content being posted on their platforms. But these lawsuits focus on claims of product liability, arguing that the AI systems used to maximize engagement caused the harm, not the content. Whether these tech firms' AI systems can be considered a "defective product" will play out in the courts in the coming years. But as one parent, whose fourteen-year-old daughter killed herself and is now suing TikTok, said of social media companies: "[Their goal] is to get as much time from these kids on their products, but there's no safeguards." And she added, "They need to change what they're feeding these children— change the algorithm, so it doesn't take them into these dark places."[29]

While Section 230 of the CDA may protect tech companies in the US, Big Tech will likely not be protected overseas. For example, in October 2022, a London coroner found that social media posts contributed to the death of fourteen-year-old Molly Russell. The coroner said that the online material Molly viewed on Instagram and Pinterest "was not safe" and "should not have been available for a child to see."[30]

Predation and cyberbullying

Online services strive to have a network effect where their platform gains more value as more people use it. As such, these services are motivated to nudge users to invite and connect with other users with whom they may share common interests or connections. This lets unknown adults "friend with" or "connect" with kids. UK-based 5Rights Foundation, an advocacy group founded by Baroness Beeban Kidron, found in 2020 that "75 percent of the top 12 most popular social media platforms used AI to recommend children's profiles to strangers."[31]

In addition, many online services either set children's profiles public by default or nudge them to make their profiles public versus private. Again, it is in these services' interests to get as many users as possible to sign up and use their platforms, and having public profiles facilitates a social graph being built via additional sign-ups and connections. But children having public profiles can facilitate unwanted contact with strangers, including adults.[32]

Children don't understand the consequences of oversharing on social media platforms. They also don't realize that there is not necessarily an "erase" button and that their postings can remain on the internet. Considering that many online services nudge children to share, this could lead to loss of privacy and intimate details being exposed to adults or weaponized by cyberbullies.[33]

Furthermore, many online services and apps nudge and encourage kids to turn on location tracking so that their friends and connections can know where they are. But this also makes it easier for strangers to track and contact children.[34]

When you combine these design choices, you can see why 25 percent of nine- to seventeen-year-olds have reported "online sexually explicit interaction" with people they believed to be adults. Research has also shown how prevalent online predation has become. For example, the 5Rights Foundation conducted research in 2021 that utilized avatars that simulated children with new accounts on Facebook, Instagram, and TikTok. Within hours these accounts were targeted with messages from adults asking to connect and offering pornography.[35]

Oversharing and connecting with strangers can also lead to "sextortion," in which someone threatens to share intimate images that may have been shared or hacked. A US study found that one in twenty teens has been the victim of this.[36]

Finally, these design choices, such as the lack of an erase button, oversharing, how sensational content gets amplified, the ability to comment on videos featuring minors, and so on, have also helped exacerbate online harassment and cyberbullying. In addition, most postings on social media can be permanent and may become viral among classmates, thus increasing exposure. Sadly, Pew Research has found that 60 percent of US teens have experienced cyberbullying, while 50 percent of girls aged eleven to eighteen in the UK have experienced online abuse. Furthermore, research has shown that victims of cyberbullying are "twice as likely to self-harm as their peers." Unfortunately, there can be no respite from cyberbullying because it follows children home, given it is on the internet and the internet does not sleep.[37]

Legislation

There has been increased activity in Europe and the US to protect kids online. As has been the case with privacy, regulation of AI, and cracking down on abuses of persuasive technology, Europe is taking the lead. Still, California has also taken a significant step forward while US federal law lags.

European legislation

The regulatory environment around protecting children on the internet has increasingly centered around the concept of "age-appropriate design." Pioneered by the 5Rights Foundation, its regulatory approach to kids' online safety "is to consider the privacy and protection of children in the design of any digital product or service that children are likely to access." Thus, tech companies and Big Tech, in particular, are being asked to consider the impact and potential harms of the design of their products on children.[38]

The 5Rights Foundation championed the UK's Age Appropriate Design Code (AADC). It is not a new law per se but regulations and guidance from the UK's data protection authority—the Information Commissioner's Office (ICO)—that went into effect in 2020. It provides a set of fifteen standards that act as a set of "technology-neutral design principles and practical privacy features" aimed at protecting kids under eighteen in the digital world. The achievements by the UK's AADC have been impressive, and a wide range of online services have made hundreds of changes, including these by Big Tech firms:[39]

- Google's YouTube turns off autoplay for under-eighteens and has turned on by default break and bedtime reminders.
- The Google Play Store prevents under-eighteens from being able to view and download apps rated as adult-only.
- Google lets anyone under eighteen request their images be removed from Google's image search.
- TikTok and Meta's Instagram have disabled direct messaging between kids and adults they do not follow.
- TikTok does not push notifications after nine p.m. to children aged thirteen to fifteen and after ten p.m. to sixteen- and seventeen-year-olds.
- Meta has updated its policies limiting ad targeting for kids under eighteen based on age, gender, and location.

In addition, enforcement of the UK AADC has begun, as evidenced by the announcement by the UK ICO in the fall of 2022 that it intends to fine TikTok £27 million for alleged children's violations.

Moving on to the European Union, Europe's comprehensive privacy law—the General Data Protection Regulation or GDPR—requires parental consent for data collection of kids under sixteen. Furthermore, European regulators are now cracking down on privacy and other online child safety issues. For example, Ireland's Data Protection Commission (DPC), the regulatory agency responsible for enforcing the GDPR in Ireland, fined Meta €405 million in the fall of 2022 for making children's Instagram accounts public by default based on an inquiry it made in 2020. In response to this investigation, Meta made updates in 2021 to Instagram to make kids' accounts private by default and to block adults from messaging children who don't follow them.[40]

Finally, the European Union passed the Digital Services Act (DSA) in 2022, which enforces more strict content moderation, bans "dark patterns" and other persuasive techniques that trick users, and entirely bans behavioral advertising to children under eighteen years of age. The DSA will come into effect by 2024.

US state legislation

The most significant state law for kids' online safety that has passed is the California Age Appropriate Design Code (Cal AADC). It was signed into law in the fall of 2022 and will go into effect in 2024. It was also sponsored by the 5Rights Foundation and is modeled on the UK's code with the same name. Key to the bill is a focus on online services that are "likely to be accessed by children," not just services specifically aimed at kids. In addition, the Cal AADC puts significant "privacy by design" obligations on online services, including the following:[41]

- Stop selling kids' data and restrict data from being collected from them.
- Restrict profiling of children in ways that are either risky or harmful to kids.
- Set the highest level of privacy settings by default.
- Switch off geolocation by default for kids.
- Document in a data protection impact assessment whether the service uses persuasive technologies that extend the use of the service

via autoplay, rewards for time spent (e.g., streaks), and notification or nudging.

• Provide tools to report privacy concerns and flag inappropriate behavior.

This landmark law also extends the protection of children using online services beyond what is currently offered by the federal children's privacy law that is now in place—the Children's Online Privacy Protection Rule (COPPA). For example, the Cal AADC protects children up to eighteen, while COPPA applies only to kids under thirteen. Cal AADC also ensures that kids receive better protection regarding data collection and default privacy settings. It also provides visibility into the impact of AI systems that can cause addictive behavior.[42]

The Cal AADC is another example of the "California effect." It will likely force Big Tech firms to offer these kid-friendly designs in their products for the entire US, as it will be costly to offer one solution for kids in California versus the rest of the US. However, Big Tech is not going quietly in terms of accepting the Cal AADC. NetChoice, an industry trade group representing tech companies such as Amazon, Google, Meta, and TikTok, sued the State of California in December 2022 over the AADC. NetChoice claimed in its lawsuit that the AADC was unconstitutional in allegedly violating these companies' First Amendment rights by infringing on the editorial rights over their websites and apps.[43]

US federal legislation

The Children's Online Privacy Protection Act (COPPA) was enacted in 1998 and empowered the Federal Trade Commission (FTC) to issue and enforce regulations concerning kids' online privacy. The goal of COPPA is to give parents consent over what personal information is collected from their children under the age of thirteen. Parents can also request their kids' data be deleted or made available for review and request that their kids' data not be made available to third parties. COPPA applies to online services and websites directed to children under thirteen or to "general audience" online services and websites that have "actual knowledge" the user is under thirteen. These services must enforce data minimization by collecting only reasonably necessary data and retaining collected data for only as long as needed to fulfill the purpose for which it is collected.[44]

The FTC has only enforced COPPA forty times through 2022. The vast majority of the fines have been in the sub-$1 million range. However, the largest COPPA penalty of $275 million was levied in December 2022 against Epic Games, the maker of the Fortnite video game, for illegally collecting personal information from children without parents' consent. The second largest fine of $170 million was imposed in 2018 against Google's YouTube for a similar allegation.[45]

Privacy advocates have many concerns with COPPA, including that it does not cover kids from thirteen to eighteen, does not address addictive design issues, and has had spotty enforcement; plus, many "general audience" online services are claiming they don't have "actual knowledge" of kids using their service. Hence COPPA "version 2"—the Children and Teens' Online Privacy Protection Act—was proposed in 2021. One of the sponsors of this new bill, Senator Ed Markey, was one of the authors of the original COPPA. It would cover teens up to sixteen and outright ban behavioral advertising for those under sixteen. It would also close the "actual knowledge" loophole by creating a new "constructive knowledge" standard that requires online services to determine if kids are accessing their services. It would also set up a Youth Marketing and Privacy Division at the FTC to put more weight behind enforcement. And it would create an "eraser button" that would make it easier to delete information.[46]

The Kids Online Safety Act (KOSA) was proposed in 2022 by Senators Richard Blumenthal and Marsha Blackburn. Like the AADC, it would require online services to prioritize kids' well-being and best interests when designing their services and have the most robust default privacy settings for kids. In addition, it would require audits that assess the risks to children of online services' AI systems and would need those services to provide parents with more tools to protect their kids' privacy. And these online services would need to reduce the impact of potentially harmful content on their platforms. Finally, online services would be required to open up "black box" algorithms to academics and nonprofits to assist in research on the harms of AI systems to kids.[47]

The Protecting the Information of our Vulnerable Children and Youth (PRIVCY) Act was introduced in 2021 by Representative Kathy Castor. It also builds upon the AADC by requiring sites likely to be accessed by children to have the best interests of children in mind and also requires risk assessments of AI systems. Like the COPPA version 2 proposal, it too establishes a Youth Marketing and Privacy Division at the FTC and bans behavioral advertising for kids under eighteen. Finally, it lets parents sue tech firms if they violate kids' privacy rights.[48]

Lastly, the Kids Internet Design and Safety (KIDS) Act was introduced in 2021 by Senators Ed Markey and Richard Blumenthal and Representative Kathy Castor. It would "stop online practices such as manipulative marketing, amplification of harmful content, and damaging design features, which threaten young people online." For example, it would ban persuasive and addictive technologies such as autoplay, nudges, and streaks while eliminating likes and follower counts for children.[49]

Despite strong support from consumer protection groups, all of these federal bills have failed to move forward as of the end of 2022.

Road map to contain the impact of Big Tech on kids

One may conclude that the best way forward to protect kids online is to avoid having kids use technology. But in today's modern age, that is not practical or possible, especially given our dependence on products from Big Tech firms and the reality that the digital world is a necessary and significant part of our kids' lives. To prepare young people for a world in which AI will automate many jobs, we want and need kids to be tech literate and savvy. But we also want to keep them safe.

The good news is that the need for kids' online safety has reached national consciousness, and laws are being passed in Europe and at the US state level. In addition, there is a push to get laws passed at the US federal level, as evidenced by President Biden's 2022 State of the Union speech. He stated, "We must hold social media platforms accountable for the national experiment they're conducting on our children for profit." He added, "It's time to strengthen privacy protections, ban targeted advertising to children, demand tech companies stop collecting personal data on our children."[50]

I agree. We should pass comprehensive privacy legislation that, among the other capabilities I list in appendix 2, limits data collection to what is needed to perform the necessary task, bans selling kids' data, and bans behavioral advertising targeting children. President Biden also added to his list the need for safety by design for kids in his 2023 State of the Union address, which I agree also needs addressing. For children, this means that autoplay and notifications are off by default, included is support for save buttons (so kids don't have to continue to stay online to complete a given task), and no more encouraging or rewarding streaks or the number of likes and followers. In addition, kids' geolocation should be off by default, and their privacy settings should be set to the highest levels. And, of course, eliminate dark patterns for everyone. So, implementing the AADC at the national level makes sense.

Online services should also be required to perform childhood impact assessments and audit their AI systems for potential harm if their products are likely to be accessed by children. Furthermore, the data sets from these "black boxes" should be accessible to academics and nonprofits to facilitate research regarding the harm to the well-being and safety of kids.

We also need to fund more research on the mental health impact of technology use and kids. The passage of the Children and Media Research Advancement Act (CAMRA) bill at the end of 2022 is a significant first step. This law requires the Department of Health and Human Services (HHS) to study the impact of social media and smartphones on children and teens.

We should raise awareness of screen addiction and cyberbullying by having public service announcements (PSA) akin to the PSAs for tobacco. School districts should also seek to add discussions of screen addiction and cyberbullying to their health courses taught at schools.

In summary, strengthening our privacy laws and requiring online platforms to design their services with kids in mind would shift Big Tech and other tech firms from focusing on kids' time spent on their platforms to time well spent. And we need to redesign digital services that children use with their vulnerabilities in mind to support their well-being versus interfering with it. We have booster seat laws for children in cars, lead paint laws, and countless other regulations for childhood safety in the physical world, so it makes sense to have the same in the digital world, and it should start with the most prominent tech players.[51]

In this chapter and the last, I analyzed how AI can be used to change our behavior, facilitate screen addiction, and be exploited in a manner that can threaten kids' online safety. In the next chapter, I will examine how Big Tech's use of AI has enabled extremism and disinformation on their platforms, which has exacerbated polarization and weakened our democracy.

CHAPTER 7

Extremism and Disinformation

*One of the biggest reasons for democracies weakening
is the profound change that's taking place in how we
communicate and consume information.*

—Barack Obama, former US president[1]

From 2012 to 2021, there have been an estimated 443 total deaths due to extremism in the US. Tragically, in the last few years, we have seen shootings by extremists at an Orlando nightclub, a Pittsburgh synagogue, a high school in Florida, a supermarket in Buffalo, and a Walmart in El Paso, among others. Moreover, some analysts have claimed that there has been a "clear nexus" between these attacks and hatred being spread online via social media and other platforms.[2]

This nexus is not just a US phenomenon. The Christchurch, New Zealand, massacre in 2019, in which fifty-one people died, was live streamed on Facebook. The gunman was radicalized on YouTube, and his actions inspired the shootings in El Paso and Buffalo. Two years after the shooting, the *New York Times* found over fifty online clips of the gunman's video on social media platforms within twenty-four hours. The family of Nohemi Gonzalez, a twenty-three-year-old US citizen who was one of 130 people killed by ISIS terrorists in 2015 in a series of attacks in Paris, claimed in a lawsuit against Google that YouTube was used as a platform by ISIS to recruit members and plan terrorist attacks. Furthermore, the lawsuit claims that YouTube shared advertising revenue with ISIS-affiliated user accounts. While decided in favor of Google, the case is on appeal to the US Supreme Court as of early 2023.[3]

Besides significant criticism that online platforms are fostering extremism, there is also vocal criticism regarding online platforms' dissemination of disinformation. False information being deliberately spread to influence public opinion has heavily shaped our politics since 2016. For example, in the 2016 US presidential election, there was, per Special Counsel Robert Mueller's report, "sweeping" and "systemic" Russian social media disinformation. After Meta CEO Mark Zuckerberg initially brushed off as a "pretty crazy idea" that "fake news" on his platform influenced the 2016 US election, Meta subsequently admitted in late 2017 that over 126 million Americans saw Russian-linked posts that were designed to sway the election. This number represents nearly half the number of US voters at the time.[4]

Another example is that scientists were able to develop safe and highly effective vaccines within a year of the Covid outbreak. Still, as of September 2022, only 70 percent of Americans have gotten the two-dose series of vaccines. So, one could argue that people are dying because of disinformation. And as of fall 2022, most Republicans still bought into Donald Trump's false claims regarding the 2020 election.[5]

As the Anti-Defamation League (ADL) notes, QAnon conspiracy theories, White supremacist "replacement theory," #StopTheSteal, and Covid disinformation have become "increasingly normalized and mainstreamed." This is mainly due to their viral spread through online platforms and social media. An example they cite is that in the fall of 2020, a single "Stop the Steal" Facebook group gained over three hundred thousand members in just a day.[6]

The combination of extremism and disinformation with AI-based amplification of content designed to maximize user engagement has significantly contributed to society's hyperpolarization. This type of content plays on our prejudices and is being constantly reinforced. As a result, online platforms are increasingly leading us into "personal information bubbles" that block off alternative viewpoints. Or, even worse, it can put individuals into "rabbit holes" filled with conspiracy theories or act as a breeding ground for radicalization. And the platforms' use of our personal and behavioral data to fuel the engagement algorithms can keep people in these bubbles and rabbit holes.

The impact of this hyperpolarization on our society includes the loss of shared truths and scorn for the facts; making the extreme acceptable or normal; distrust in expertise and institutions; and weakening democratic norms. It can even help incite violence, such as the January 6 assault on the US Capitol.[7]

Furthermore, as Barack Obama noted in a 2021 speech at Stanford on how disinformation is a threat to our democracy, the reality is that purveyors of extremism and disinformation also know that if they flood our public square of social media with enough "raw sewage," many people will also "no longer know what to believe."[8]

To be clear, the problems of racism, bigotry, misogyny, and radicalization existed well before Big Tech came into being. Globalization and increasing automation via AI are displacing jobs, often leading to lower wages, thereby accelerating inequality. So, elements of our society may be more receptive to extremism and disinformation as they feel both betrayed and angry at our democracy and institutions. This trend also predates the rise of Big Tech.[9]

That said, companies like Meta know they are making matters worse. For example, the Facebook Files revealed that Meta was aware that it promoted "combustible election misinformation," which they then amplified and gave "broader distribution." Meta also had "evidence from a variety of sources that hate speech, divisive political speech, and misinformation on Facebook and the family of apps are affecting societies around the world." Meta's internal research also noted that "our core products' mechanics, such as virality, recommendations, and optimizing for engagement, are a significant part of why these types of speech flourish."[10]

If this were occurring on some random website with a few visitors, it would not be as big of a concern. But Big Tech's online services, such as video sharing and social media, are not just billboards on the internet highway that we speed by. Instead, they have become the leading pit stops of information and news, and their grip on what information we consume is increasing. For example, the Pew Research Center has found that Meta's Facebook is now a significant news source for 30 percent of Americans.[11]

I covered the concept of algorithmic amplification in the chapters on persuasive technology and kids' online safety, and this chapter will provide specific examples as it relates to disinformation and extremism. I will also discuss how the behavioral advertising model can fund website publishers that peddle extremism and disinformation. Furthermore, I will analyze how online ads are often not monitored for disinformation.

A key focus of this chapter will be on content moderation and whether Big Tech should be made accountable and liable for hate speech and extremism on their platforms. Specifically, I will look at Section 230 of the Communications Decency Act—which gives online platform providers immunity from claims regarding harmful content posted on their platforms—and discuss the associated issues and the proposals to kill or reform it.

I will conclude with recommendations on containing extremism and disinformation on online platforms. Doing so is crucial to protecting our democracy. As Barack Obama noted in his Stanford speech, "Solving the disinformation problem won't cure all that ails our democracies or tears at the fabric of our world, but it can help tamp down divisions and let us rebuild the trust and solidarity needed to make our democracy stronger."[12]

Algorithmic amplification of extremism and disinformation

As previously discussed, Big Tech firms like Meta and Google use AI to maximize user engagement on their social media platforms. So naturally, this facilitates the collection of more data and the serving of more ads. But in doing so, their services can promote content that favors controversy, disinformation, and extremism. The result is that hate speech and conspiracy theories can end up at the top of people's news feeds on Face-book or are autoplayed as recommended videos on YouTube.

An example is an internal experiment performed by a Meta researcher in July 2019. The researcher created a Facebook account for an imaginary forty-one-year-old "conservative mother" from North Carolina named Carol Smith. After being set up to follow pages for Sinclair Broadcasting and Fox News, "Carol" was recommended to Facebook pages and groups associated with the militia group The Three Percenters and the QAnon conspiracy within a few weeks. Another internal Meta research report found that "64 percent of people who joined an extremist group on Facebook only did so because the company's algorithm recommended it to them."[13]

A tragic example involves the country of Myanmar. Hate speech and fake news about the Rohingya Muslim minority spread in 2016 and 2017 through social media sites like Meta's Facebook. It eventually escalated into a full-blown genocide. Meta subsequently admitted that it had not done enough "to help prevent our platform from being used to foment division and incite offline violence."[14]

Another tragic example occurred in Ethiopia. In a $2 billion class-action lawsuit filed in December 2022, it was alleged that Meta monetized hate and violence in war-torn Ethiopia, leading to militants killing an Ethiopian professor. According to the son of the slain professor, Meta allowed "multiple posts with threats and misinformation about his father" to stay on the site and spread widely, even after being flagged for removal. Meta did not act on the posts until after the professor was killed.[15]

The problem of amplified disinformation and extremism on online platforms is more acute for non–English language content. For example, four years after the Myanmar genocide, the Facebook whistleblower testified in 2021 that 87 percent of Meta's spending on taking down disinformation on the Facebook service was for English language content. Yet only 9 percent of Facebook users speak English. In addition, YouTube appears to also have a content moderation problem for non-English videos, as evidenced by the discovery in October 2022 of dozens of Spanish-language videos with over 1.6 million views promoting election fraud conspiracies.[16]

Given these and other examples, it is not surprising that an internal Meta report "found that the company was well aware that its product, specifically its recommendation engine, stoked divisiveness and polarization." The report also noted that if left unchecked, the recommendation engine would continue to present "more and more divisive content in an effort to gain user attention & increase time on the platform." Despite the report submitted to Meta executives detailing their system's impact on society, Meta elected to ignore the report because it feared the changes would "disproportionately affect conservatives and might hurt engagement."[17]

Ironically, even after Meta was aware of what happened on its platform with the 2016 election and #StopTheSteal, when Mark Zuckerberg announced in March 2021 that his company would help get fifty million people the Covid-19 vaccine, his platform was flooded with a "cesspool" of anti-vaccine comments and content. Thus, anti-vaxxers could use his platform to sow doubt about the threat of the Covid virus and the safety and efficacy of the Covid vaccine, paralleling what Russians did in 2016, the Myanmar military in 2017, and so on. So, in effect, Zuckerberg got to personally experience opening up a Pandora's box that he designed. It got so bad that President Biden criticized Meta in the summer of 2021, saying that the falsehoods on the platform were "killing people."[18]

Another example is after Meta vowed in November 2021 to ban "organized hate groups, including white supremacist organizations, from the platform," an investigation by the Tech Transparency Project (TTP) in 2022 found that eighty white supremacist groups still had a presence on the platform. Further, when searching for the names of these groups on the platform, it appears that ads were placed on these search terms, meaning that Meta was profiting from these ads. TTP's research also showed that the "platform continues to auto-generate pages for white supremacist organizations and direct users who visit white supremacist pages to other extremist content." So, the problems of amplifying extremism and disinformation continue, as further witnessed by the Facebook Files revealing that Meta researchers were estimating that the company was removing less than 5 percent of all hate speech.[19]

Finally, it should be pointed out that the Facebook Files also revealed that Meta gives millions of celebrities, politicians, and other "VIP" users "special treatment" regarding the moderation of their content. The "XCheck" (or cross-check) program grew to at least 5.8 million users in 2020, allowing these "elite" people to bypass some of Meta's terms of use. These VIP users are likely to have their content go viral, thus representing another way disinformation may spread. Internal reports showed that in 2020 XCheck allowed "posts that violated its rules to be viewed at least 16.4 billion times, before later being removed." Note this XCheck type of program is not unique to Meta, as it was revealed in the fall of 2022 that TikTok has a similar program.[20]

There is a clear political aspect to this type of program. Namely, if a politician or political party is pumping out disinformation or indirectly inciting violence, the platforms want to avoid being criticized for censoring and are naturally reluctant to act. But as was the case with Donald Trump and the January 6 insurrection, sometimes their hand is forced. As will be discussed later, in response to Donald Trump being banned from some online platforms, right-wing politicians are taking legislative initiatives to block online platforms from cracking down on disinformation by political leaders.

Behavioral advertising funding extremism and disinformation

Researchers have found that behavioral advertising also facilitates funding website publishers that promote conspiracy theories, medical hoaxes, foreign propaganda, and extremist content. This is because behavioral advertising targets users wherever they go versus on what websites or pages they are on (i.e., contextual advertising).[21]

For example, say you were shopping for red sneakers on a shoe vendor's website but abandoned that purchase after putting the sneakers in the website's online shopping cart. Advertisers like the shoe vendor will want to retarget you on other websites to have you complete the purchase by using an ad exchange like Google's to serve ads to you and other past website visitors. Each of those ads will be personalized to each user based on what they are shopping for. Then say you subsequently visit a website filled with disinformation regarding Covid vaccines, and the publisher of that website has signed up to be on Google's ad platform. If you click on the retargeted sneaker ad on that website, the publisher will get a cut of the cost-per-click that Google charges the sneaker vendor. So now the shoe vendor is unwittingly funding Covid vaccine disinformation.[22]

This is not a few one-off ads being inadvertently placed. For example, the nonprofit organization Global Disinformation Index (GDI) published a report in 2019 that looked at twenty thousand websites that third-party organizations have found to publish disinformation. It found that Google's ad network served approximately 70 percent of the websites sampled, and GDI estimated that $235 million annually was spent running ads on those websites. Thus, GDI estimated that website publishers trafficking in disinformation were making nearly $100 million annually from serving ads. For example, it was estimated that a Russian disinformation site made millions of dollars in 2019 by serving ads from name brands such as Amazon, PayPal, Walmart, and Kroger. Thus, it is not surprising that behavioral advertising is referred to as the "lifeblood" of these sites.[23]

This funding of disinformation and extremist sites through behavioral advertising has further led to legitimate news sites losing revenue. This is because advertisers will add blocks to words like "racism," "white nationalist," and "discrimination" to avoid funding potentially controversial sites that have content with those words. But those exact words are used in legitimate news sites that report on these issues, so they get blocked too. As the *Guardian* reported in 2020, this issue cost UK newspaper and magazine publishers an estimated £170 million in digital revenue.[24]

Much like applying content moderation to political leaders, this also puts Big Tech's ad platforms in a political quandary. Namely, should they block political sites that push disinformation from their ad networks or block ads on specific pages? If the latter, how can ad networks keep up with new pages? One suggestion is to put websites in time-based penalty boxes after a certain number of violations.

Ads are often not monitored for disinformation

Applying the behavioral advertising model to political ads has also been problematic. Political ads can be highly personalized and micro-targeted to small groups. Furthermore, these ads can rile up voters with controversial content and disinformation tailored to users' behavior and profile, meaning that, unlike newspaper or TV ads that everyone can see, these personalized ads can fly under the radar.[25]

Because of past abuses, social media platforms like TikTok, Twitter, and Twitch (Amazon's video streaming service) no longer carry political ads, and Google's YouTube has strict limits on political ads. According to *Bloomberg*, this leaves Meta "the only game in town for digital political ads." But critics have claimed that Meta regularly misidentifies political ads and neglects to disclose relevant information to researchers. Furthermore, humans are not reviewing every ad submitted, meaning Meta relies heavily on AI to assess ads in combination with voluntary compliance. Thus, there have been reports of abuse, with ads containing disinformation slipping through or Meta's AI systems blocking legitimate ads.[26]

In addition, while Meta has recently blocked political ads from using sensitive information such as interests in social issues or political figures, critics say campaigns use interest-based proxies (e.g., listeners of a type of music) to target specific demographics such as race or ethnicity.[27]

Furthermore, just weeks before the 2022 midterms, a human rights watchdog published research claiming that both TikTok and Meta failed to block ads with "blatant" misinformation regarding when and how to vote in the US midterms. TikTok had approved 90 percent of advertisements with misleading and false information, while Facebook approved a "significant number" of ads containing misinformation.[28]

Accountability and liability for content

As Barack Obama noted, "For more and more of us, search and social media platforms aren't just our window into the internet; they serve as our primary source of news and information." So not surprisingly, plat-forms like Meta and Google have come under intense scrutiny regarding the content on their platforms that is either illegal (e.g., online sex traf-ficking and drugs) or harmful (e.g., disinformation, hate speech, and violent extremism).[29]

The large online platform providers have historically called them-selves "neutral platforms" and claimed they are not making editorial decisions. They have pushed back on government regulation and claimed they can self-regulate. And every time an incident occurs (e.g., Russian interference in the 2016 election), they apologize and announce new ini-tiatives that they say will fix or improve content moderation. In parallel, per Obama, they have "insisted that the content people see on social media has no impact on their beliefs or behavior—even though their business models and their profits are based on telling advertisers the exact opposite." Or they have said problems of racism or inequality pre-date them, or they may blame the scale of the problem.[30]

But Big Tech's arguments ignore that they built highly scalable plat-forms designed to maximize engagement by promoting and amplifying controversy. In other words, this is a feature, not a bug. Their "whack-a-mole" iterations since 2016 to content moderation have not been working. For example, a Covid conspiracy video called America's Front-line Doctors was viewed over twenty million times before the online platform providers removed it. And QAnon, the militia movement, and #StopTheSteal were able to draw millions of users before they were con-tained online.[31]

Section 230

Fortunately for the tech companies, they do have a "get out of jail free card" for being held liable for illegal and harmful content. The twenty-six words of Section 230 of the Communications Decency Act—passed in 1996—give online platform providers immunity from claims regarding harmful content posted on their platforms. In other words, content cre-ators are liable for the content they post online, not the content's host providers (e.g., websites, search engines, or social media services). As

Slate notes, this protection "also provides important procedural bene-fits in litigation: It enables defendants to kick a suit out of court before discovery, which is often the most expensive phase of litigation." While the current legal interpretation of Section 230 does immunize algorith-mic amplification of content, technology companies can be liable if they create their own content.[32]

Partisan views of section 230

Even though Section 230 is referred to as the "Internet's Magna Carta," and many experts believe it provides the "cornerstone of online expres-sion," it has come under heavy criticism from both the right and left, albeit for different reasons. For example, during the 2020 election, for-mer President Trump tweeted "REVOKE 230" after Twitter started putting fact-checking labels on his tweets, and then-candidate Biden told the editorial board of the *New York Times* that Meta should have civil liability like newspapers. The Biden administration in September 2022 has called for the removal of "special legal protections" under Section 230 that "broadly shield the companies from liability even when they host or disseminate illegal, violent conduct or materials."[33]

Republicans believe that Section 230 gives online platforms too much leeway in moderating what people say online. They feel these platforms disproportionately suppress conservative speech, partly due to their belief that tech companies' content moderation policies are influenced by their more liberal employees. For some Republicans, there are also ill feelings toward online platforms for the decision to ban former President Trump. Democrats believe these platforms are not doing enough to stop extremists from organizing online, prevent the spread of disinformation, reduce misogyny, and crack down on illegal activity such as drug sales.[34]

So, both Republicans and Democrats have introduced legislation that addresses their concerns. The Republican bills force platform providers to be more "neutral" regarding content moderation. The Democratic bills limit the scope of Section 230 protections in terrorism and civil rights cases. Furthermore, there have been some bipartisan proposals that "raise the bar" and make the tech companies meet certain conditions before getting the legal protection of Section 230, such as requiring the platforms to report to law enforcement when they see illegal activity. Additional proposals "create more exceptions," such as restricting tech companies from using Section 230 as a defense in cases involving child sexual abuse imagery and wrongful death. For example, one bipartisan bill was passed in 2018 that removes the Section 230 "liability shield" for sites that facilitate online sex trafficking.[35]

Section 230 and the First Amendment

But the colossal elephant in the room is that these proposals collide with the First Amendment. The Electronic Frontier Foundation has said that Section 230 is "one of the most valuable tools for protecting freedom of expression and innovation on the internet." In effect, revoking Section 230 and treating online platform providers like traditional publishers would force online platforms to check every post. This could lead to significant moderation to avoid lawsuits and be cost-prohibitive for smaller tech companies. The proposals to limit online content moderation in the name of making them more "neutral" could create a "free-for-all" that would make these platforms even more toxic (e.g., more QAnon, election conspiracies, Covid vaccine disinformation, etc.).[36]

Section 230 will be closely scrutinized by the US Supreme Court with their taking up the case of the family of *Nohemi Gonzalez v. Google*. While this case involves terrorist content, it could narrow Section 230 with regard to terrorism, or it could lead to a broader ruling that may impact algorithmic amplification or Section 230 altogether. This case will be decided in 2023.[37]

Elon Musk's acquisition of Twitter also may significantly influence content moderation in the public square of social media. Before the deal closed, Musk had said he would reinstate former President Trump on Twitter and generally loosen up content moderation policies in favor of more "free speech." He reinstated Trump on Twitter in November 2022, and Meta followed suit in January 2023. Musk may find that the content moderation policies he puts in place at Twitter may cause conflict with foreign nations where Tesla does business or even advertisers who may not want their brands associated with an app that has lax content moderation regarding hate speech or disinformation.

Legislation to contain extremism and disinformation

European legislation

Not surprisingly, Europe is leading the charge with regulations that curb the distribution and dissemination of illegal and harmful content. The Digital Services Act (DSA), passed in 2022 and taking effect by 2024, will require online businesses to be more aggressive in monitoring their platforms for illicit content or otherwise risk fines. The DSA will hold online platforms liable if they do not swiftly remove hate speech, child sexual abuse, terrorist propaganda, commercial scams, and other content deemed illegal by member countries of the EU. Furthermore, online platforms must give end users tools to flag this content easily. Finally, companies will need to be more transparent by providing independent researchers and regulators with internal data on how their algorithms work and overall content moderation efforts. According to the Associated Press, an example could be requiring Google's YouTube to "turn over data on whether its recommendation algorithm has been directing users to more Russian propaganda than normal."[38]

US state legislation

At the US state level, there has been a lot of activity to address online content moderation efforts, and the laws reflect if the states are more Republican or Democratic. For example, in Republican Florida, Senate Bill 7072 was passed in 2022. This law stops online platforms from banning politicians under almost any circumstance, even if, for example, the politician fomented insurrection. In addition, online platforms cannot censor, deplatform, or shadow ban a "journalistic enterprise" based on the content they publish. But the definition of a journalistic enterprise is any website that publishes one hundred hours of videos, so in theory, it could include pornography sites. This law was ruled unconstitutional by the Eleventh Circuit Court of Appeals.[39]

In Republican Texas, House Bill 20 was passed into law in 2022. It significantly limits online platforms from content moderation on the "basis of a viewpoint." It also provides the right for individuals to sue the tech platforms if they disagree with content moderation decisions. It seemingly applies to political "viewpoints" but also viewpoints on the Holocaust, women's rights and place in society, LGBTQ, and so on, and would likely make any online platform with no moderation an undesirable place to visit. Furthermore, this right to sue would empower "aggrieved users" from filing "an unending stream of lawsuits," thus putting more pressure on online platforms to not moderate most content. A federal appeals court suspended enforcement of the Texas law in October 2022, pending the likelihood that the US Supreme Court will review the case.[40]

In Democratic California, Assembly Bill 587 was signed into law in 2022. The law would require online platforms to publicly post their policies on disinformation and hate speech. It would also require online platforms to report quarterly details on their content management policies and enforcement activities to state regulators.[41]

US federal legislation

At the US federal level, dozens of Section 230–related bills have been proposed in the 2019–22 time frame to either repeal it, limit its scope, or impose new obligations. For example, the Platform Accountability and Transparency Act (PATA) was introduced in December 2021 by Senators Amy Klobuchar, Robert Portman, and Chris Coons. It is a bipartisan bill requiring online platforms to provide independent researchers and the public with access to platform data regarding content postings and the moderation of those postings. The idea is that, like the California bill and Europe's DSA, this bill would provide more transparency into algorithms that may amplify disinformation and extremism as well as policies and activities regarding content moderation. Unfortunately, the bill has yet to move forward as of the end of 2022.[42]

Road map to contain online extremism and disinformation

One of the biggest contributors to the spread of online extremism and disinformation is the surveillance-based advertising model that provides the behavioral data fueling the AI-powered user engagement that amplifies extremism and disinformation. So, the less behavioral data, the less likely platforms can create a digital voodoo doll of us that can rile us up or lead us into a rabbit hole or bubble. So, pressuring the Big Tech companies to reduce online tracking is critical, as is passing legislation that, at the very minimum, bans the collection of children's behavioral data and the use of sensitive personal information for targeting.

As discussed in chapter 5 on persuasive technology, much like the EU's Digital Services Act will require online platforms to perform risk assessments of AI systems that may result in behavioral harm, we need a Food and Drug Administration (FDA) equivalent for AI in the US. This entity would allow for auditing high-risk AI systems that cause harm, which, for example, would likely include AI systems that are highly addictive or amplify content that fosters extremism and polarization.

Furthermore, much like the National Transportation Safety Board gets access to the "black box" that contains the data on airline crashes, we need transparency on the platforms' content moderation terms of services and their enforcement of those terms. Additionally, online platforms must give end users tools to flag harmful content easily and provide users with the reasons behind content moderation decisions and the right to appeal. Finally, transparency should also apply to ads placed on these platforms. Researchers should be given access to an archive of ads and corresponding data on how those ads were targeted.[43]

The Federal Trade Commission (FTC) or state attorney generals should investigate deceptive or unfair trade practices with respect to online platforms not honoring content moderation terms of services or failing to protect consumers from significant harm. An example could be Meta's XCheck program, which exempts VIP users from their content moderation standards, or the platform needing to remove commercial scams swiftly.[44]

The big question is, should Section 230 be reformed or eliminated? I am leery of eliminating Section 230, as it is a valuable tool to protect online freedom of expression. That being said, I think reform can happen to address egregious harms and unlawful activity that results in violence, but only if the platforms do not act promptly to remove when flagged. In addition, platforms need to report illegal activity to law enforcement. Lastly, Section 230 should also be reformed to require platform providers to have a higher standard of care regarding the targeted advertising they serve.[45]

Finally, one way to help contain online extremism and disinformation is to pressure online platforms to stop amplifying it and to boycott them if they don't. For example, in June 2020, a group of civil society groups created the "Stop Hate for Profit" coalition. They asked businesses to pause advertising for one month on Meta's platform in protest of the hate speech and extremism found on the platform. Eventually, over 1,200 companies joined the "pause." It is unknown to what extent this month-long boycott impacted Meta's advertising revenue. Still, this campaign raised significant awareness, and the groups claimed content associated with the boycott had over one billion views.[46]

Big Tech must be accountable for amplifying disinformation and extremism threatening our democracy. The recommendations I provided in this section would be an excellent first step. As noted by former President Obama in his Stanford speech on disinformation, "We have a choice right now. Do we allow our democracy to wither, or do we make it better?"[47]

The first three chapters of this book focused on the mining and collecting of our data and the negative consequences that have emerged because of this. Chapters 4 through 7 analyzed how Big Tech consumes and processes this data via artificial intelligence (AI) and how that has created its own unique threats, including how it has enabled extremism and disinformation on its platforms. In the next and final chapter, I will examine how Big Tech's dominant market positions have harmed entrepreneurship and innovation and undermined journalism and a vibrant free press. This chapter will also show how Big Tech's monopoly positions have worsened the overcollection of our data and the use of AI for exploitative purposes.

CHAPTER 8

Competition

When companies don't face robust competition, or when they're allowed to just squash out competition, they can become too big to care. They can impose all sorts of terms or contractual provisions that really just leave Americans in a position of take it or leave it.

—FTC Chairperson Lina Khan[1]

In 2020, lawmakers with the US House Judiciary Subcommittee on Antitrust grilled the CEOs of Amazon, Apple, Google, and Meta in a six-hour hearing regarding how their firms "have exploited, entrenched, and expanded their power over digital markets in anticompetitive and abusive ways." After the hearing, the subcommittee concluded that the testimony of the CEOs was "evasive and non-responsive." Their testimony also left lawmakers and critics concerned about whether these companies believed they were "beyond the reach" of meaningful oversight.[2]

This hearing was part of a bipartisan investigation into the state of competition in important "digital markets" that play a significant role in our economy. The investigation considered ten large and important markets, including online search, e-commerce, social media, mobile app stores, web browsers, and digital advertising. In doing so, it examined the dominance of Amazon, Apple, Google, and Meta in these digital markets and how these four firms' business practices affected the US economy and its democracy. The investigation examined over 1.3 million documents, interviewed over 240 people, held seven hearings—including the 2020 hearing with the CEOs of these four firms—and in 2022 published a comprehensive 350-plus page report with detailed recommendations.[3]

The investigation highlights that competition has always been critical to the health and growth of our economy. This is especially true in our new digital economy, where "software is eating the world," creating new markets and transforming existing ones. Silicon Valley is the epicenter of our digital economy, with start-ups acting as the scrappy underdogs that challenge the status quo with their disruptive technology. This start-up ecosystem has generated millions of new jobs and created incredible wealth for entrepreneurs, investors, and employees. In addition, start-ups spur fellow market participants to improve their products' quality and functionality, be more customer-centric, and not overprice.

But lack of competition in a market results in incumbents not investing in innovation and instead focusing on building features to lock in customers and protect their preexisting revenue streams. When incumbents become too dominant in a digital market, venture capitalists (VCs) see these big digital markets as "kill" or "no-fly" zones. This means they are unwilling to invest in start-ups that would go head-to-head against these gorillas. For example, very few VCs have invested in mobile operating systems, web browsers, and online search engines. Furthermore, the lack of competition means incumbents are not inclined to invest and innovate in areas such as privacy that start-up competitors would push them in the market to improve.[4]

The subcommittee found in investigating the four companies that the digital markets they dominated were "winner-take-all." This means that these markets "tip" toward one or two large companies, leading to high degrees of concentration. The six-hundred-plus acquisitions these firms have made in the last ten years—many of which were potential or nascent competitors—have contributed to this concentration. None of these acquisitions were blocked by regulators.

Based on this concentration in strategic digital markets and perceived anticompetitive practices, regulators in the US and EU have concluded that the four have evolved into "gatekeepers" to large swathes of our digital economy, controlling key distribution channels, including direct access to customers. As gatekeepers, they can uniquely extract concessions or dictate terms to third parties and consumers that likely would not be tolerated in a competitive market. For example, mobile app developers are forced to only use the mobile platform provider's payment platform for in-app purchases, or consumers must consent to the increasingly intrusive collection of behavioral data to use their services. And because of their position as gatekeepers of key digital markets, one analyst projects that by 2030 over 30 percent of the world's gross domestic output may flow through Big Tech firms and a few others.[5]

Furthermore, as these firms have branched into other markets with integrated offerings, they now act as both the marketplace owner and competitors to third parties who participate in the marketplace. This "dual role" in a "multisided" market means they can write rules for others while they play by their own rules. This has led to critics claiming that these firms can self-preference their apps and products in their marketplaces, appropriate data from third parties to offer their competitive solutions, block off direct access by third parties to consumers, and make sudden changes to platform policies that can punish third-party competitors. Thus, regulators now see the gatekeepers resembling the railroad monopolies of the late 1800s. Federal Trade Commission (FTC) Chair Lina Khan used the same analogy when she wrote about Amazon, "The thousands of retailers and independent businesses that must ride Amazon's rails to reach market are increasingly dependent on their biggest competitor."[6]

Even if a VC were willing to fund a start-up in one of these markets or an established company were to try to go head-to-head against a Big Tech vendor, the reality is that competing directly against Big Tech is quite challenging. The barriers to entry are enormous. For example, Big Tech's products have billions of users with strong network effects that make their products more valuable as more and more users enter Big Tech's walled gardens. This is not easily replicated.

In addition, Big Tech's products have high switching costs, making it difficult for consumers to switch to alternatives. For example, the lack of data portability makes it nearly impossible to move your connections, messages or chats, purchase histories, address books, and so on. Furthermore, Big Tech's products need interoperability, so even if you could move to another provider, you would not be able to communicate online with your friends who stay behind on the Big Tech platforms. Because of this lock-in, to no one's surprise, Big Tech firms have diminished motivation to address consumer protection concerns, as they know that consumers are stuck and have no other places to go.[7]

In this chapter, I will give an overview of some of the anticompetitive practices of Amazon, Apple, Google, and Meta. I will show how they act as gatekeepers by controlling access to their respective markets and then use that position to maintain and even abuse their market dominance. While the subcommittee did not consider Microsoft a gatekeeper, I will provide an update on Microsoft and what anticompetitive concerns regulators have with them.

I will also discuss the effects of Big Tech's durable market power. One may argue that some of Big Tech's products are free to consumers, so why is this a problem, as there is no consumer harm? This "consumer-welfare standard" is the current school of thought in antitrust policy, born out of the shift in antitrust policy championed by Robert Bork and the "Chicago School" during the Reagan administration. But as FTC Chair Khan noted in her groundbreaking 2017 *Yale Law Journal* paper, "The long-term interests of consumers include product quality, variety, and innovation—factors best promoted through both a robust competitive process and open markets." I will examine how these firms' market dominance has impacted entrepreneurship and innovation, weakened privacy, and undermined journalism and a vibrant press.[8]

I will then review legislative proposals to rein in Big Tech's market dominance, and provide recommendations that would provide more oversight and enforcement to foster more competition in digital markets.

Amazon

Amazon now controls about 40 percent of US online retail sales due to a first-mover advantage and successfully executing a dual-part strategy.

First, Amazon has been willing to invest heavily in growth while forgoing profits. Second, it has delivered vertical integration by making aggressive acquisitions in adjacent markets to add to its "stockpile of customer data" and shore up "competitive moats" to gain advantages in one sector of e-commerce to help boost its fortunes in another. However, critics say this strategy has enabled Amazon to become a gatekeeper, with an inherent advantage to undermine competitors because of its ability to sell its products and compete against others while owning the underlying platform where the transactions are done.[9]

Amazon Prime is an excellent example of its willingness to sustain losses to establish market dominance. Prime is the company's loyalty program that is offered as an annual subscription and provides free two-day delivery and other perks, including access to Amazon's video and music streaming service. One analyst estimated in 2015 that Amazon lost $1 to $2 billion per year on the Prime program. But the upside for Amazon is that it is estimated that now nearly two-thirds of US households have Prime membership, with a typical Prime member spending $1,600 annually on Amazon compared to $600 per year for nonmembers. In addition, the Prime renewal rate by consumers is estimated at 98 percent.[10]

Prime has also contributed to the estimate that over 60 percent of all online product searches begin on Amazon's website in the US. And Prime has further cemented consumer lock-in to Amazon, especially since in 2019, Amazon Prime began to offer same-day delivery, so there are now even fewer reasons to go to a brick-and-mortar store, let alone other online retailers. As noted by one market participant who told the subcommittee, "Prime members will continue to use Amazon and not switch to competing platforms, despite higher prices and lower-quality items on Amazon compared to other marketplaces, and despite recent increases in the price of a Prime membership." Not only are consumers less likely to switch, but third-party sellers do not have a comparable marketplace option to turn to in light of the fact that Amazon has over 150 million Prime users in the US.[11]

Amazon has also acquired over one hundred companies in the last twenty years, allowing it to expand aggressively into multiple lines of business. For example, acquisitions of Whole Foods, MGM, Zappos, Ring, and others have enabled Amazon to evolve from an online retailer to, per FTC Chair Khan, "a marketing platform, a delivery and logistics network, a payment service, a credit lender, an auction house, a major book publisher, a producer of television and films, a fashion designer, a hardware manufacturer, and a leading provider of cloud server space and computing power." Besides taking out direct competitive threats (e.g., Quidsi, the parent company of Diapers.com), this has further led to Amazon's competitors being its customers; for example, rivals such as Netflix rely on Amazon Web Services (AWS) for cloud computing, and other retailers use Amazon's delivery service. This reliance by competitors on Amazon's platform creates a scenario where critics contend there is an inherent conflict of interest.[12]

It has also led to Amazon being able to gather more behavioral data (e.g., purchases online on Amazon's website and in-person purchases at Whole Foods) to facilitate the selling of more products, as well as data on its competitors that sell or operate on its platform. For example, the subcommittee heard concerns that "Amazon leverages its access to third-party sellers' data to identify and replicate popular and profitable products from among the hundreds of millions of listings on its marketplace." This allegedly lets Amazon copy products and create rival offerings (e.g., under the private label Amazon Basics) or contact the manufacturer directly and cut out the seller. Critics claim this data exploitation effectively lets Amazon increase sales without the corresponding risk. As FTC Chair Khan noted, "It is third-party sellers who bear the initial costs and uncertainties when introducing new products; by merely spotting them, Amazon gets to sell products only once their success has been tested." In addition, Amazon locks out third-party sellers from even knowing who the purchasing customers are.[13]

Another criticism of Amazon is its self-preferencing of its products. Critics have pointed out that Amazon will give its products "featured placement under a given search." Furthermore, Amazon will not let competitors buy ads on its platform for keywords associated with Amazon's devices while allowing advertisements to run on searches involving competitors' products. Even Alexa, Amazon's voice assistant, will default to Amazon's services with specific voice commands. Self-preferencing is another example critics point to of the inherent problems with Amazon's dual position as both the "operator" and "seller" in its marketplace.[14]

Apple

Apple is the leading mobile device vendor in the US, with over 50 percent market share as of late 2022. Apple also dominates the worldwide premium smartphone market, with over 75 percent of the $1,000-plus market segment. There are over one billion iPhone users worldwide. Apple's iOS mobile operating system is one of the two dominant platforms in the mobile operating system market, with the other being Google's Android. Apple installs iOS on its mobile devices (e.g., iPhones and the iPad tablet), does not license iOS to other mobile vendors, and does not support other mobile operating systems.[15]

Apple has created a robust mobile ecosystem—including its App Store for software distribution—that has delivered incredible benefits for consumers and app developers. But despite this, critics believe that Apple's dominant market position and hegemony over this ecosystem have enabled Apple to become a gatekeeper controlling software distribution and in-app purchases (IAP) of "digital goods and services" on its devices. Furthermore, they claim that Apple leverages this control to create barriers to competition and self-preference its offerings. This includes charging app developers "supra-competitive" prices via the App Store—fees significantly higher than what would be found in normal competition. Thus, the Subcommittee on Antitrust and the European Commission have concluded that Apple's monopoly power in software distribution and in-app purchases has caused competitive harm, increased prices, and reduced consumer choices.[16]

Apple's App Store is the only way consumers are allowed by Apple to install apps on their iOS devices. Apple blocks apps from being installed on its devices outside the App Store (a practice known as "sideloading") and does not allow for alternative app stores. Apple takes a 30 percent commission for third-party apps sold through the App Store. However, based on regulatory pressure, starting in 2021, it created a 15 percent commission for small developers up to the first $1 million sold.[17]

In addition, Apple charges a similar commission model for in-app purchases (IAP), including subscriptions. All apps must use Apple's payment system to process transactions. Furthermore, Apple does not let third-party apps tell consumers that apps or IAPs may be available at a lower price elsewhere. Moreover, Apple bars developers from providing links to alternative payment methods or offering their own payment processing system inside their app.

Apple has stated that control over app distribution and IAPs allows it to ensure high levels of security and protect against fraud. But this control of app distributions and purchases has allowed Apple to generate about $24 billion in annual App Store sales with little overhead. The former senior director of App Store review told the subcommittee that Apple's yearly cost for running the App Store is $100 million.[18]

Critics, such as the Coalition for App Fairness, claim that this "app tax" increases consumer prices and suppresses developer revenue. One example they highlight is that an upgrade to the video game Fortnite costs $9.99 in the Apple App Store, but the same upgrade costs only $7.99 if purchased directly through the developer Epic Games. So, the consumer bears the extra cost burden, and Apple does not let Epic tell the consumer within its app of the lower prices available elsewhere. As a result, Epic Games filed an antitrust lawsuit against Apple in the US in 2020. That case is on appeal as of the end of 2022.

Furthermore, the coalition has drawn attention to the fact that the 15–30 percent commission is especially burdensome on app developers, especially those that compete with one of Apple's apps—such as Music, Mail, or Books—as Apple does not have to pay the tax. A case in point is Spotify, which is trying to compete against Apple in audiobooks. For a consumer to buy an audiobook on the iOS app, Spotify would have to pay Apple a 30 percent commission, while the same audiobook offered by Apple would not have that same cost structure.[19]

Another example the coalition points to is Apple's 30 percent commission fees from IAPs. This is akin to a payment processing fee, but in almost any other industry, payment processing fees are in the 2–5 percent range. Spotify filed an antitrust complaint in Europe in 2019, arguing that app developers should be free to tell consumers how they can purchase services and subscriptions outside Apple's payment system. The EU investigation is ongoing as of the end of 2022.[20]

The Subcommittee on Antitrust also investigated whether Apple self-preferences its apps by not allowing consumers to delete Apple's apps installed on devices by default and by giving its app higher search rankings in the App Store search results. Their conclusion was yes. For example, the *Wall Street Journal* reported in 2019 that Apple's apps "ranked first in more than 60 percent of basic searches, such as for 'maps'" and that "Apple apps that generate revenue through subscriptions or sales, like Music or Books, showed up first in 95 percent of searches related to those apps."[21]

Finally, developers also expressed their concern to the subcommittee that Apple is a competitor and operator of its marketplace and can exploit data of purchases of apps to determine what apps to build next or functionality to add to iOS. The only way for app developers to avoid these and other concerns today is to forgo participation in the App Store and thus forgo half the smartphone market.[22]

Google

According to an antitrust lawsuit filed in 2020 by the US Department of Justice (DoJ) and over a dozen states, Google started as a "scrappy startup" and the "darling of Silicon Valley" that delivered an "innovative way to search the emerging internet." But the lawsuit concludes "that Google is long gone." This lawsuit, three other state-initiated antitrust cases directed at Google, and the US House Judiciary Subcommittee on Antitrust's final report on *Competition in Digital Markets* all peg Google as a "monopoly gatekeeper for the internet." Google does dominate multiple digital markets, with a market share of 90 percent in internet search, 65 percent in web browsers, over 80 percent in navigation mapping services, 70 percent in worldwide mobile operating systems, and over 85 percent in online advertising exchanges. To achieve that dominance, critics have pointed to numerous anticompetitive tactics that have resulted in Google becoming a walled garden of multiple interlocking monopolies.[23]

Let's first look at online search. It is alleged that Google has repeatedly undermined vertical search providers (e.g., search sites for travel) by preferencing search results for its competitive offerings. For example, when Google released its local business directory with user reviews, Google put its reviews at the top, above the organic results from companies such as Yelp. Another example is from the *Wall Street Journal*, which reported in 2019 that Google gave videos hosted on YouTube higher search results than videos with more views and engagement hosted on competing platforms.[24]

Google also scrapes content from publisher sites (e.g., news organizations' websites) and summarizes it in their search results. Critics say this often reduces the need for consumers to click on the link and visit the publisher's site, thus depriving the publisher of user traffic and corresponding advertising revenue. This is counter to Google founder Larry Page's comment in 2004 that Google did not want to be a portal but instead was focused on wanting users to come to Google and be quickly and efficiently sent to other sites.[25]

Furthermore, not only has Google increasingly added its own content to its search results page—often appropriated from other publishers— but it has also added additional advertising at the top and bottom of the search results page. As one market participant told the subcommittee, Google "consistently reserves the top of the [search engine results page] for its own vertical products or advertisements paid for through search engine marketing, pushing its rivals' organic results to the bottom, regardless of how relevant or useful they might be." Thus by "siphoning off traffic from the rest of the web" and by taking up more and more real estate on its search results page, critics say that Google is compelling businesses who depend on traffic from Google to pay for more ads, as those parties' organic content is now getting pushed farther down in search results. Thus, instead of investing in high-quality web content that would lead to better organic search results, they now increasingly need to pay Google for ads. For consumers, if Google's vertical search offering is not superior to an organic search result, it means Google is directing consumers to inferior results.[26]

Another way Google allegedly maintains its monopoly in search is via "exclusionary agreements" that Google makes with other technology providers. Unsurprisingly, Google is the default search engine for the Google Chrome browser. But Google also pays Apple an estimated $15 billion per year to make Google search the default for Apple's Safari browser and pays Mozilla hundreds of millions of dollars to have Google search be the default for Mozilla's Firefox browser. Google's contracts with mobile device manufacturers who want to use Android require that those manufacturers must make Google search their devices' default search. And some of Google's contracts forbid the preinstallation of any competing search engine. Furthermore, critics claim that it could be more intuitive for users to switch many of these browsers' default search engines.[27]

Paying billions of dollars to be the default search engine for the vast majority of internet searches is worth it to Google, given their ability to make much more than what they pay out via their monetization of advertising. It also gives Google massive amounts of additional search data to provide leading indicators and actionable insight for the rest of its business, gather more behavioral data to improve ad targeting and increase engagement within its walled garden, and further differentiate its search results compared to competitors.[28]

Anticompetitive concerns about these contracts led to the US DoJ and many states filing an antitrust lawsuit against Google in 2020 that is still active as of the end of 2022. The case alleges that Google's actions have eliminated competition in search, thereby letting Google charge its advertisers significantly more than it could in a competitive market. The suit further claims that Google's search engine contracts impact consumers by impeding innovation, including in privacy and data protection, and reducing the quality of search results that consumers get.[29]

There is also concern about Google having a monopoly position in digital advertising. Through acquisitions of companies such as Double-Click and internal development, Google owns the entire ad tech stack. This means that their technology represents the advertisers who want to buy ads (i.e., the demand side), the publishers who want to sell ad space on their websites and mobile apps (i.e., the supply side), and the underlying advertising exchange where these transactions occur. In effect, critics allege Google acts as the "pitcher, batter, and umpire, all at the same time" in the ad tech market, which would be an inherent conflict. Furthermore, there is concern that Google combines the data from its ad tech solutions (e.g., browsing activity) with personal information collected through Google's services, which gives it an advantage in the market compared to other ad tech solutions. For example, when Google purchased DoubleClick, it told the FTC it would not combine the data, but the company reneged on its commitment.[30]

In a 2020 antitrust lawsuit filed by seventeen states against Google, with the state of Texas taking the lead, the Texas attorney general claimed that Google's control over the ad tech market let it "charge monopoly prices—19 to 22 percent on every transaction . . . . That would be similar to the NYSE charging $22,000 on every $100,000 stock trade on its exchange." The case claims that "all of Google's most important rivals for ad servers have exited the market" because of Google's anticompetitive position. A US federal judge allowed the case to proceed in the fall of 2022. Furthermore, the US DoJ filed its own antitrust lawsuit in January 2023 with similar allegations against Google and its monopoly position in the digital advertising market. The *Wall Street Journal* had reported in July 2022 that Google would be willing to split its ad-tech business into a separate entity under the Alphabet holding company to head off a possible US antitrust lawsuit in this part of its business, but clearly the DoJ was not interested in that offer.[31]

Finally, Google is facing similar criticism of Android and its Play Store that Apple met with iOS and the App Store. Namely, Google's monopoly power on Android—in software distribution and in-app purchases, its self-preferencing of its applications in its marketplace, its onerous commissions, and its monitoring of competing apps to get "near-perfect" market intelligence—have caused competitive harm, increased prices, and reduced consumer choices. As a result, Google is facing yet another antitrust lawsuit from over thirty-six states, with this one focused on Android and the Play Store filed in July 2021. This case is pending. In addition, Epic Games has also sued Google with an antitrust similar to the one it filed against Apple.[32]

Meta

Meta is the world's largest online social network, with nearly three billion users. According to market analysis firm Comscore, Meta's social media market share has been more than 70 percent since 2016. The acquisitions of Instagram in 2012 and WhatsApp in 2014 have significantly contributed to this dominant market share. Both purchases were made to shore up Meta's position in the then-new and rapidly growing mobile market with its focus on text messaging and its use of integrated digital cameras that could facilitate the taking, sharing, and commenting on photos.[33]

The Subcommittee on Antitrust and US DoJ have asserted that Meta is a monopoly and that it has maintained its market dominance through a series of anticompetitive measures, including implementing CEO Mark Zuckerberg's strategy, expressed in 2008, that "it is better to buy than compete." This was especially true when Meta worried that its desktop-centric approach would miss the "mobile wave" that was happening a few years after the release of iPhone and Google Android in the 2007–8 time frame. Critics claim that Meta facilitated this strategy by identifying potential competitive threats and aiming to "acquire, copy, or kill" these firms. Thus, competitors were pressured into selling to Meta or risked being crushed by them. Further, critics have also claimed that Meta has implemented platform policies that weaken potential competitors. Therefore, critics believe that Meta's conduct has harmed competition, left consumers with fewer choices in the market, and negatively impacted advertisers by not allowing the benefits of having alternative social network sites to advertise with.[34]

Based on this criticism and the investigation done by the subcommittee, the FTC and forty-six states sued Meta in December 2020 for illegally maintaining a monopoly by implementing a "systematic strategy" of acquiring "up-and-coming" rivals such as Instagram and

WhatsApp. The relief sought in this lawsuit included the divestiture of Instagram and WhatsApp, the removal of anticompetitive prohibitions on developers, and the requirement that Meta seeks "prior notice and approval of any future mergers and acquisitions."[35]

The lawsuit alleges that "after repeated failed attempts to develop innovative mobile features for its network," Meta instead "resorted to an illegal buy-or-bury scheme to maintain its dominance." For example, Zuckerberg wrote an internal note in early 2012 that the then-independent Instagram would leave his company "very behind in both functionality and brand on how one of the core use cases of Facebook will evolve in the mobile world." For Zuckerberg, this would be a "really scary" outcome for his company, as advertisers would move to a mobile-first competitive social network that would threaten Meta's advertising profits. He then wrote, "We might want to consider paying a lot of money" for Instagram, which they subsequently did.[36]

In addition, the suit claims that Meta imposes anticompetitive measures for software developers. For example, the complaint claims that Meta only allows access to application programming interfaces (APIs) to the Meta platform if developers "refrain from developing competing functionalities" and if their apps do not connect to or promote other social media apps. In other words, Meta was also being accused of implementing policies that do not let third parties reduce the inherent consumer lock-in or high switching costs that Meta has for its service.[37]

In June 2021, a federal judge threw out the antitrust case against Meta, saying that the FTC had failed to provide enough facts to back up the claims in the complaint and that the states waited too long to file their case, given that the acquisitions had happened seven to nine years prior. In August 2021, the FTC filed an amended complaint with additional evidence. The judge ruled in January 2022 that the antitrust case could move forward but dismissed the charges that Meta had violated antitrust laws by implementing policies that cut off developers. The *New York Times* noted, "While the judge's decision was a big victory for the agency, ultimate success with the suit is far from certain and it will be years before there is any final resolution."[38]

Microsoft

The 1990s antitrust lawsuit against Microsoft is the example given on the FTC's website in their definition of the word "monopolization." In the mid-1990s, Microsoft bundled its Internet Explorer browser with Windows 95 and prevented hardware manufacturers from bundling non-Microsoft web browsers on the Windows operating system. This tactic allowed Internet Explorer to reach 95 percent market share by the late 1990s. The DoJ sued Microsoft in 1998, claiming this violated a consent decree that Microsoft had signed with the DoJ in 1994. The court ruling for this case ordered Microsoft to split into two separate entities—one for Windows and one for everything else—but the DoJ and Microsoft settled the lawsuit in 2002. In the end, Microsoft was not split up. Instead, Microsoft paid billions in fines, agreed to make it seamless for non-Microsoft software to run on Windows, was barred from preventing hardware manufacturers from bundling non-Microsoft products on Windows computers, and was required to be under government oversight for ten years.[39]

This settlement opened the door for Google Chrome and other software vendors by not having a gatekeeper control internet browsing in the early days of the internet. So, this is a great case study of how innovation can be unleashed when a gatekeeper's grip is loosened.[40]

This experience of being under the antitrust microscope led Microsoft to become quite careful in its business practices to not run afoul of regulators. Microsoft also evolved since the 1990s to have a significant portion of its revenue focused on selling software and cloud services to businesses, so many of its product offerings are less well-known to consumers than those of the other Big Tech firms. So even though Microsoft has the second largest market cap of the five Big Tech companies—behind Apple—it avoided the antitrust scrutiny by the US House Judiciary Subcommittee on Antitrust, as it was not considered a gatekeeper in the ten digital markets the subcommittee looked at. Instead, Microsoft was interviewed as part of the investigation to gather information about the business practices of the other Big Tech firms.[41]

But even though Microsoft has been flying under the antitrust radar for the last decade, it announced in early 2022 that it planned to acquire Activision Blizzard for $69 billion, making this deal the largest acquisition in Microsoft's history. Doing so put Microsoft back on the antitrust radar with regulators. Activision is one of the market leaders in video games and would become part of Microsoft's gaming business, including Xbox. In late 2022 it was reported that the European Commission (EC) would investigate the transaction, and in early 2023 the EC issued a statement of objection to the deal. The FTC in December 2022 sued to block the acquisition, citing concerns including whether Activision's popular games would only become available on the Xbox platform. Some analysts believe the deal could eventually go through, as the combined entity will only have approximately 15 percent market share. Still, if it does pass the European and FTC gauntlet, Microsoft will likely have to sign on to restrictions to potential anticompetitive practices in the video game market.[42]

The threats of Big Tech's anticompetitive practices

Impact on innovation

One of the main effects of Big Tech's dominant market power is that there has been a steep decline in the funding of start-ups. Start-ups have been the historic engine that enabled the US to become the leader in the Third Industrial Revolution—today's digital and computer era. But research by the Kauffman Foundation and others has shown that the share of jobs held at newly created companies has fallen over the last twenty years, and the number of new technology firms has also declined. In addition, the number of seed-stage funding deals (i.e., less than $1 million invested in a new venture) in the US has dropped from its high in 2014.[43]

This is partly because many VCs will not fund start-ups in the ten digital markets that Big Tech dominates, seeing those as "kill" zones. Given these markets' significant sizes, a massive chunk of our digital economy is essentially off-limits to new entrants. As one VC noted to the subcommittee about Amazon, "I think of Amazon as the sun. It is useful but also dangerous. If you're far enough away, you can bask. If you get too close, you'll get incinerated. So, you have to be far enough from Amazon and be doing something that they wouldn't do."[44]

Apple's and Google's "app tax" should also not be ignored in terms of impact on companies trying to create a business developing and selling mobile apps. A commission and payment processing fee of 30 percent is high compared to any other online marketplace. This puts app developers in a dilemma. Because they have to pay this high tax to Apple and Google, they could forgo hiring more engineers to build out more innovative and competitive solutions. Or they could accept lower profits, making them less attractive to potential investors or acquirers, thus diminishing their ability to have a lucrative "exit." Or the developers could charge more for their apps, which passes on the "app tax" to consumers.

Not only are tech companies feeling the impact, but local "brick-and-mortar" businesses are less likely to form, as they can easily be undercut by online retail giants such as Amazon. This is of concern, as starting local businesses has historically been a "pathway" to the middle class. Furthermore, some of the anticompetitive advertising practices I discussed can make it more expensive for local merchants to advertise on those platforms, thus requiring those businesses to direct more money to those two companies versus investing in their own businesses.[45]

Looking to the future, the massive investment in AI by Big Tech, combined with their hoard of data and their elastic cloud-based computing environments, lends itself to these same Big Tech firms cornering the market for AI and automation. However, this consolidation may not favor innovation as we embark on the Fourth Industrial Revolution—the fusion of advances in AI, robotics, IoT, and so on that blur the lines between the biological, physical, and digital spheres. Moreover, Big Tech's inside track on winning the next industrial revolution may further exasperate societal inequality, as it won't be a country broadly winning Industry 4.0 but just a handful of highly concentrated companies.[46]

Impact on consumer privacy

Even though many of the Big Tech products are free to consumers, these firms monetize their products through attention and data collection. In light of how Big Tech is so essential to navigating our daily life, and we are locked into their products due to network effects, high switching costs, and lack of alternatives, we must accept the terms of usage they give us. These terms include the increasingly intrusive collection of our personal and behavioral data. In other words, because Big Tech lacks competition, it can continue extracting more data from us, as there is no market pressure to do otherwise. In the past, this data was used for behavioral advertising, but as discussed, this data can now be weaponized against us or lead us into rabbit holes when combined with AI. The unchecked collection of more and more of our data lets Big Tech further entrench its market position as it gains more insight into our buying and browsing habits. Regulators see this exploitation as "equivalent to a monopolist's decision to increase prices or reduce product quality."[47]

Impact on the press and journalism

Per the subcommittee, a free and healthy press is "essential to a vibrant democracy," but the news industry has been in free fall for over two decades. The lifeblood of the news industry is advertising, and newspaper advertising revenue in the US has dropped from a high of nearly $50 billion in 2000 to $9.6 billion in 2020. In addition, the number of US newsroom employees has fallen from over seventy-one thousand in 2004 to slightly over thirty thousand in 2020. Long-term trends such as the consolidation of newspapers by private equity firms, online advertising sites like Craigslist taking over the lucrative classified advertising business, and so on have significantly impacted those numbers. Furthermore, how consumers receive and digest news via the internet has also affected the news industry's business model that historically delivered a hard copy newspaper to people's doorsteps.[48]

But in recent years, the trend toward content aggregation on Big Tech platforms—whereby content from multiple news sources is consolidated in a social media platform's news feed—has accelerated the decline of the news industry, especially with local news. The Big Tech firms, most notably Meta and Google, scrape news articles and summarize the articles by presenting, per the subcommittee, "attention-grabbing quotes from high points of stories." In many instances, this is sufficient for consumers to get the news they want. Therefore, web traffic back to the news publishers' websites does not occur, thus depriving them of advertising revenue. This also incentivizes news organizations to write more sensational or exploitive stories to play to aggregated news feeds' algorithms. Thus, the overall quality of our news diminishes as "click-bait" is favored. Google's and Meta's positions as gatekeepers of news also creates a significant power imbalance when news publishers negotiate revenue-sharing agreements with these two firms, further diminishing publishers' ability to monetize and invest in content.[49]

Impact on our politics

The Big Tech firms have dramatically increased their influence in the political process to protect their monopoly positions. Technology firms have increased lobbying expenditures from slightly over $1 million in 1998 to nearly $75 million in 2019. Furthermore, Big Tech firms have funded think tanks and nonprofit advocacy groups to help direct policy discussions. For example, in 2021, the trade group Chamber of Progress was formed with funding from Amazon, Apple, Meta, and others. Its mission is to support progressive and left-leaning causes, yet it opposed many of the antitrust bills that progressive Democratic lawmakers put forth in 2022. Of course, one could argue that Big Tech is looking to protect its interests, much like the railroad robber barons tried to influence legislators and regulators over a hundred years ago. But, as Subcommittee Chair David Cicilline noted in his antitrust investigation, the stakes for our democracy are pretty high in this battle of influence. He stated, "Because concentrated economic power also leads to concentrated political power, this investigation also goes to the heart of whether we, as a people, govern ourselves, or whether we let ourselves be governed by private monopolies."[50]

Legislation to address competition in digital markets

There is a lot of legislative activity both in Europe and the US to force Big Tech to break open their walled gardens. But, as usual, Europe is taking the lead.

European legislation

The European Commission's Digital Markets Act (DMA) was passed in 2022, with enforcement starting in 2024. This significant legislation cracks down on Big Tech and addresses many of the anticompetitive practices I have detailed in this chapter.

The DMA introduces rules for "gatekeepers" that control direct access to consumers and have a dominant market position in ten "core platform services" such as online search, social networking services, messaging services, web browsers, operating systems, app stores, and virtual assistants. Determination of which vendors are considered gatekeepers will occur by the spring of 2023, and an estimated ten companies will get this designation. The criteria for gatekeeper status is based on a multiple-part test that includes having EU revenue of €7.5 billion in each of the last three years or at least a €75 billion market capitalization in the previous financial year, presence in at least three EU countries, and over forty-five million monthly active users in one or more of the core platform services.[51]

The DMA rules are aimed "at preventing gatekeepers from imposing unfair conditions on businesses and end users and ensuring the openness of important digital services." Examples of the "dos" that are imposed on gatekeepers include the following:[52]

- Let consumers easily uninstall preinstalled apps and change any default settings that force consumers to use the gatekeeper's products.

- Let consumers install third-party app stores (e.g., not have to use the App Store on an iPhone or Google Play on an Android device).

- Let consumers unsubscribe from a service from the gatekeeper just as easily as they subscribe to it (e.g., easily cancel an Amazon Prime membership, which was the subject of a lawsuit in Norway).

- Let third parties interoperate with gatekeepers' services (e.g., require Meta's WhatsApp to receive messages from Signal or Telegram).

- Let developers be able to promote offers and conclude contracts outside the gatekeepers' services (e.g., to address Spotify's concern that it could not tell consumers inside their app of the ways to purchase an audiobook from the Spotify website).

Examples of "don'ts" imposed on gatekeepers include the following:

- Ban using marketplace data on third parties that compete with them.
- Ban self-preferencing their own products (e.g., in search results).
- Ban the requirement that third parties use the gatekeeper's payment system or other services.
- Ban tracking consumers outside the gatekeepers' walled gardens without user consent (e.g., technology like the Meta Pixel that can collect behavioral data on third-party websites).

As you can see, the DMA will significantly change how Big Tech does business by tearing down many walls in Big Tech's gardens and further restricting behavioral advertising. If the gatekeeper does not follow the rules, they can face fines of up to 10 percent of worldwide revenue or even up to 20 percent if they are repeat offenders.[53]

The threat of the DMA is already changing Big Tech's behavior well before enforcement of the DMA begins in 2024. For example, *Bloomberg* reported in December 2022 that Apple would allow alternative app stores on iPhones and iPads in Europe by the end of 2023. And Amazon reached a legally binding agreement in December 2022 with European Commission antitrust regulators to stop using non-public seller data to benefit its retail e-commerce business and its branded and private label products. Furthermore, Amazon agreed not to give preference to its offerings in the Amazon.com special buy-it-now "Buy Box" and will offer a second "Buy Box" to be displayed if a different seller provides a differentiated product based on price, delivery, or both. But these changes by Apple and Amazon will likely only be available for consumers in the European Union.[54]

Europe is by no means done regulating Big Tech. The Digital Service Act (DSA) was passed in 2022, which Big Tech will also need to grapple with when its enforcement begins by 2024. For example, the DSA requires risk assessments of specific categories of algorithms, applies content moderation requirements to social media sites, and bans targeted advertising that profiles children or is based on sensitive personal information such as ethnicity or sexual orientation. And in 2023, Europe may pass its Artificial Intelligence Act, which will likely ban or limit specific uses of AI.[55]

US legislation

As the 2022 legislative session ended in Congress, two Big Tech antitrust bills had strong bipartisan support but could not come up for a vote in the Senate. Both were written in response to the investigation by the Subcommittee on Antitrust.

The first is the Open App Markets Act (OAMA), introduced in the Senate by Senators Richard Blumenthal, Amy Klobuchar, and Marsha Blackburn and in the House by Representatives Johnson, Cicilline, and Buck. The OAMA would do the following:[56]

- Let consumers choose which default apps they want and delete any preinstalled apps they did not want.
- Let consumers be able to install third-party app stores on their mobile devices (including support for sideloading).
- Let app developers be able to communicate directly with consumers.
- Let app developers use alternative payment systems for in-app purchases, including subscriptions.
- Ban gatekeepers from self-preferencing their apps.
- Ban using non-public data regarding third-party apps to build competing apps.

The second Big Tech antitrust bill of significance that was considered in the 2022 legislation session was the American Innovation and Choice

Online Act (AICOA). It was introduced in the Senate by Senators Amy Klobuchar and Charles Grassley and in the House by Representative David Cicilline. The bipartisan and bicameral bill would, among other things, prevent gatekeepers from doing the following:[57]

- Self-preferencing their own products.
- Discriminating against direct competitors.
- Using non-public data regarding third-party sellers or apps to advantage the gatekeeper's products.

Like all the other consumer protection bills proposed in 2022 to rein in Big Tech, these antitrust bills have also not moved forward in the 2022 legislative session.

Road map to contain Big Tech's anticompetitive business practices

As much as we think of Big Tech's massive install base and network effects, their innovation and first-mover advantages, and the moats they have built up via acquisitions and vertical integration, the reality is that an equally key contributor to them becoming gatekeepers was that they rapidly grew when antitrust policy was at its most lax in decades. The focus of antitrust policy currently being based on the standard of considering "consumer welfare" in terms of whether consumer prices are low (or free in the case of many Big Tech products) has allowed Big Tech to make six-hundred-plus acquisitions without any of them being blocked, to control multiple sides of a market, and to self-preference their products.[58]

But Big Tech's grip on vital digital markets is causing a welcome rethink of antitrust policy. Lawmakers and regulators are starting to view monopolistic harm not solely from a consumer pricing perspective but also considering the impact on innovation and whether we have a fair and robust economy, as well as the impact on our democracy, which includes privacy and having a vibrant press.[59]

Restore competition

We need to reinvigorate competition in digital markets. For example, we saw incredible innovation after AT&T was broken up, including cheaper options for long-distance phone calls as well as a highly competitive telecommunications infrastructure taking root that not only let the internet grow and flourish but enabled the mobile revolution. In addition, forcing Microsoft to let other web browsers be installed on the Windows platform opened the door for Google and others. I understand that antitrust cases may take decades, but legislation can now be passed to restore competition.

The first step would be to implement rules that prevent discrimination. As recommended by the Subcommittee on Antitrust, nondiscrimination rules "would require dominant platforms to offer equal terms for equal service and would apply to price as well as to terms of access." For example, self-preferencing should be banned. This would let developers use alternative in-app purchasing payment methods, let consumers use alternative app stores, allow consumers to uninstall gatekeepers' default apps, stop gatekeepers from favoring their products in search results, permit developers to communicate with consumers, and more. Furthermore, data exploitation should also be banned, including using non-public data regarding third-party sellers or apps to advantage the gatekeeper's products. And consumers should be able to easily unsubscribe from a service from the gatekeeper just as easily as they subscribe to it. Passing OAMA and AICOA, or anything comparable to Europe's DMA, would be a significant first step.

The second is to pass legislation that requires the structural separation of certain businesses, such as digital advertising. For example, financial brokers such as Goldman Sachs and Citibank are barred from owning stock exchanges such as the NYSE or NASDAQ. Given that Google's DoubleClick is the equivalent of a stock exchange but for digital advertising, and Google also acts as a broker for buyers and sellers for ads, legislation could pass that requires structural separation in this market. For example, in 1906, Congress passed a law prohibiting railroads from "transporting any goods that they had produced or in which they held an interest," thereby blocking railroads from owning subsidiaries and other entities that competed with its customers. Requiring a similar prohibition in digital advertising would likely reduce prices, as the anti-trust lawsuit filed by various states claims that Google charges twice as much as rivals in ad deals.[60]

The high switching costs associated with Big Tech products must also be addressed to improve competition and increase consumer choice. Requiring interoperability would, per the subcommittee, "break the power of network effects" by letting new market entrants interconnect with gatekeepers' services and facilitate consumers' communication across platforms. For example, the DMA has an interoperability obligation for gatekeepers that provide messenger services requiring them to allow text messages between platforms. There should also be a data portability requirement. This is a standard feature among privacy laws such as Europe's GDPR and California's CPRA, but it should be available at the federal level. Data portability would let consumers fully move their data (e.g., social connections, purchase histories, etc.) out of walled gardens to competitive offerings. Both interoperability and data portability would break the consumer lock-in we have now with Big Tech platforms by reducing the high switching costs.[61]

And as discussed, having a healthy press is key to a vibrant democracy. The subcommittee recommended legislation that would give news publishers a "safe harbor" to better and more fairly negotiate with gatekeepers concerning revenue from content distribution. A bill such as the Journalism Competition and Preservation Act of 2019 would be needed legislation to protect journalism, especially the local press.

Strengthen antitrust laws and enforcement

Antitrust laws and enforcement should also be strengthened. For example, none of the six-hundred-plus acquisitions by Big Tech over the last two decades were blocked. So, besides legislation that could clarify the intent of existing antitrust laws—such as the Sherman Act and the Clayton Act—that antitrust should not be solely factoring in harm to consumer welfare, there need to be more aggressive anticompetitive actions taken by the DoJ and FTC.

The Biden administration agrees. For example, it put in place Lina Khan to run the FTC. Khan is best known for her law school journal article that examined the Amazon "antitrust paradox," which represented a "scorching indictment" of Robert Bork's and the Chicago School's theories of antitrust. Based on her initial work at the FTC, including amending the complaint against Meta that would have WhatsApp and Instagram divested from Meta and the FTC's lawsuit to block the Microsoft acquisition of Activision, the FTC under her leadership is taking a harder line on Big Tech's anticompetitive practices than it did under her predecessors. Combined with the DoJ's January 2023 antitrust lawsuit against Google over its online advertising business, the antitrust heat is being felt by Big Tech. Whether or not federal antitrust suits will also target Amazon (e.g., requiring it to divest its AWS cloud computing business) or Apple (e.g., its App Store practices that bar using alternative app stores and payment systems) is to be seen.[62]

Next steps

When it comes to Big Tech, we often focus on their products, brands, go-to-market, and founder stories when we consider how they became the internet giants they are now. But we must recognize that Big Tech's anticompetitive practices have also significantly contributed to them becoming these giants who act as gatekeepers to our digital economy. As much as we may like their brands or fondly recall how they started as scrappy start-ups and the darlings of Silicon Valley, having such high degrees of concentration is not healthy for our economy or democracy. As the subcommittee notes, when too much economic power is in the hands of a few, "the result is less innovation, fewer choices for consumers, and a weakened democracy." Justice Louis Brandeis wrote over a century ago, "We must make our choice. We may have democracy, or we may have wealth concentrated in the hands of a few, but we cannot have both."[63]

In the conclusion, I will summarize the choices we need to make concerning containing Big Tech.

Conclusion

Companies that once were scrappy, underdog startups that challenged the status quo have become the kinds of monopolies we last saw in the era of oil barons and railroad tycoons. Although these firms have delivered clear benefits to society, the dominance of Amazon, Apple, Facebook, and Google has come at a price.

—Majority Report on Competition in Digital Markets, US House Judiciary Subcommittee on Antitrust[1]

In late October 2022, Meta announced that its revenue had declined 4 percent year over year in its third fiscal quarter of 2022 (Q3 22). The day after that earnings announcement, Meta's stock dropped 22 percent. But Meta's share price slide had been happening all of 2022. From the beginning of 2022 through October 31, 2022, Meta's stock price was down 73 percent. In comparison, in that same period, the S&P 500 was down 20 percent, and Meta's stock price was down over two times the average of its Big Tech peers. As a result, Meta lost over $700 billion in market capitalization in that period. As one industry pundit noted in November 2022, if you had purchased Meta stock in 2015, you would have lost money, and if you had bought shares of General Motors or IBM at the same time, it would have been a better investment.[2]

Approximately two weeks after its disappointing Q3 22 earnings announcement, Meta CEO Mark Zuckerberg announced layoffs of over eleven thousand employees. He cited in his message to employees that "the macroeconomic downturn, increased competition, and ads signal loss" were the causes for Meta's revenues to be "much lower" than expected.[3]

"Increased competition" was a reference to TikTok eating into Meta's revenue. Meta is trying to catch up to TikTok with its "Reels" short-form video. But in doing so, Meta is no longer relying on its core strength as a social network but trying to match TikTok's strength as an in-the-moment entertainment platform. Because TikTok does not require your friends to join its platform to distract and engage with you, it does not need to build a social graph and can sidestep the network effects game. Nor are TikTok users' friends required to generate content. So, to chase advertising dollars, TikTok is forcing Meta to branch out beyond its social networking model and pursue new models of engagement and attention-seeking.[4]

By "ads signal noise," Zuckerberg was referring to the impact of Apple's App Tracking Transparency (ATT), which was introduced as part of Apple's iOS 14.5 update in April 2021. According to Apple, ATT "allows you to choose whether an app can track your activity across other companies' apps and websites for the purposes of advertising or sharing with data brokers." It is estimated that as of mid-2022, approximately 75 percent of Apple iOS users opted out of tracking. Meta told financial analysts in February 2022 that this loss of tracking data from Apple devices would cause a $10 billion revenue shortfall in 2022, as less behavioral and "interaction" data is being collected, thereby diminishing their ability to target ads.[5]

Beyond competition from TikTok and Apple's ATT, Meta also faces other challenges. For example, its Metaverse—Meta's virtual reality world that Meta says is "the next evolution in social connection and the successor to the mobile internet" and the basis for rebranding the company from Facebook to Meta—is not taking off. In 2015, Zuckerberg outlined in an internal email that they "need to own a computing platform" to hedge against Google's and Apple's gatekeeper status in the mobile space. So, Meta has been trying to build its computing platform with its Metaverse. But this initiative is not going too well as the "successor" to mobile. And it is likely too late for Meta to create a "Facebook Phone." Ironically, Apple's gatekeeper status in mobile has kneecapped Meta six years after Zuckerberg sent that email.[6]

And regulators are circling Meta. An antitrust lawsuit filed by the Department of Justice (DoJ) and several states is trying to break off WhatsApp and Instagram from Meta. California's privacy law will begin enforcement in 2023, thus raising the "user consent" bar for collecting and processing personal data. The EU also passed the Digital Markets Act to put tighter regulations on "gatekeepers," which will be enforced by 2024. The Irish Data Protection Commission (DPC) fined Meta over $400 million in the fall of 2022 for the past practice of making kids' Instagram profiles public by default. The Irish DPC also fined Meta $235 million in November 2022 for a 2021 data breach that led to the personal information of over five hundred million Facebook users being leaked online. And in 2021, Australian lawmakers passed legislation forcing Meta and Google to make payments to news organizations.[7]

But the most significant regulatory action against Meta was taken in January 2023 by Ireland's DPC. Besides fining Meta over $400 million, the DPC ruled that Meta violated EU privacy law by not allowing consumers in Europe the ability to say yes or no to the collection of personal data to facilitate the serving of personalized ads when using Meta's products. Instead, the DPC alleges that Meta buried the consent clause in the terms and conditions of its services. Thus, the DPC concluded that Meta broke European privacy law by not giving European consumers the legal right to opt out of personal data collection and only offering "forced consent," meaning that consumers must agree to their data being collected or not be able to use Meta's services. Meta publicly said it would appeal the ruling, and it may be years for adjudication. But much like the high percentage of opt outs seen with Apple's App Tracking Transparency, this could significantly dent Meta's revenue. While some EU users will accept data collection and Meta can still provide contextual ads (based on page content), one analyst estimates that this judgment could eventually put 5 to 7 percent of Meta's revenue at risk. As Big Tech critic Jason Kint noted in a tweet, all these actions clearly show that tech regulators and the law are now catching up with consumer privacy and data protection expectations.[8]

One is temporarily down, and none of them are out

So, is Meta the new Myspace and destined for the ash heap of history? The answer is no. For all of Meta's challenges, the company is still a gatekeeper and has a dominant market position. For example, in its Q3 22 earnings announcement, Meta stated that it is still adding users. Its platform grew by fifty million users to 2.93 billion daily active users (DAUs). It also increased monthly active users (MAUs) by sixty million to 3.71 billion. That is nearly four billion users that use Meta's services every month, which is half the world's population.[9]

In addition, time spent on Meta's platforms is increasing. Meta Chief Strategy Officer Dave Wehner said in the Q3 2022 earnings call, "In terms of aggregate time spent on Instagram and Facebook, both are up year-over-year in both the US and globally." Furthermore, Meta said that Meta's Reels, its short-form video format, increased usage by 50 percent in just six months and is on a $3 billion revenue run rate, so it is gaining on TikTok. In addition, Meta is making considerable investments in areas beyond the Metaverse with significant upside, specifically in AI. As one industry watcher noted, "Meta the metaverse company may be a speculative boondoggle, but that doesn't change the fact that the old Facebook is still a massive business with far more of its indicators pointing up-and-to-the-right than its Myspace-analogizers want to admit."[10]

Nor is Meta the canary in the Big Tech coal mine, signaling the downfall of Big Tech. For example, Apple reported solid third quarter of 2022 financial results and passed two billion active devices at the end of 2022. Moreover, even though Amazon, Google, and Microsoft had layoffs in the late 2022 and January 2023 time frame (e.g., Amazon laid off 18,000 out of 1.5 million employees), with none announced by Apple in a similar time frame, the layoffs by Amazon, Google, Meta, and Microsoft still leave them above their respective 2021 headcount levels. Furthermore, Wall Street rewarded Big Tech for these job cuts. While the four Big Tech firms that had layoffs incurred $10 billion in cumulative expenses related to their cost-cutting moves, their combined market caps rose $800 billion from November 2022 to February 2023. In the case of Meta, in that period, its stock rose over 100 percent, and it added $250 billion in market capitalization, showing investor confidence that the worst is behind Meta.[11]

Big Tech will likely come out of 2023 even more potent, especially as the few potential start-up competitors willing to fly in Big Tech's "kill zones" will face funding challenges, with the general downward trend in VC funding in 2022 going into 2023. So, some of Big Tech's competitors may be killed off because they don't have the substantial cash balances that the Big Tech firms have to weather the storm. Or, as funding and exit opportunities dry up, innovative start-ups may be forced into being acquired at discounted rates. Furthermore, because VCs avoided investing in the markets dominated by the Big Tech firms, they put a lot of money into markets like cryptocurrency, which melted down in 2022. The result is that some VCs may not get limited partners to invest more money into any of their new funds, thus further drying up the money available to start-ups that could conceivably compete with Big Tech.[12]

Big Tech's continued strength is also represented by its successful lobbying against attempts to regulate it in the US. For example, the major bipartisan antitrust bills proposed in 2022, the American Innovation and Choice Online Act (AICOA) and the Open App Markets Act (OAMA), did not come up for a vote in the Senate in that legislative session. In addition, all the bills proposed in 2022 to protect kids' online safety, such as the Children and Teens' Online Privacy Protection Act and Kids Online Safety Act (KOSA), also languished. This was also true of the American Data Privacy and Protection Act (ADPPA), an omnibus and bipartisan privacy bill. That being said, regulatory progress was made in Europe with the passage of the Digital Markets Act (DMA) and the Digital Services Act (DSA). Still, critics have pointed out that European regulators have not historically been as punitive regarding enforcing their tech regulations. And while California has progressed with its Age Appropriate Design Act (AADC), a trade group representing Big Tech immediately sued California to stop it. So, even with successes in Europe and California, the issue remains that no significant legislation has passed at the US federal level to contain Big Tech in any meaningful manner.

And let's remember that Big Tech's monopolistic businesses produce high returns on capital. With high margins and low customer acquisition costs, the Big Tech firms have massively profitable businesses that generate a lot of cash. As a result, the five Big Tech firms have five of the seven largest cash balances of any S&P 500 company as of 2022. So, Big Tech can buy or invest its way into a seat at the table of the ensuing technology wave or even the next industrial revolution, in which AI will play a leading role. For example, Microsoft has invested $13 billion in OpenAI, a leading provider of AI-based solutions for text-to-image generation and chatbots. Google invested over $300 million in an AI start-up called Anthropic, which competes with OpenAI. And for AI to be effective, it requires massive amounts of computing power, which Big Tech uniquely has.[13]

So, the unique combination of Big Tech's dominant market positions, the lax regulatory environment at the US federal level, their huge cash war chests, and their industry-leading investments in cutting-edge technology like AI and cloud computing remain even after the economic downturn experienced in 2022. Thus, the Big Tech firms are well-positioned to continue their leadership in 2023 and beyond. And the issues and threats associated with these modern-day robber barons will continue if left unchecked.

There is a better path

But there is good news. We can contain the threats of Big Tech that weaken our civil rights, economy, and democracy. It won't be easy, but there is a path to do it.

Containing digital surveillance

We live in a world where our online activity is constantly being tracked, and a dossier of every one of us is increasing in breadth and depth. For some, that dossier is equivalent to three million documents' worth of data. In effect, firms like Google and Meta have incredible insight into our day-to-day routines, as if we are in a reality TV show and the cameras are on us all the time. For example, I am in a world where my online activity and location data are logged on average every six minutes by Google. In the past, this digital surveillance was focused on serving targeted ads, but now it can be used to erode our rights and be weaponized against us.

It does not have to be that way. We can pass a comprehensive privacy law, as spelled out in appendix 2, to give us the right to know what data is being collected on us and give us the right to say no to its collection, sale, and sharing. If personal information is collected, a comprehensive privacy bill would then limit its use to the minimum needed to achieve the purposes for its collection. We can also create a world where digital surveillance is banned for children, and our most sensitive data is prohibited from being used for behavioral advertising and used to discriminate against us. In effect, we as consumers can have an "Online Bill of Rights." And we can have a government entity whose sole job is to ensure businesses are following these privacy rules and respecting our privacy rights and, if companies are not, to fine them and prevent them from breaking the rules moving forward.

We live in a world where shadowy data brokers collect all our online activity and merge it with our credit purchase history, property records, location data, and more. And anyone with a credit card can buy this information about us. Data brokers also profile and score us, which is then used by others to make crucial decisions impacting our lives, such as loans, housing, and jobs, despite the underlying data being incorrect half the time.

But it, too, does not have to be this way. We can pass a data broker law that, by letting us do a simple registration on a government web page, would tell every data broker to delete our data and, moving forward, never collect, sell, or share it again.

We live in a world where our data is constantly hacked, and identity theft is rampant.

This, too, does not have to be. If less data is collected and stored, there is less data that can be breached. So having a comprehensive privacy and data broker law in place can empower us to say no to these and other companies having too much of our data. Likewise, businesses should be required to have reasonable data security practices in place for sensitive data. And we can have a Federal Aviation Administration (FAA) equivalent that can be the central government agency that can holistically catalog and investigate data breaches and levy fines for poor cybersecurity practices. That same agency could also provide guidance and best practices to help make consumers and businesses more secure.

Containing artificial intelligence

We live in a world where AI is increasingly automating human decision-making and is also being used to influence our behavior. AI can significantly benefit society, but we are experiencing AI that can be biased and used for exploitative means, such as what we have seen with deepfakes. Thus, AI can be the equivalent of Pandora, who brought with her powerful gifts but also unleashed mighty plagues and evils.

Suppose Google CEO Sundar Pichai is right that AI will have a more profound impact on humanity than fire or electricity. In that case, just as we have firefighters and we regulate electric utilities, we should seek to regulate AI—especially biased or exploitative AI that can be used to discriminate against or harm us. We should have a Federal Drug Administration (FDA) equivalent to ensure the most impactful AI systems are safe, just like the FDA does for drugs. And like for our privacy, we should have an "AI Bill of Rights" that lets us know how AI systems contribute to outcomes that impact us.

We also live in a world where Big Tech uses increasingly AI-based persuasive technologies to maximize our engagement and suck up more and more of our attention. Unfortunately, this persuasive technology has led to addiction, which is highly troublesome for the most vulnerable in society, namely children. Not only are children exposed to addictive technologies, but they are bombarded with harmful or inappropriate content, unsolicited contact from adults, and cyberbullying.

We don't have to accept persuasive technology and can ban the worst examples of it—dark patterns that purposely try to trick us. And we can require Big Tech to design products that don't constantly autoplay content to keep kids on their platforms. We can have their products support save buttons so that kids don't have to stay online to complete a task, and we can require that these products stop the encouragement and reward of streaks. Furthermore, we can require that kids' profiles are not public by default. In other words, we can insist that digital products are designed with the equivalent child safety features for products in the physical world.

We also live in a world where social media and other online platforms are filled with toxic and harmful content, including disinformation and extremism. This content gets promoted and amplified by online platforms' AI-based recommendation systems to encourage us to return to their platforms. Doing so has created polarization in our society and weakened our democracy. And it has led some people down rabbit holes of conspiracy theories that are hard to climb out of.

But we can have a healthier democracy with less polarization while giving people freedom of speech but not guaranteed freedom of reach. We can have laws that require platforms' content moderation policies to be transparent and AI-based recommendation systems to be open to assessment for harm. We can investigate deceptive or unfair trade practices relating to online platforms not honoring content moderation terms of services or failing to protect consumers. And we can require online platforms to report illegal behavior and have a higher standard of care regarding targeted advertising.

Containing tech monopolies

We live in a world with monopolists dominating our largest and most consequential digital markets. Unfortunately, the start-up engine that propelled our economy in the past is seeing decreased funding, as investors are unwilling to fund companies in these important digital markets that the Big Tech firms dominate. As a result, vast swathes of the economy are now forced to ride and depend on Big Tech's rails to market and must pay for it through high commission fees or be forced to use Big Tech's payment systems. And Big Tech is preferencing its products, further decreasing the ability for competitors to compete in the Big Tech marketplaces. Finally, consumers are locked into the Big Tech products, given the lack of interoperability, meaning they have to accept the terms of service from Big Tech, which increasingly lets them gather more and more personal data and weaken our privacy.

We can make our economy more competitive. Like in the past, we either regulated or broke up monopolies in railroads, oil production, telecommunications, and the bundling of a browser with an operating system—and innovation flourished because of this. We can do the same in digital markets that Big Tech dominates. For example, we should not let Big Tech self-preference their products or be able to use marketplace data on competitors to inform their own decisions. We should reduce the "app tax" on app developers by allowing alternative app stores and payment systems. And we should let third parties be able to interoperate with gatekeepers' services, so consumers are not locked into Big Tech's less consumer-friendly products in privacy and data protection.

We did it in the past. We can do it again.

Big Tech has enriched our lives by building incredible products that let us create, locate, shop, learn, entertain, work, and communicate with others. So, we should not be dismissive of their positives.

But we must rein in Big Tech's negatives. If we don't, our civil rights are at risk, our economy is stifled, and our democracy is vulnerable. Senator John Sherman, the author of the landmark 1890 antitrust law that is named after him, remarked over one hundred years ago, "If we will not endure a king as a political power, we should not endure a king over the production, transportation, and sale of the necessaries of life."[14]

The question is whether this generation will continue to accept the threats associated with today's "kings" of technology, or will we usher in a new era of reforms to counter these more powerful modern versions of the nineteenth-century robber barons. I am confident that increased awareness, coupled with a straightforward road map like what I have laid out in this book, will motivate more people to insist we can and must contain Big Tech, thus enabling us to strengthen our society, economy, and democracy.

Acknowledgments

I want to thank my family for supporting me on this project. I would also like to thank our dog, Chloe, for keeping me company on a nearby couch as I worked late nights on this. And thanks to the folks at Greenleaf Book Group for helping me turn my Word documents into a finished book.

I would also like to acknowledge the trailblazers who have astutely written and evangelized on critical aspects of the impact of Big Tech on our society, economy, and democracy. People and their works that immediately come to mind that have influenced this book include Shoshanna Zuboff and her groundbreaking book on digital surveillance, Roger McNamee and his book on the threat of Facebook, Tristan Harris and his Center for Humane Technology and their writings on persuasive technology, Baroness Beeban Kidron and her 5RightsFoundation and their work and research on kids' online safety, Cory Doctorow and his blogs on digital surveillance and monopolies, Scott Galloway and his weekly musings on topics such as TikTok and weapons of mass distraction, Jason Kint and his tweets on the latest Big Tech happenings, and Lina Khan and her groundbreaking antitrust article on Amazon plus her work at the FTC.

There are many journalists whose reporting on Big Tech has been quite insightful and helpful. I want to give a special shoutout to the team at *The Markup*, including its co-founder and former editor-in-chief Julia Angwin, for all their excellent investigative work on Big Tech. Other journalists whose reporting has been a vital resource in this book include Karen Hao, Sam Schechner, Georgia Wells, Keach Hagey, and Jeff

Horwitz at the *Wall Street Journal*; Geoffrey Fowler, Cristiano Lima, and Will Oremus at the *Washington Post*; Celia Kang, Tripp Mickle, Shira Ovide, Natasha Singer, and Adam Satariano with the *New York Times*; Sara Morrison with *Vox*; Johana Bhuiyan at the *Guardian*; Will Evans and Gilad Edelman with *Wired*; Ina Fried at *Axios*; and Joseph Cox at *Vice*. Several blogs were quite beneficial, including the writings of Bennett Cyphers, Katharine Trendacosta, Gennie Gebhart, and others at the Electronic Frontier Foundation, plus Justin Hendrix's *Tech Policy Press* with its great posts from Jennifer King, Charlotte Slaiman, and others. This is not an exhaustive list, and I apologize if I overlooked someone. Thank you to everyone whose content I referenced in the notes.

I would also like to acknowledge and thank the whistleblowers and policy advocates who are making Big Tech more accountable. The whistleblowers include Cambridge Analytica whistleblowers Christopher Wylie and Brittany Kaiser and Facebook whistleblower Frances Haugen. Thank you to European Commissioner for Competition Margrethe Vestager and the folks behind the Digital Markets Act and Digital Services Act. In California, thanks to my fellow Prop 24 and California Privacy Rights Act (CPRA) teammates Alastair Mactaggart, Robin Swanson, Celine Mactaggart, and Rick Arney. Alastair was the driving force behind both of California's privacy laws and deserves all the credit for leading the charge for privacy laws in the US. Now that the CPRA is in effect, I wish the California Privacy Protection Agency the best of success, including its executive director Ashkan Soltani, board member Lydia de la Torre, and the rest of the team and board. Thanks also to California state Senator Josh Becker, who introduced various bills to regulate data brokers that I proposed to him.

At the federal policy level, I am excited we have FTC Chair Lina Khan moving the ball forward with the FTC and Jonathan Kanter reinvigorating antitrust at the DoJ. Thanks to President Biden for putting both in place and advocating for improved online safety for kids, enhanced privacy, and more competition. Thanks to Tim Wu for his insightful writing on competition and his productive stint at the National Economic Council. Thanks to Representative David Cicilline and the staff members on the US House Judiciary Subcommittee on Antitrust, which published its comprehensive final report in 2022 on competition in digital markets that provides a road map for needed antitrust actions. And shoutouts to President Obama for his speech on disinformation at Stanford, Representative Kathy Castor and Senators Ed Markey and Richard Blumenthal for their work on protecting kids online, Senator Ron Wyden for his AI Act, and Senator Amy Klobuchar for her antitrust work. And thanks to Representative Ro Khanna for his Online Bill of Rights and his book *Dignity in a Digital Age*.

Finally, I want to acknowledge and extend my deepest sympathies to the families who have lost loved ones in part due to the excesses of Big Tech. So many are bravely challenging the status quo via the judicial system, including the family of fourteen-year-old Molly Russell, who sadly died of self-harm while suffering from depression and the harmful effects of online content. Another example is the family of American law student Nohemi Gonzalez, who was tragically killed in a 2015 ISIS terrorist attack in Paris and whose family claims YouTube's algorithms recommended and amplified ISIS videos to others. In addition, I know there are dozens of lawsuits against Big Tech firms filed by other grieving families across the US and other parts of the world. Hopefully, these legal actions will spur changes, and we citizens, in turn, will also encourage policymakers and regulators to do their part, thus pressuring Big Tech to curb its excesses and minimize its negative impact on people.

APPENDIX 1

Protecting Your Online Privacy

Here are some suggestions for protecting your online privacy. I will first provide general recommendations on limiting third parties from tracking you. I will next discuss tips on reducing your overall data footprint. I will then describe how you can get data brokers to delete your data and stop tracking you, as well as the steps you can take to protect yourself again identity theft. Finally, I will suggest changes to various default settings inside Big Tech's products that you can configure to limit your data being shared with them.

Limit tracking

You can change your web browser privacy settings to limit online tracking via third-party cookies. All browsers let you see what third-party cookies are on your computer. You can delete these cookies, but this does not stop future tracking by third-party cookies. But from there, you can configure the browser to "Block Third-Party Cookies" and send a "Do Not Track" request with your browsing traffic. For example, you control this on Google Chrome by going to Settings → Privacy and Security → Cookies and Other Site Data. You can also turn on "private browsing mode," such as Google Chrome's Incognito mode, which results in your browser not saving your browsing history, cookies, and any information entered in forms. But the drawback of Incognito mode is that websites can still track that a consumer visited their website.

There are also third-party browser extensions that can reduce third parties from tracking you. For example, Privacy Badger from the Electronic Frontier Foundation (EFF) can stop "advertisers and other third-party trackers from secretly tracking where you go and what pages you look at on the web." In addition, privacy-centric browsers such as Brave, Avast Secure Browser, DuckDuckGo, and Apple's Safari combine many of the capabilities of third-party browser extensions and address the shortcomings of Incognito mode. For example, the Apple Safari browser has a feature called Intelligent Tracking Prevention (ITP) that, per Apple, can obscure data such as "device and browser configuration, and fonts and plug-ins you have installed." ITP can also hide your IP address from trackers and block social widgets (e.g., Facebook Like buttons) from tracking you. In addition, ITP also provides a "Privacy Report" that shows all the cross-site trackers that were blocked.[1]

Mobile devices also have settings that let you configure whether ads will target you based on your browsing activity or app usage. For example, you can reset or delete your Mobile Advertising ID (MAID) by selecting the Privacy setting on your phone and selecting Advertising. You can also turn off "Ad Personalization" to stop ad targeting based on your past activity. You can view "Location" in your settings and disable apps that may have been granted location privileges that may only be using that permission to feed data brokers your precise geolocation.[2]

Apple's App Tracking Transparency (ATT) lets you set, per Apple, "whether an app can track your activity across other companies' apps and websites for the purposes of advertising or sharing with data brokers." Apple also requires mobile app developers to create a "Privacy Nutrition Label" that you can view to assess what data is being collected about you by the app developer. Google's Android does not natively provide an ATT equivalent to block third-party trackers in your apps. Privacy vendor DuckDuckGo offers App Tracking Protection (ATP) that is equivalent to ATT but for Android. It is a feature of the free DuckDuckGo app for Android, but you do not have to use the DuckDuckGo internet browser inside their app to take advantage of

ATP. DuckDuckGo's research found that the average Android user has thirty-five apps, and those apps can experience between one thousand and two thousand daily tracking attempts that contact over seventy tracking companies and data brokers.[3]

You can also install personal virtual private networks (VPNs) that help you hide your online identity. A VPN lets your traffic go through a secure communication channel to the VPN provider's servers, so your web traffic appears to be coming from the VPN server versus your device. In addition, messaging services such as Signal utilize end-to-end encryption that encodes your message so it can only be unlocked by the intended receiver's device, making it difficult for anyone to intercept your messages.[4]

Finally, different services offer email masking or even credit card masking. For example, Apple claims that its Mail Privacy Protection "hides your IP address so senders can't link it to your other online activity or determine your location" and "prevents senders from seeing if you've opened the email they sent you." In addition, software vendor IronVest has a "Masked Cards" product that lets you create a "burner" credit card for every purchase, stopping data brokers from collecting your purchase history.[5]

Reducing your data footprint

There are other ways to reduce the amount of data exhaust that can be vacuumed up. At the top of the list is to make your social media accounts private versus public so data brokers cannot "web crawl" your profiles and posts. Additionally, if you have been doxxed, you can request content removal from Google via https://support.google.com/websearch/troubleshooter/3111061?hl=en or Bing via https://www.microsoft.com/en-ca/concern/bing. Furthermore, for a given Google search result that has your address, email address, or phone number, you can request removal from Google's search engine index by tapping the menu item for the search result (represented as three dots to the right of the search result) and select Remove Result in the About This Search window.[6]

You can reduce the number of inbound marketing calls by adding your name to the FTC's Do Not Call registry. You should also consider contacting your phone company to see if they can stop listing your phone number on Caller ID or if there is an option to opt out of the sale of your phone numbers. Consider registering with DMAChoice. com to opt out of email marketing databases. You can additionally put a freeze on creditors checking your credit report by contacting each of the Big 3 credit reporting agencies. Another action is to use the website https://www.optoutprescreen.com/ to opt out of being solicited for new credit cards or insurance. Finally, you can say no to loyalty programs that sell your purchase history to data brokers.[7]

Getting data brokers to opt you out or delete your data

You can go directly to the data brokers themselves and request the deletion of your data. In addition, you can ask that they never sell any new data on you. But it is a daunting task, given that there are four thousand data brokers worldwide, and most people need help knowing where to start. Yael Grauer, an investigative reporter with Consumer Reports, has created a "Big Ass Data Broker Opt-Out List" that you can search for that provides directions on how to opt out for some of the largest data brokers. Privacy Rights Clearinghouse has a good listing at https://privacyrights.org/data-brokers. As discussed in chapter 2, California and Vermont have data broker registries that list registered data brokers. Or you can use an internet search engine to search for your name and address, create a list of the websites you appear on, and work through that list.

But once you find the data brokers you want to target, making one-by-one requests to get your data deleted can be a long and painful process. As discussed, in light that we do not have a federal privacy law, a data broker may reject or not reply to your requests if you live in a state without a privacy law. Furthermore, even if you were to identify a data broker you want to have your data deleted from, and you live in a state that gives you the privacy right of deletion, many data brokers make it very difficult to exercise that right. For example, Consumer Reports asked volunteers to exercise their CCPA data subject rights with various data brokers, and many consumers found it to be a "scavenger hunt." This means that it may take dozens of hours to have one's personal information deleted from just a handful of data brokers' databases.[8]

Some software products are available that act as authorized agents on your behalf and will search for and delete your data across multiple data broker websites that do "people search." Their range of coverage is between a dozen to a few hundred data brokers. Often referred to as "opt-out services," most charge a monthly subscription fee, but some may have a freemium offering for a limited number of data brokers. Examples of companies in this space include Atlas Privacy, Confidently, DeleteME, and PrivacyBee.[9]

Protecting against identity theft

Considering that hackers can use the data collected by data brokers to facilitate identity theft in terms of phishing attacks or guessing security questions, consumers should be aware of some best practices to protect themselves. It starts with not relying just on a password but also having multifactor authentication set up for critical online accounts. Then, if the password is phished, guessed, or stolen, the hacker will still not be able to access your account, as they lack the second factor for access. Password managers are also good tools to ensure that your passwords are not easily guessed. And subscribing to alerts on https://haveibeenpwned.com/ will notify you if your password for a given online account has been caught up in a known breach and is floating around the dark web.

Big Tech product settings

Below are suggested settings and controls inside various products from Apple, Google, Meta, Microsoft, and Amazon that can limit data sharing with them. Note that the vendors will occasionally change or reorganize their Settings menu or app, so if you need help finding the controls I suggest configuring, you can search for the topic.

Apple

As previously discussed, I highly recommend globally enabling App Tracking Transparency. You can do this by going to the Settings app and then to the Privacy & Security menu. From there, select Tracking and switch off Allow Apps to Request to Track. You can also turn off targeted advertising on Apple's App Store and its News and Stocks apps. You do this within Privacy & Security by going to Apple Advertising and switching off Personalized Ads.

You can turn off the sharing of data with Apple that is used to improve its products. To do so, under Privacy & Security, go to Analytics & Improvements, and switch off Share iPhone Analytics. And to prevent your iPhone from sharing your geolocation data to improve Apple Maps, under Privacy & Security, go to Location Services and System Services, and then turn off iPhone Analytics and Routing & Traffic.[10]

Finally, you can turn on Advanced Data Protection for iCloud to enable end-to-end encryption of your iCloud backups. This means that only you—and not even Apple—can access the data you store on the iCloud service. On your iPhone or iPad that runs iOS version 16.2 or above, go to Settings, tap Your Name, then go to iCloud, select Advanced Data Protection, and then Account Recovery. You then designate a recovery contact (a friend who can help you regain access to your iCloud account and data) or a recovery key (a secret twenty-eight-character key that you use to recover your account or data). Or you can select both.[11]

Google

Go to myactivity.google.com to control tracking and to delete data collected by Google search and other Google services such as Google

Maps and YouTube. For example, you can configure auto-deletion or delete any activity over three months old. You can also turn off the collection of your device's location history. In addition, you can switch off "ad personalization" for Google services and Google partners. Google's ad personalization serves you with targeted ads based on the behavioral data that Google collects on you.

Google also provides a Privacy Checkup. To access this, go to Google .com, and assuming you are logged in with your Google account, you can select Manage Your Google Account. Then choose Data & Privacy. Select the Privacy Checkup. You can also use the Data & Privacy option page to turn off Personalized Ads and see what third-party apps can access your account.

On Android, you can go to the Settings app, then to the Google menu, then to the Ads menu, and then turn off Opt Out of Ads Personalization. You can delete your Advertising ID that apps have used to track you. Android's Settings app also has a Privacy menu where you can configure the Permission Manager to granularly control what apps have what permissions on your device. For example, you can configure what apps should be allowed access to your location or camera.

Meta

As discussed in chapter 1, the Meta Pixel is widely deployed across hundreds of thousands of websites. It captures your interactions with websites—for example, the information you put into online forms such as your name, address, what items you put in a shopping cart, and so on—and transmits that information back to Meta's Facebook service. You can view what recent activity Meta has collected by going to https://www.facebook.com/off_facebook_activity/. You can clear past activities, but more importantly, you can disconnect the collection of any future activity.

You can control which ads you see by going to Settings & Privacy → Ads. This takes you to your Ad Preferences page, where you can select Ad Settings to turn off ads from advertisers who use the Meta platform for advertising or stop ads based on your social media interactions with businesses. Note this does not delete any data, so you still need to configure Off-Facebook Activity.

You should also perform a Privacy Checkup under Settings & Privacy. This will give you a guided tour of how to configure Ad Settings. It will also suggest ways you can keep your Facebook account more secure and limit who can find you on Facebook.

Amazon

The first thing you should do is make sure your Amazon Wish Lists are private. On the Amazon.com website, log in with your Amazon account and go to Help & Settings → Your Account → Your Lists. Then, click on the three dots to the right for each list, select Manage List, and configure the Privacy setting to Private. You can also stop Amazon from saving your search history by going to https://www.amazon .com/gp/history, selecting Manage History, and configuring Turn Browsing History on/off to Off.[12]

Another suggestion is to turn off Amazon Sidewalk from your devices. Sidewalk lets Amazon products share network connections with nearby devices. To turn it off, within the Alexa app on your phone, go to the More icon → Settings → Account Settings → Amazon Sidewalk and then switch off Enabled. You can also stop and clear any Alexa voice recordings by going into the Alexa app on your phone to Settings → Alexa Privacy → Manage Your Alexa Data → Choose How Long to Save Voice Recordings, and then tapping Don't Save Recordings.[13]

Microsoft

If you have an account with Microsoft, Microsoft offers a privacy dashboard at https://account.microsoft.com/privacy. You can review your account safety settings, manage your activity data, and manage privacy settings across products such as Windows, Xbox, Office, and Teams. You can also go to https://account.microsoft.com/privacy/ad-settings and turn off personalized ad settings.

On Windows PCs, you can turn off letting apps on your PC track you via an advertising ID. Go to Settings → Privacy and turn off Let Apps Use Advertising ID. In addition, you can turn off letting Microsoft track your app launches on your PC. You can also go to Activity History and clear any activity your PC has captured about you.

APPENDIX 2

Ingredients for a Comprehensive US Privacy Law

So, what should go into a comprehensive US privacy law to protect against the digital surveillance we see from Big Tech? It would need to take the best of Europe's GDPR and California's CPRA and allow for flexibility for states to innovate and experiment with adding to it. It should have three key pillars: comprehensive consumer rights, strict business obligations, and enforcement with teeth.

Consumer rights should include, at the minimum, the following:[1]

- *Right to Be Informed* (also known as "Right to Know" or "Right to be Notified")—the right to be informed of the purpose of the collection of your data and if your data will be sold or shared.
- *Right to Access*—the right for you to access the categories of personal data, the recipients of the data, the purposes of collection and processing, and the actual data itself.
- *Right to Correct* (also known as "Right to Rectification")—the right to correct the personal data a business has on you.
- *Right to Delete* (also known as "Right to Erasure" or "Right to Be Forgotten")—the right for you to tell a business to delete data they have on you.

- *Right to Data Portability*—the right to get your data in a standard format so you can move it from one service to another (e.g., your emails or contacts).
- *Right to Reject Automated Decision-Making and Profiling*—the right not to be subject to decisions based solely on automated processing, including profiling. An example would be objecting to a loan approval done exclusively by automated means.[2]
- *Right to "Opt Out" of Sale and Sharing of Personal Information* (also known as the "Right to Say No")—the right for you to tell the business they can't sell or share your information.
- *Right of No Retaliation* (also known as "Right to Not Be Discriminated Against")—the right not to be discriminated against by the business if you exercise any of these rights.
- *Right to Limit Use of Sensitive Personal Information*—the right for you to direct a business that collects your sensitive personal information (e.g., sexual orientation, health information, union membership, race, ethnic origin, religion, precise geolocation, etc.) to limit its use to solely what is necessary to perform the service. So, if the service asks you for your location to get picked up in a car, it should not use your location to send you ads of nearby businesses.

Business obligations should include, at the minimum, the following:[3]

- *Data Minimization*—businesses should limit the collection, use, retention, and sharing of your data to what is reasonably necessary and proportionate to achieve the purposes for which it was collected or processed.[4]
- *Heightened Protections Concerning Sensitive Data*—businesses must employ stricter data minimization rules for sensitive personal data (e.g., it cannot be collected or used beyond strict necessity to provide service.)
- *Prohibition of Discriminatory Uses of Data*—businesses may not collect, process, or transfer personal data in a discriminatory manner based on race, religion, color, sex, national origin, or disability.

- *Limitations on Targeted Advertising*—businesses should not be able to knowingly target children or utilize sensitive personal data such as religious beliefs, sexual orientation, and ethnicity with regard to online behavioral advertising.
- *Responsiveness to Rights Requests*—businesses must respond in a timely manner to the above consumers' rights.
- *Support for Global Privacy Control*—businesses must support consumers' use of Global Privacy Control (GPC). GPC is a browser plug-in that sends a signal to a website that a consumer visits with their browser, instructing the website that the consumer wants to opt out of any selling and sharing of their personal information.
- *Appropriate Security Measures*—businesses must implement reasonable security procedures to safeguard personal information from unauthorized or illegal access. Also, they must notify you if your data has been breached.[5]
- *Data Protection Impact Analysis*—businesses must perform a cybersecurity audit annually and do risk assessments of the processing of personal data.
- *Data Protection Officers*—businesses must have a person responsible for overseeing the businesses' privacy program.

Finally, essential enforcement requirements in a comprehensive privacy law should include, at the minimum, the following:[6]

- *Dedicated Supervisory Authority*—we should have a dedicated agency that monitors privacy in the US and has sufficient funding. It could be akin to the Federal Drug Administration (FDA), which oversees the safety and security of food, drugs, and biological products. Considering that the Federal Trade Commission (FTC) has historically been responsible for consumer protection, it is a logical place to have as the home for this agency.
- *Penalties*—the enforcement agency should be able to levy significant fines for businesses violating our privacy rights. In addition,

the agency should be able to force the offenders to stop processing data altogether or change the way they are doing it.

- *Private Right of Action*—consumers should have the right to file a lawsuit if their privacy rights are violated.

This is not a comprehensive listing but should be the "floor" for any federal privacy law in the US and not preempt more robust state provisions.

Notes

About the Cover

1. George Frederick Keller, "The Curse of California," *The Wasp*, August 19, 1882. Image from Wikimedia Commons, https://commons.wikimedia.org/wiki/File:The_Curse_of_California.jpg; Udo J. Keppler, "Next!" Puck, September 7, 1904. Image from the repository of the Library of Congress, https://www.loc.gov/pictures/item/2001695241/.

Introduction

1. The White House, "Readout of White House Listening Session on Tech Platform Accountability," September 8, 2022, https://www.whitehouse.gov/briefing-room/statements-releases/2022/09/08/readout-of-white-house-listening-session-on-tech-platform-accountability/.

2. Kevin Starr, *California: A History* (New York: Modern Library, 2007), 81; Wikipedia, "Central Pacific Railroad," updated January 24, 2023, https://en.wikipedia.org/wiki/Central_Pacific_Railroad.

3. Starr, *California: A History*, 117, 154–155; CPI Inflation Calculator, accessed January 10, 2023, with the start year of 1890 and the end year of 2023, https://www.in2013dollars.com/.

4. The Geography of Transport Systems, "Automobile Production, Selected Countries, 1950–2021," accessed January 3, 2023, https://transportgeography.org/contents/chapter1/the-setting-of-global-transportation-systems/automobile-production-world/.

5. In light of the fact that Google is 99 percent of Alphabet's revenue, I will refer to Alphabet as Google. Alphabet is a holding company that was created through the restructuring of Google in 2015, with Google becoming a subsidiary of Alphabet. In light of Meta Platforms Inc. doing business as Meta, I will refer to the company as Meta. Meta was formerly named Facebook, with the renaming occurring in 2021. Unless otherwise indicated, Facebook will refer to Meta's flagship social media networking service, which Meta offers alongside other products and services such as Instagram, WhatsApp, and Messenger.

6. Slickcharts, "S&P 500 Companies by Weight," accessed December 31, 2022, https://www.slickcharts.com/sp500; World Population Review, "GDP Ranked by

Country, 2022," accessed December 31, 2022, https://worldpopulationreview
.com/countries/countries-by-gdp.

7. Al Root, "Tesla Isn't the Most Valuable American Car Company Yet," *Barrons*,
    January 9, 2020, https://www.barrons.com/articles/tesla-stock-gm-1950s-was
    -richer-51578510312.

8. Klaus Schwab, "The Fourth Industrial Revolution: What It Means, How to
    Respond," World Economic Forum, January 14, 2016, https://www.weforum.org
    /agenda/2016/01/the-fourth-industrial-revolution-what-it-means-and-how-to
    -respond/.

9. Shelley Walsh, "50 Google Search Statistics & Facts," *Semrush Blog*, May 25, 2021,
    https://www.semrush.com/blog/google-search-statistics/; World Population Review,
    "Facebook Users by Country, 2022," accessed January 3, 2023, https://world
    populationreview.com/country-rankings/facebook-users-by-country; Anyron
    Copeman, "Windows Now Has 1.4 Billion Users, but How Many Are on Windows
    11?" *Tech Advisor*, January 26, 2022, https://www.techadvisor.com/article/745681
    /windows-now-has-1-4-billion-users-but-how-many-are-on-windows-11.html;
    William Gallagher, "There Are 1B iPhones in Use Worldwide, Apple Says," *Apple
    Insider*, January 27, 2021, https://appleinsider.com/articles/21/01/27/there-are-1b
    -iphones-in-use-worldwide-apple-says; Wallaroo, "TikTok Statistics—Updated
    January 20, 2022," updated January 20, 2022, https://wallaroomedia.com/blog
    /social-media/tiktok-statistics/; Katharina Buchholz, "The Road to One Billion
    Users," Statista, October 14, 2021, https://www.statista.com/chart/25974/social
    -networks-time-spent-to-reach-one-billion-mau/; Jay Traughott, "Guess How Many
    Cars GM Has Built in Its 106-Year History," *CarBuzz*, May 5, 2015, https://carbuzz
    .com/news/guess-how-many-cars-gm-has-built-in-its-106-year-history.

10. Statista, "Number of Instagram Users Worldwide from 2020 to 2025," accessed
    January 3, 2023, https://www.statista.com/statistics/183585/instagram-number-of
    -global-users/; Daniel Threlfall, "27 Facebook Messenger Statistics That Will
    Change the Way You Think About Marketing," *MobileMonkey*, updated May
    2021, https://mobilemonkey.com/blog/facebook-messenger-statistics-facebook
    -messenger-marketing; ThinkImpact, "WhatsApp Statistics," accessed January 3,
    2023, https://www.thinkimpact.com/whatsapp-statistics/; Shawn Knight, "Google
    Photos Passes the One Billion User Mark, Ninth Product in Google's Roster to Do
    So," *TechSpot*, July 24, 2019, https://www.techspot.com/news/81119-photos
    -becomes-ninth-google-product-pass-one-billion.html; Statista, "User Population
    of Selected Internet Browsers Worldwide from 2014 to 2021 (in Millions),"
    accessed January 3, 2023, https://www.statista.com/statistics/543218/worldwide
    -internet-users-by-browser/; Statista, "YouTube – Statistics & Facts," accessed
    January 10, 2023, https://www.statista.com/topics/2019/youtube/; SaaS Scout,
    "Gmail Statistics, Users, Growth and Facts for 2021," accessed January 3, 2023,
    https://saasscout.com/statistics/gmail-statistics/.

11. Kashmir Hill, "I Tried to Live Without the Tech Giants. It Was Impossible," *New
    York Times*, July 30, 2020, https://www.nytimes.com/2020/07/31/technology
    /blocking-the-tech-giants.html.

12. Simon Kemp, "Digital 2022: Global Overview Report," DataReportal, January
    26, 2022, https://datareportal.com/reports/digital-2022-global-overview-report;
    Justin Scheck et al., "Facebook Promised Poor Countries Free Internet. People Got
    Charged Anyway," *Wall Street Journal*, January 24, 2022, https://www.wsj.com
    /articles/facebook-free-india-data-charges-11643035284; Domo, "Data Never
    Sleeps 9.0," accessed January 3, 2023, https://www.domo.com/learn/info
    graphic/data-never-sleeps-9; John Gramlich, "10 Facts About Americans and

Facebook," Pew Research Center, June 1, 2021, https://www.pewresearch.org/fact-tank/2021/06/01/facts-about-americans-and-facebook/.

13. Federal Trade Commission, "Commercial Surveillance and Data Security Rulemaking," August 11, 2022, https://www.ftc.gov/legal-library/browse/federal-register-notices/commercial-surveillance-data-security-rulemaking; Standard Oil analogy quoted from Alastair Mactaggart in "Californians for Consumer Privacy's Proposition 24 Webinar," October 1, 2020, https://www.youtube.com/watch?v=66UZB9tFmdA.

14. Peter Thiel, "Competition Is for Losers with Peter Thiel," Y Combinator, YouTube video, 50:27, March 22, 2017, https://www.youtube.com/watch?v=3Fx5Q8xGU8k.

15. Gramlich, "10 Facts About Americans and Facebook."

16. Geoffrey Fowler (@geoffreyfowler), "I don't care about privacy," Twitter, June 24, 2022, 8:49 a.m., https://twitter.com/geoffreyfowler/status/1540361470176702464.

17. Wikiquote, "Dan Patrick (sportscaster)," updated July 26, 2021, https://en.wikiquote.org/wiki/Dan_Patrick_(sportscaster); Barry Popik, "You can't stop him, you can only hope to contain him," *The Big Apple*, March 20, 2022, https://www.barrypopik.com/index.php/new_york_city/entry/you_cant_stop_him_you_can_only_hope_to_contain_him.

Chapter 1

1. CBS News (@CBSNews), "Sen. Hatch: 'If [a version of Facebook . . . ,'" Twitter, April 10, 2018, 12:31 p.m., https://twitter.com/CBSNews/status/983789635406004224.

2. Jeannie Suk Gersen, "Why the 'Privacy' Wars Rage On," *New Yorker*, June 20, 2022, https://www.newyorker.com/magazine/2022/06/27/why-the-privacy-wars-rage-on-amy-gajda-seek-and-hide-brian-hochman-the-listeners; Samuel Warren and Louis Brandeis, "The Right to Privacy," *Harvard Law Review*, December 15, 1890, https://groups.csail.mit.edu/mac/classes/6.805/articles/privacy/Privacy_brand_warr2.html.

3. U.S. Const. amend. IV.

4. Alphabet, Form 10-Q, July 26, 2022, https://abc.xyz/investor/static/pdf/20220726_alphabet_10Q.pdf; Alphabet, "Alphabet Announces Third Quarter 2021 Results," October 26, 2021, https://abc.xyz/investor/static/pdf/2021Q3_alphabet_earnings_release.pdf?cache=f1ba3f6; Alphabet, "Alphabet Announces Fourth Quarter and Fiscal Year 2021 Results," February 1, 2022, https://abc.xyz/investor/static/pdf/2021Q4_alphabet_earnings_release.pdf?cache=d72fc76; Meta Platforms, Inc., Form 10-Q, July 28, 2022, https://d18rn0p25nwr6d.cloudfront.net/CIK-0001326801/f657a197-fe9f-4414-81d3-b56c02701886.pdf; Meta Platforms, Inc., Form 10-K, February 3, 2022, https://d18rn0p25nwr6d.cloudfront.net/CIK-0001326801/14039b47-2e2f-4054-9dc5-71bcc7cf01ce.pdf.

5. Amazon.com, Inc., "Amazon.com Announces Fourth Quarter Results," February 3, 2022, https://www.businesswire.com/news/home/20220202005957/en/; Amazon.com, Inc., "Amazon.com Announces Second Quarter Results," July 28, 2022, https://ir.aboutamazon.com/news-release/news-release-details/2022/Amazon.com-Announces-Second-Quarter-Results-fe1df2b70/; Seb Joseph and Ronan Shields, "The Rundown: Google, Meta, and Amazon Are on Track to Absorb More Than 50% of All Ad Money in 2022," *Digiday*, February 4, 2022, https://digiday.com/marketing/the-rundown-google-meta-and-amazon-are-on

-track-to-absorb-more-than-50-of-all-ad-money-in-2022/amp/; Ronan Shields, "Microsoft's Ad Revenue Hit $10B, and It's Investing—Is It a Sleeping Giant About to Wake?" *Digiday*, January 27, 2022, https://digiday.com/media/microsofts-ad -revenue-hit-10b-and-its-investing-is-a-sleeping-giant-about-to-wake/amp/; David Cohen, "LinkedIn Collective Community for B-to-B Marketers Debuts," *Adweek*, July 27, 2022, https://www.adweek.com/social-marketing/linkedin-collective -community-for-b-to-b-marketers-debuts/. For Microsoft's ad revenue, I added Microsoft's search and news advertising with the LinkedIn Marketing Solutions revenue to calculate the $15 billion in revenue; Ben Lovejoy, "Apple's Ad Business Sees Windfall; Is Accused of Breaking Its Own Privacy Rules," *9to5Mac*, October 18, 2021, https://9to5mac.com/2021/10/18/apples-ad-business-windfall/.

6. Statista, "Average Daily Time Spent per Capita with the Internet Worldwide from 2011 to 2021," accessed January 3, 2023, https://www.statista.com/statistics /1009455/daily-time-per-capita-internet-worldwide/; Kemp, "Digital 2022: Global Overview Report"; Ethan Cramer-Flood, "Worldwide Digital Ad Spending Year -End Update," *Insider Intelligence*, November 23, 2021, https://www.insider intelligence.com/content/worldwide-digital-ad-spending-year-end-update.

7. MySudo, "What Is Digital Exhaust and Why Does It Matter?" August 17, 2020, https://mysudo.com/2020/08/what-is-digital-exhaust-and-why-does-it-matter/; Shoshana Zuboff, *The Age of Surveillance Capitalism: The Fight for a Human Future at the New Frontier of Power* (New York: Public Affairs, 2019).

8. Jeremy Bullmore, "Why It's Time to Say Goodbye to IKTHTMISOAIW*," *WPP Annual Report & Accounts 2013*, accessed January 3, 2023, https://reports.wpp .com/annualreports/2013/what-we-think/why-its-time-to-say-goodbye-to -ikthtmisoaiw.

9. Vishveshwar Jatain, "The Walled Gardens of Ad Tech, Explained," *Blockthrough Blog*, June 16, 2021, https://blockthrough.com/blog/the-walled-gardens-of-the-ad -tech-industry-explained/.

10. Eduardo Abraham Schnadower Mustri et al., "Behavioral Advertising and Consumer Welfare: An Empirical Investigation," Federal Trade Commission, November 1, 2022, https://www.ftc.gov/system/files/ftc_gov/pdf/PrivacyCon-2022 -Acquisiti-Mustri-Behavioral-Advertising-Consumer-Welfare.pdf; IAB Europe, "Digital Advertising & Marketing," accessed January 10, 2023, https://iabeurope .eu/the-value-of-digital-advertising/; Statista, "Digital Advertising – Worldwide," accessed January 10, 2023, https://www.statista.com/outlook/dmo/digital -advertising/worldwide.

11. Brian McCullough, "A Revealing Look at the Dot-com Bubble of 2000—and How It Shapes Our Lives Today," *Ideas.Ted.Com*, December 4, 2018, https://ideas.ted. com/an-eye-opening-look-at-the-dot-com-bubble-of-2000-and-how-it-shapes-our -lives-today/.

12. Google, Form S-1, April 29, 2004, https://www.sec.gov/Archives/edgar /data/1288776/000119312504073639/ds1.htm.

13. Shoshana Zuboff, "The Threat of Surveillance Capitalism, and the Fight for a Human Future," *ABC*, August 21, 2019, https://www.abc.net.au/religion /shoshana-zuboff-threat-of-surveillance-capitalism/11433716.

14. Google, Form S-1, April 29, 2004.

15. Google, Form S-1, April 29, 2004; Zuboff, "The Threat of Surveillance Capitalism."

16. Jeff Pelline, "Excerpts from Google Co-founders' Playboy Interview," *ZDNet*, August 12, 2004, https://www.zdnet.com/article/excerpts-from-google-co-founders -playboy-interview/.

17. 10k Reader, "The Greatest Acquisitions of All Time," July 2022, https://www
.10kreader.com/blog/the-greatest-acquisitions-of-all-time.

18. Daisuke Wakabayashi, "Google Will No Longer Scan Gmail for Ad Targeting,"
New York Times, June 23, 2017, https://www.nytimes.com/2017/06/23/technology
/gmail-ads.html.

19. 10k Reader, "The Greatest Acquisitions of All Time."

20. Slintel, "Market Share of Google DoubleClick," August 3, 2022, https://www
.slintel.com/tech/ad-exchange/google-doubleclick-market-share.

21. Dylan Curran, "Are You Ready? Here Is All the Data Facebook and Google Have
on You," *The Guardian*, March 30, 2018, https://www.theguardian.com/comment
isfree/2018/mar/28/all-the-data-facebook-google-has-on-you-privacy.

22. Facebook, Inc., Form S-1, February 1, 2012, https://www.sec.gov/Archives/edgar
/data/1326801/000119312512034517/d287954ds1.htm; Wikipedia, "On the
Internet, nobody knows you're a dog," updated December 19, 2022, https://en
.wikipedia.org/wiki/On_the_Internet,_nobody_knows_you%27re_a_dog.

23. 10k Reader, "The Greatest Acquisitions of All Time"; At the time of Meta's IPO, it
claimed 845 million monthly users. Facebook, Inc., Form S-1, February 1, 2012.

24. Geoffrey A. Fowler, "There's No Escape from Facebook, Even If You Don't Use
It," *Washington Post*, August 29, 2021, https://www.washingtonpost.com
/technology/2021/08/29/facebook-privacy-monopoly/.

25. Angie Waller and Colin Lecher, "Help Us Investigate Facebook Pixel Tracking,"
The Markup, January 21, 2022, https://themarkup.org/pixel-hunt/2022/01/21
/help-us-investigate-facebook-pixel-tracking; Julia Angwin, "Facebook's Pervasive
Pixel," *The Markup*, August 20, 2022, https://themarkup.org/newsletter/hello
-world/facebooks-pervasive-pixel; Fowler, "No Escape from Facebook."

26. An analogy from Geoffrey A. Fowler, "Facebook Will Now Show You Exactly
How It Stalks You—Even When You're Not Using Facebook," *Washington Post*,
January 28, 2020, https://www.washingtonpost.com/technology/2020/01/28/off
-facebook-activity-page/.

27. Statista, "Market Share of Leading Retail E-commerce Companies in the United
States as of June 2022," accessed January 3, 2023, https://www.statista.com
/statistics/274255/market-share-of-the-leading-retailers-in-us-e-commerce/.

28. Matt Burgess, "All the Ways Amazon Tracks You and How to Stop It," *Wired*,
June 19, 2021, https://www.wired.co.uk/article/amazon-history-data.

29. Kate O'Flaherty, "The Data Game: What Amazon Knows About You and How to
Stop It," *The Guardian*, February 27, 2022, https://www.theguardian.com
/technology/2022/feb/27/the-data-game-what-amazon-knows-about-you-and-how
-to-stop-it.

30. Ina Fried, "What Amazon Knows About You," *Axios*, May 2, 2019, https://www
.axios.com/2019/05/02/what-amazon-knows-about-you.

31. Reuters, "A Look at the Data Amazon Collects on Consumers Through Its
Services," *Indian Express*, November 20, 2021, https://indianexpress.com
/article/technology/tech-news-technology/a-look-at-the-data-amazon-collects-on
-consumers-through-its-services-7632364/.

32. O'Flaherty, "The Data Game."

33. Fried, "What Amazon Knows About You."

34. Microsoft, "Earnings Release FY22 Q4," November 30, 2022 https://www
.microsoft.com/en-us/Investor/earnings/FY-2022-Q4/segment-revenues.

35. Wikipedia, "Usage Share of Operating Systems," updated February 7, 2023, https://en.wikipedia.org/wiki/Usage_share_of_operating_systems; Statista, "Market Share of Major Office Productivity Software Worldwide as of February 2022," accessed January 3, 2023, https://www.statista.com/statistics/983299/worldwide-market-share-of-office-productivity-software/; Felix Richter, "Amazon, Microsoft & Google Dominate Cloud Market," Statista, November 15, 2022, https://www.statista.com/chart/18819/worldwide-market-share-of-leading-cloud-infrastructure-service-providers/; Oberlo, "Most Popular Browsers in 2022," accessed January 3, 2023, https://www.oberlo.com/statistics/browser-market-share.

36. StatCounter, "Search Engine Market Share Worldwide," accessed January 3, 2023, https://gs.statcounter.com/search-engine-market-share; Wikipedia, "Microsoft Advertising," updated February 5, 2023, https://en.wikipedia.org/wiki/Microsoft_Advertising; Statista, "Annual Revenue of LinkedIn from 2017 to 2022," accessed January 3, 2023, https://www.statista.com/statistics/976194/annual-revenue-of-linkedin/; LinkedIn, "About LinkedIn," accessed January 3, 2023, https://about.linkedin.com/.

37. Jules Bonnard, "France Fines Microsoft 60 Million Euros over Advertising Cookies," *Agence France-Presse*, December 22, 2022, https://www.yahoo.com/now/france-fines-microsoft-60-million-081512167.html.

38. Wikipedia, "Apple Inc.," updated February 6, 2023, https://en.wikipedia.org/wiki/Apple_Inc.

39. Johana Bhuiyan, "Apple Says It Prioritizes Privacy. Experts Say Gaps Remain," *The Guardian*, September 23, 2022, https://www.theguardian.com/technology/2022/sep/23/apple-user-data-law-enforcement-falling-short; Parmy Olson, "Can Apple Be a Privacy Hero and an Ad Giant?" *Washington Post*, September 14, 2022, https://www.washingtonpost.com/business/can-apple-be-a-privacy-hero-and-an-ad-giant/2022/09/14/360e214c-33ea-11ed-a0d6-415299bfebd5_story.html; Apple, "Apple Advances User Security with Powerful New Data Protections," December 7, 2022, https://www.apple.com/newsroom/2022/12/apple-advances-user-security-with-powerful-new-data-protections/.

40. Apple, "Apple Advances User Security."

41. Sam Schechner, "Meta Fined over $400 Million in EU for Serving Ads Based on Online Activity," *Wall Street Journal*, January 4, 2022, https://www.wsj.com/articles/meta-fined-411-million-for-sending-ads-based-on-online-activity-11672844441.

42. Kinshuk Jerath, "Mobile Advertising and the Impact of Apple's App Tracking Transparency Policy," Apple, April 26, 2022, https://www.apple.com/privacy/docs/Mobile_Advertising_and_the_Impact_of_Apples_App_Tracking_Transparency_Policy_April_2022.pdf; Flurry, "App Tracking Transparency Opt-In Rate—Monthly Updates," May 2, 2022, https://www.flurry.com/blog/att-opt-in-rate-monthly-updates/; Kif Leswing, "Facebook Says Apple iOS Privacy Change Will Result in $10 Billion Revenue Hit This Year," *CNBC*, February 2, 2022, https://www.cnbc.com/2022/02/02/facebook-says-apple-ios-privacy-change-will-cost-10-billion-this-year.html.

43. Cory Doctorow, "How to Destroy Surveillance Capitalism," *OneZero*, August 25, 2020, https://onezero.medium.com/how-to-destroy-surveillance-capitalism-8135e6744d59; European Commission, "Ethics Guidelines for Trustworthy AI," April 8, 2019, https://www.aepd.es/sites/default/files/2019-12/ai-ethics-guidelines.pdf.

44. Angwin, "Facebook's Pervasive Pixel"; Surya Mattu and Colin Lecher, "Applied for Student Aid Online? Facebook Saw You," *The Markup*, April 28, 2022, https://themarkup.org/pixel-hunt/2022/04/28/applied-for-student-aid-online

-facebook-saw-you; Simon Fondrie-Teitler, "Tax Filing Websites Have Been Sending Users' Financial Information to Facebook," *The Markup*, November 22, 2022, https://themarkup.org/pixel-hunt/2022/11/22/tax-filing-websites-have-been -sending-users-financial-information-to-facebook.

45. Jason Koebler and Anna Merlan, "This Is the Data Facebook Gave Police to Prosecute a Teenager for Abortion," *Vice*, August 9, 2022, https://www.vice.com /en/article/n7zevd/this-is-the-data-facebook-gave-police-to-prosecute-a-teenager-for -abortion. Meta announced in January 2023 that it would start rolling out support for end-to-end encryption as a default setting of Messenger chats.

46. Jeremy B. Merrill, "Google Has Been Allowing Advertisers to Exclude Nonbinary People from Seeing Job Ads," *The Markup*, February 11, 2021, https://themarkup .org/google-the-giant/2021/02/11/google-has-been-allowing-advertisers-to-exclude -nonbinary-people-from-seeing-job-ads.

47. Craig Silverman, "Google Allowed Sanctioned Russian Ad Company to Harvest User Data for Months," *ProPublica*, July 5, 2022, https://arstechnica.com /information-technology/2022/07/google-allowed-sanctioned-russian-ad-company -to-harvest-user-data-for-months; Christianna Silva and Elizabeth de Luna, "It Looks Like China Does Have Access to US TikTok User Data," *Mashable*, July 2, 2022, https://mashable.com/article/tiktok-china-access-data-in-us.

48. NATO StratCom COE, "Data Brokers and Security," 2021, https://stratcomcoe.org /cuploads/pfiles/data_brokers_and_security_20-01-2020.pdf; Justin Sherman, "Data Brokers and Sensitive Data on US Individuals," Duke University, Sanford Cyber Policy Program, 2021, https://sites.sanford.duke.edu/techpolicy/wp-content /uploads/sites/17/2021/08/Data-Brokers-and-Sensitive-Data-on-US-Individuals -Sherman-2021.pdf.

49. Tom Kemp, "Looking at US Data Protection Laws in the Context of the CCPA," May 14, 2020, https://tomkemp.blog/2020/05/14/looking-at-us-data-protection -laws-in-the-context-of-the-ccpa/; European Court of Human Rights, "European Convention on Human Rights," accessed January 3, 2023, https://www.echr.coe .int/Documents/Convention_ENG.pdf; European Commission, "Charter of Fundamental Rights of the European Union," October 26, 2012, https://eur-lex .europa.eu/legal-content/EN/TXT/?uri=CELEX:12012P/TXT.

50. Tom Kemp, "GDPR's Key Data Processing Principles and Individual Rights," November 14, 2019, https://tomkemp.blog/2019/11/14/revisiting-the-gdprs-key -data-processing-principles-and-individual-rights/.

51. European Commission, "Questions and Answers: Digital Services Act," May 20, 2022, https://ec.europa.eu/commission/presscorner/detail/en/QANDA_20_2348; European Commission, "Questions and Answers: Digital Markets Act: Ensuring Fair and Open Digital Markets," April 23, 2022, https://ec.europa.eu/commission /presscorner/detail/en/QANDA_20_2349.

52. The author is proud to have volunteered and led the marketing efforts to pass the Prop 24 ballot initiative.

53. Categorization of sector-specific laws comes from Lauren Steinfeld, "Privacy Law and Data Protection," Coursera, April 28, 2020, https://www.coursera.org/learn /privacy-law-data-protection; The description of the various laws in the bullets comes from Tom Kemp, "Looking at US Data Protection Laws in the Context of the CCPA."

54. Tom Kemp, "Big Tech Wolf in Sheep's Clothing? Californians Unite in Opposition to the ADPPA 'Trap,'" August 10, 2022, https://tomkemp.blog/2022/08/10/big -tech-wolf-in-sheeps-clothing-californians-unite-in-opposition-to-the-adppa-trap/.

55. Nico Grant, "Google Says It Will Delete Location Data When Users Visit Abortion Clinics," *New York Times*, July 1, 2022, https://www.nytimes.com/2022/07/01 /technology/google-abortion-location-data.html.

56. Gilad Edelman, "Why Don't We Just Ban Targeted Advertising?" *Wired*, March 22, 2020, https://www.wired.com/story/why-dont-we-just-ban-targeted-advertising/.

Chapter 2

1. Tim Cook, "2019 Commencement Address by Apple CEO Tim Cook," Stanford, June 16, 2019, https://news.stanford.edu/2019/06/16/remarks-tim-cook-2019 -stanford-commencement/.

2. *The Pillar*, "Pillar Investigates: USCCB Gen Sec Burrill Resigns After Sexual Misconduct Allegations," July 20, 2021, https://www.pillarcatholic.com/p/pillar -investigates-usccb-gen-sec?s=r; Joseph Cox, "Data Broker Is Selling Location Data of People Who Visit Abortion Clinics," *Vice*, May 2, 2022, https://www.vice.com /en/article/m7vzjb/location-data-abortion-clinics-safegraph-planned-parenthood. After the story was published, the data broker said it would no longer sell location data for visits to Planned Parenthood.

3. Acxiom, Global Data Navigator datasheet, accessed January 3, 2023, https: //marketing.acxiom.com/rs/982-LRE-196/images/Fact_Sheet_Global_Data _Navigator.pdf; WebFX, "What Are Data Brokers – And What Is Your Data Worth?" March 16, 2020, https://www.webfx.com/blog/internet/what-are-data -brokers-and-what-is-your-data-worth-infographic/; Knowledge Sourcing Intelligence, "Global Data Broker Market Size," June 2021, https://www .knowledge-sourcing.com/report/global-data-broker-market.

4. NATO StratCom COE, "Data Brokers and Security"; Federal Trade Commission, "Data Brokers: A Call for Transparency and Accountability," 2014, https://www.ftc .gov/system/files/documents/reports/data-brokers-call-transparency-accountability -report-federal-trade-commission-may-2014/140527databrokerreport.pdf.

5. US Senate Committee on Commerce, Science, and Transportation, "A Review of the Data Broker Industry: Collection, Use, and Sale of Consumer Data for Marketing Purposes, Staff Report for Chairman Rockefeller," December 18, 2013, http: //educationnewyork.com/files/rockefeller_databroker.pdf; Wikipedia, "LiveRamp," updated December 29, 2022, https://en.wikipedia.org/wiki/LiveRamp.

6. Harvey Rosenfield and Laura Antonini, "Opinion: Data Isn't Just Being Collected from Your Phone. It's Being Used to Score You," *Washington Post*, July 31, 2020; Federal Trade Commission, "Data Brokers."

7. Wolfie Christl, "Corporate Surveillance in Everyday Life," *Cracked Labs*, June 2017, https://crackedlabs.org/en/corporate-surveillance.

8. Statista, "Number of Internet of Things (IoT) Connected Devices Worldwide from 2019 to 2030," March 17, 2022, https://www.statista.com/statistics/1183457/iot -connected-devices-worldwide/.

9. California Privacy Rights Act, accessed January 15, 2023, https://www.caprivacy. org/annotated-cpra-text-with-ccpa-changes/#1798.140(c); Antonio Regalado, "More than 26 Million People Have Taken an At-Home Ancestry Test," *MIT Technology Review*, February 11, 2019, https://www.technologyreview.com/2019/02/11/103446 /more-than-26-million-people-have-taken-an-at-home-ancestry-test/.

10. Aaron Riecke et al., "Data Brokers in an Open Society," *Open Society Foundations*, November 2016, https://www.opensocietyfoundations.org/uploads/42d529c7 -a351-412e-a065-53770cf1d35e/data-brokers-in-an-open-society-20161121.pdf;

Federal Reserve Bank of San Francisco, "2022 Findings from the Diary of Consumer Payment Choice," May 5, 2022, https://www.frbsf.org/cash/publications/fed-notes/2019/june/2022-findings-from-the-diary-of-consumer-payment-choice/.

11. Scott Galloway, "WMDs," May 6, 2022, https://www.profgalloway.com/wmds/; Joshua Benton (@jbenton), "Put another way: Americans spend 67% more time . . . ," Twitter, June 3, 2022, 7:09 a.m., https://twitter.com/jbenton/status/1532726113700564994.

12. Christl, "Corporate Surveillance in Everyday Life."

13. NATO StratCom COE, "Data Brokers and Security."

14. Federal Trade Commission, "Data Brokers."

15. Federal Trade Commission, "Data Brokers."

16. Federal Trade Commission, "Data Brokers."

17. NATO StratCom COE, "Data Brokers and Security"; Federal Trade Commission, "Data Brokers"; Joseph Cox, "The California DMV Is Making $50M a Year Selling Drivers' Personal Information," *Vice*, November 25, 2019, https://www.vice.com/en/article/evjekz/the-california-dmv-is-making-dollar50m-a-year-selling-drivers-personal-information.

18. Sherman, "Data Brokers and Sensitive Data."

19. Sherman, "Data Brokers and Sensitive Data"; Chris Chmura, "Your Pay Stub Is Probably in the Cloud," *NBC Bay Area*, May 6, 2022, https://www.nbcbayarea.com/investigations/consumer/your-pay-stub-is-probably-in-the-cloud-silicon-valley-startup-recommends-a-vault-instead/2883933/; WPP, "WPP's Data Alliance and Spotify Announce Global Data Partnership," November 15, 2016, https://www.prnewswire.com/news-releases/wpps-data-alliance-and-spotify-announce-global-data-partnership-300362733.html; Lois Beckett, "Everything We Know About What Data Brokers Know About You," *ProPublica*, June 13, 2014, https://www.propublica.org/article/everything-we-know-about-what-data-brokers-know-about-you.

20. Federal Trade Commission, "Data Brokers"; Robots.net, "How Data Brokers Profit from Your Data," February 22, 2022, https://robots.net/fintech/general-fintech/how-data-brokers-profit-from-your-data-a-guide/; Christl, "Corporate Surveillance in Everyday Life."

21. Christl, "Corporate Surveillance in Everyday Life"; Bennett Cyphers and Gennie Gebhart, "Behind the One Way Mirror: A Deep Dive into the Technology of Corporate Surveillance," Electronic Frontier Foundation (EFF), December 2, 2019, https://www.eff.org/wp/behind-the-one-way-mirror.

22. Molly McGuane, "First-Party Cookies vs. Third-Party Cookies (Biggest Differences)," *Terakeet*, February 4, 2021, https://terakeet.com/blog/first-party-cookies-vs-third-party-cookies/.

23. McGuane, "First-Party Cookies."

24. Cyphers and Gebhart, "Behind the One Way Mirror."

25. Cyphers and Gebhart, "Behind the One Way Mirror."

26. Tatum Hunter and Jeremy Merrill, "Health Apps Share Your Concerns with Advertisers. HIPAA Can't Stop It," *Washington Post*, September 22, 2022, https://www.washingtonpost.com/technology/2022/09/22/health-apps-privacy/.

27. Jon Keegan and Alfred Ng, "There's a Multibillion-Dollar Market for Your Phone's Location Data," *The Markup*, September 30, 2021, https://themarkup.org/privacy/2021/09/30/theres-a-multibillion-dollar-market-for-your-phones-location-data.

28. Jon Keegan and Alfred Ng, "Who Is Policing the Location Data Industry?" *The Markup*, February 24, 2022, https://themarkup.org/ask-the-markup/2022/02/24/who-is-policing-the-location-data-industry.

29. Cyphers and Gebhart, "Behind the One Way Mirror."

30. Federal Trade Commission, "Data Brokers"; Cambridge research summarized by Christl, "Corporate Surveillance in Everyday Life"; Experian, "Collection Triggers," accessed January 11, 2023, https://www.experian.com/assets/consumer-information/product-sheets/collection-triggers.pdf.

31. NATO StratCom COE, "Data Brokers and Security."

32. Epsilon, "Niches 5.0 Brochure," July 22, 2019, https://www.epsilon.com/us/insights/resources/niches-5.0-brochure; Cyphers and Gebhart, "Behind the One Way Mirror"; Shoshana Wodinsky, "Experian Is Tracking the People Most Likely to Get Screwed Over by Coronavirus," *Gizmodo*, April 15, 2020, https://gizmodo.com/experian-is-tracking-the-people-most-likely-to-get-scre-1842843363.

33. Federal Trade Commission, "Data Brokers"; Atlas Privacy, "Does Starbucks Know If I Wet the Bed," February 9, 2022, https://atlasprivacy.medium.com/does-starbucks-know-if-i-wet-the-bed-37a7d9a9487f.

34. US Senate Committee on Commerce, Science, and Transportation, "A Review of the Data Broker Industry."

35. Consumer Financial Protection Bureau (CFPB), "What Is a FICO Score?" September 4, 2020, https://www.consumerfinance.gov/ask-cfpb/what-is-a-fico-score-en-1883/.

36. Harvey Rosenfield and Laura Antonini, "Opinion: Data Isn't Just Being Collected from Your Phone. It's Being Used to Score You"; Drew Harwell, "A Face-Scanning Algorithm Increasingly Decides Whether You Deserve the Job," *Washington Post*, November 6, 2019, https://www.washingtonpost.com/technology/2019/10/22/ai-hiring-face-scanning-algorithm-increasingly-decides-whether-you-deserve-job/; Paul Boutin, "The Secretive World of Selling Data About You," *Newsweek*, May 30, 2016, https://www.newsweek.com/secretive-world-selling-data-about-you-464789.

37. Tableau, "The Big View: All Sentinel Reports by Federal Trade Commission," May 5, 2022, https://public.tableau.com/app/profile/federal.trade.commission/viz/TheBigViewAllSentinelReports/TrendsOverTime; Bree Fowler, "Your Digital Footprint: It's Bigger Than You Realize," *CNet*, April 4, 2022, https://www.cnet.com/news/privacy/features/your-digital-footprint-its-bigger-than-you-realize/; ITRC, "2021 Consumer Aftermath Report," accessed January 16, 2023, https://www.idtheftcenter.org/wp-content/uploads/2021/09/ITRC_2021_Consumer_Aftermath_Report.pdf.

38. Yael Grauer, "What Are 'Data Brokers,' and Why Are They Scooping Up Information About You?" *Vice*, March 27, 2018, https://www.vice.com/en/article/bjpx3w/what-are-data-brokers-and-how-to-stop-my-private-data-collection; Boutin, "The Secretive World."

39. Kaitlyn Tiffany, "Doxxing Means Whatever You Want It To," *The Atlantic*, April 22, 2022, https://www.theatlantic.com/technology/archive/2022/04/doxxing-meaning-libs-of-tiktok/629643/; Michael Balsamo and Colleen Long, "Report: Officers' Personal Information Leaked Online," *San Jose Mercury News*, June 10, 2020, https://www.mercurynews.com/2020/06/10/report-officers-personal-information-leaked-online/.

40. Senator Amy Klobuchar, "Klobuchar, Murkowski Urge FTC to Protect Domestic Violence Victims' Information Online," March 4, 2021, https://www.klobuchar .senate.gov/public/index.cfm/2021/3/klobuchar-murkowski-urge-ftc-to-protect -domestic-violence-victims-information-online.

41. Boutin, "The Secretive World"; US Department of Justice, "Marketing Company Agrees to Pay $150 Million for Facilitating Elder Fraud Schemes," January 27, 2021, https://www.justice.gov/opa/pr/marketing-company-agrees-pay-150-million -facilitating-elder-fraud-schemes.

42. Justin Sherman, "Data Brokers Are a Threat to Democracy," *Wired*, April 13, 2021, https://www.wired.com/story/opinion-data-brokers-are-a-threat-to-democracy/; Lauren Kirchner, "When Zombie Data Costs You a Home," *The Markup*, October 6, 2020, https://themarkup.org/locked-out/2020/10/06/zombie-criminal-records -housing-background-checks; Steven Melendez, "When Background Checks Go Wrong," *Fast Company*, November 17, 2016, https://www.fastcompany.com /3065577/when-background-checks-go-wrong; NATO StratCom COE, "Data Brokers and Security."

43. Sherman, "Data Brokers and Sensitive Data"; Boutin, "The Secretive World."

44. House Committee on Oversight and Reform, "Warren, Maloney, Wyden, DeSaulnier Probe Data Broker's Collection of Data on Black Lives Matter Demonstrators," August 4, 2020, https://oversight.house.gov/news/press-releases /warren-maloney-wyden-desaulnier-probe-data-brokers-collection-of-data-on -black; Jon Keegan and Alfred Ng, "Gay/Bi Dating App, Muslim Prayer Apps Sold Data on People's Location to a Controversial Data Broker," *The Markup*, January 27, 2020, https://themarkup.org/privacy/2022/01/27/gay-bi-dating-app-muslim -prayer-apps-sold-data-on-peoples-location-to-a-controversial-data-broker; Joseph Cox, "More Muslim Apps Worked with X-Mode, Which Sold Data to Military Contractors," *Vice*, January 28, 2021, https://www.vice.com/en/article/epdkze /muslim-apps-location-data-military-xmode.

45. Joseph Cox, "Data Marketplace Selling Info About Who Uses Period Tracking Apps," *Vice*, May 17, 2022, https://www.vice.com/en/article/v7d9zd/data-market place-selling-clue-period-tracking-data.

46. Bennett Cyphers, "Inside Fog Data Science, the Secretive Company Selling Mass Surveillance to Local Police," Electronic Frontier Foundation, August 31, 2022, https://www.eff.org/deeplinks/2022/08/inside-fog-data-science-secretive-company -selling-mass-surveillance-local-police.

47. House Committee on Oversight and Reform, "Warren, Maloney, Wyden, DeSaulnier Probe Data Broker's Collection."

48. Kate Cox, "Secret Service Buys Location Data That Would Otherwise Need a Warrant," *Ars Technica*, August 17, 2020, https://arstechnica.com/tech-policy /2020/08/secret-service-other-agencies-buy-access-to-mobile-phone-location -data/; Rae Hodge, "ICE Uses Private Data Brokers to Circumvent Immigrant Sanctuary Laws, Report Says," *CNet*, April 22, 2022, https://www.cnet.com/ news/politics/ice-uses-private-data-brokers-to-circumvent-immigrant-sanctuary -laws-report-says/.

49. Justin Sherman, "Data Brokers Are Advertising Data on US Military Personnel," *Lawfare Blog*, August 23, 2021, https://www.lawfareblog.com/data-brokers-are -advertising-data-us-military-personnel.

50. Sam Biddle and Jack Poulson, "American Phone-Tracking Firm Demo'd Surveillance Powers by Spying on CIA and NSA," *The Intercept*, April 22, 2022,

https://theintercept.com/2022/04/22/anomaly-six-phone-tracking-zignal
-surveillance-cia-nsa/.

51. Sherman, "Data Brokers and Sensitive Data."

52. State of California Department of Justice, "California Consumer Privacy Act
(CCPA)," accessed January 16, 2023, https://www.oag.ca.gov/privacy/ccpa;
Privacy Rights Clearinghouse, "Registered Data Brokers in the United States:
2021," February 22, 2022, https://privacyrights.org/resources/registered-data
-brokers-united-states-2021.

53. Tim Cook, "You Deserve Privacy Online. Here's How You Could Actually Get It,"
TIME magazine, January 16, 2019, https://time.com/collection/davos-2019
/5502591/tim-cook-data-privacy/.

54. Senator Bill Cassidy, "Cassidy, Ossoff, Trahan Introduce Bill to Protect Americans'
Online Privacy and Data," February 9, 2022, https://www.cassidy.senate.gov
/newsroom/press-releases/cassidy-ossoff-trahan-introduce-bill-to-protect-americans
-online-privacy-and-data.

55. Senator Ron Wyden, "Wyden, Paul and Bipartisan Members of Congress
Introduce The Fourth Amendment Is Not For Sale Act," April 21, 2022, https://
www.wyden.senate.gov/news/press-releases/wyden-paul-and-bipartisan-members
-of-congress-introduce-the-fourth-amendment-is-not-for-sale-act-.

56. Senator Bill Cassidy, "Cassidy, Warren, Rubio Introduce Protecting Military
Service Members' Data Act of 2022," May 19, 2022, https://www.cassidy.senate
.gov/newsroom/press-releases/cassidy-warren-rubio-introduce-protecting-military
-service-members-data-act-of-2022.

57. US Courts, "Judicial Security Bill Advances: Judge Who Lost Son Urges Final
Passage," December 2, 2021, https://www.uscourts.gov/news/2021/12/02/judicial
-security-bill-advances-judge-who-lost-son-urges-final-passage.

58. Senator Elizabeth Warren, "Warren, Wyden, Murray, Whitehouse, Sanders
Introduce Legislation to Ban Data Brokers from Selling Americans' Location and
Health Data," June 15, 2022, https://www.warren.senate.gov/newsroom/press
-releases/warren-wyden-murray-whitehouse-sanders-introduce-legislation-to-ban
-data-brokers-from-selling-americans-location-and-health-data.

59. Epsilon, "What a World Without Third-Party Cookies Means for Digital
Advertising," accessed January 11, 2023, https://www.epsilon.com/us/insights
/trends/third-party-cookies.

Chapter 3

1. Lorenzo Franceschi-Bicchierai, "Facebook Doesn't Know What It Does with Your
Data, or Where It Goes: Leaked Document," *Vice*, April 26, 2022, https://www
.vice.com/en/article/akvmke/facebook-doesnt-know-what-it-does-with-your-data
-or-where-it-goes.

2. Definition of data breach from US Department of Health and Human Services,
"State and Tribal Child Welfare Information Systems, Information Security Data
Breach Response Plans," July 1, 2015, https://www.acf.hhs.gov/sites/default/files
/documents/cb/im1504.pdf; *Security Magazine*, "Over 22 Billion Records Exposed
in 2021," February 10, 2022, https://www.securitymagazine.com/articles/97046
-over-22-billion-records-exposed-in-2021; IBM, "Cost of a Data Breach," accessed
January 11, 2023, https://www.ibm.com/reports/data-breach.

3. Kenneth Terrell, "Identity Fraud Hit 42 Million People in 2021," *AARP*, April 7, 2022, https://www.aarp.org/money/scams-fraud/info-2022/javelin-report.html.

4. SelfKey, "Facebook's Data Breaches – A Timeline," April 19, 2022, https://selfkey .org/facebooks-data-breaches-a-timeline/.

5. Michael X. Heiligenstein, "Amazon Data Breaches: Full Timeline Through 2022," *Firewall Times*, June 22, 2022, https://firewalltimes.com/amazon-data-breach -timeline/; Michael X. Heiligenstein, "Google Data Breaches: Full Timeline Through 2022," *Firewall Times*, January 18, 2022, https://firewalltimes.com /google-data-breach-timeline/; Michael X. Heiligenstein, "Microsoft Data Breaches: Full Timeline Through 2022," *Firewall Times*, March 23, 2022, https:// firewalltimes.com/microsoft-data-breach-timeline/.

6. Doctorow, "How to Destroy Surveillance Capitalism."

7. Doctorow, "How to Destroy Surveillance Capitalism."

8. Doctorow, "How to Destroy Surveillance Capitalism"; Chavi Mehta and Foo Yun Chee, "Amazon Hit with Record EU Data Privacy Fine," *Reuters*, July 30, 2021, https://www.reuters.com/business/retail-consumer/amazon-hit-with-886-million -eu-data-privacy-fine-2021-07-30/; Cecilia Kang, "FTC Approves Facebook Fine of About $5 Billion," *New York Times*, July 12, 2019, https://www.nytimes.com /2019/07/12/technology/facebook-ftc-fine.html.

9. District of Columbia v. Mark Zuckerberg, Case Number 2022 CA 002273 B, in the Superior Court of the District of Columbia, Complaint filed May 23, 2022, https://oag.dc.gov/sites/default/files/2022-05/2022.05%20%283%29.pdf.

10. Lesley Fair, "FTC's $5 Billion Facebook Settlement: Record-Breaking and History -Making," *FTC business blog*, July 24, 2019, https://www.ftc.gov/business-guidance /blog/2019/07/ftcs-5-billion-facebook-settlement-record-breaking-and-history -making; FTC, "FTC Imposes $5 Billion Penalty and Sweeping New Privacy Restrictions on Facebook," July 24, 2019, https://www.ftc.gov/news-events /news/press-releases/2019/07/ftc-imposes-5-billion-penalty-sweeping-new-privacy -restrictions-facebook.

11. District of Columbia v. Mark Zuckerberg Complaint.

12. District of Columbia v. Mark Zuckerberg Complaint.

13. District of Columbia v. Mark Zuckerberg Complaint.

14. District of Columbia v. Mark Zuckerberg Complaint.

15. Wikipedia, "Facebook—Cambridge Analytica Data Scandal," updated February 9, 2023, https://en.wikipedia.org/wiki/Facebook%E2%80%93Cambridge _Analytica_data_scandal.

16. District of Columbia v. Mark Zuckerberg Complaint.

17. FTC, "FTC Imposes $5 Billion Penalty."

18. FTC, "FTC Imposes $5 Billion Penalty."

19. Mike Isaac and Natasha Singer, "Facebook Agrees to Extensive New Oversight as Part of $5 Billion Settlement," *New York Times*, July 24, 2019, https://www .nytimes.com/2019/07/24/technology/ftc-facebook-privacy-data.html.

20. Paul Grewal, "Suspending Cambridge Analytica and SCL Group from Facebook," Meta Newsroom, March 16, 2018, https://about.fb.com/news/2018/03 /suspending-cambridge-analytica/.

21. Paul Grewal, "Document Holds the Potential for Confusion," Meta Newsroom, August 23, 2019, https://about.fb.com/news/2019/08/document-holds-the -potential-for-confusion/.

Containing Big Tech

22. Arjun Kharpal, "Facebook Parent Meta Agrees to Pay $725 Million to Settle Cambridge Analytica Suit," *CNBC*, December 23, 2022, https://www.nbcnews.com/tech/tech-news/facebook-parent-meta-agrees-pay-725-million-settle-cambridge-analytica-rcna63081.

23. Scott Galloway, "TikTok: Trojan Stallion," July 8, 2022, https://www.profgalloway.com/tiktok-trojan-stallion/; Alex W. Palmer, "How TikTok Became a Diplomatic Crisis," *New York Times*, December 20, 2022, https://www.nytimes.com/2022/12/20/magazine/tiktok-us-china-diplomacy.html.

24. Cecilia Kang, "ByteDance Inquiry Finds Employees Obtained User Data of 2 Journalists," *New York Times*, December 22, 2022, https://www.nytimes.com/2022/12/22/technology/byte-dance-tik-tok-internal-investigation.html; Emily Baker-White, "EXCLUSIVE: TikTok Spied on Forbes Journalists," *Forbes*, December 22, 2022, https://www.forbes.com/sites/emilybaker-white/2022/12/22/tiktok-tracks-forbes-journalists-bytedance/.

25. Sheera Frenkel and Cecilia Kang, "Exclusive Extract: How Facebook's Engineers Spied on Women," *The Telegraph*, July 12, 2021, https://www.telegraph.co.uk/news/2021/07/12/exclusive-extract-facebooks-engineers-spied-women/; Jenna Romaine, "New Report Says Facebook Fired 52 Employees Caught Spying on Users' Inboxes," *The Hill*, July 14, 2021, https://thehill.com/changing-america/resilience/smart-cities/562988-new-report-says-facebook-fired-52-employees-caught/.

26. Franceschi-Bicchierai, "Facebook Doesn't Know What It Does with Your Data."

27. Will Evans, "Amazon's Dark Secret: It Has Failed to Protect Your Data," *Wired*, November 10, 2021, https://www.wired.com/story/amazon-failed-to-protect-your-data-investigation/.

28. Evans, "Amazon's Dark Secret."

29. Evans, "Amazon's Dark Secret."

30. Tom Kemp, "GDPR's Accountability and Governance Obligations," May 10, 2020, https://tomkemp.blog/2020/05/10/revisiting-the-gdprs-accountability-and-governance-obligations/.

31. Wikipedia, "Security Breach Notification Laws," updated December 27, 2022, https://en.wikipedia.org/wiki/Security_breach_notification_laws; Tom Kemp, "Comparing Business Obligations: GDPR vs. CCPA vs. CPRA," June 1, 2020, https://tomkemp.blog/2020/06/01/comparing-business-obligations-gdpr-vs-ccpa-vs-cpra/.

32. Doctorow, "How to Destroy Surveillance Capitalism."

Chapter 4

1. Amol Rajan, "Google Boss Sundar Pichai Warns of Threats to Internet Freedom," *BBC*, July 12, 2021, https://www.bbc.com/news/technology-57763382.

2. US Department of Justice, "Justice Department Secures Groundbreaking Settlement Agreement with Meta Platforms, Formerly Known as Facebook, to Resolve Allegations of Discriminatory Advertising," June 21, 2022, https://www.justice.gov/opa/pr/justice-department-secures-groundbreaking-settlement-agreement-meta-platforms-formerly-known?s=03. *ProPublica* deserves credit for reporting on this problem with Facebook's housing ads six years before the settlement. Also, see Ariana Tobin and Ava Kofman, "Facebook Finally Agrees to Eliminate Tool That Enabled Discriminatory Advertising," *ProPublica*, June 22, 2022, https://www.propublica.org/article/facebook-doj-advertising-discrimination-settlement.

3. Dakota Foster, "Antitrust Investigations Have Deep Implications for AI and National Security," The Brookings Institution, June 2, 2020, https://www.brookings.edu/techstream/antitrust-investigations-have-deep-implications-for-ai-and-national-security/; Meta Platforms, Inc., "Second Quarter 2022 Results Conference Call," July 27, 2022, https://s21.q4cdn.com/399680738/files/doc_financials/2022/q2/Meta-Q2-2022-Earnings-Call-Transcript.pdf.

4. European Parliament, "What Is Artificial Intelligence and How Is It Being Used?" updated March 29, 2021, https://www.europarl.europa.eu/news/en/headlines/priorities/artificial-intelligence-in-the-eu/20200827STO85804/what-is-artificial-intelligence-and-how-is-it-used.

5. Karen Hao, "How Facebook Got Addicted to Spreading Misinformation," *MIT Technology Review*, March 11, 2021, https://www.technologyreview.com/2021/03/11/1020600/facebook-responsible-ai-misinformation/.

6. Paul Mozur, "One Month, 500,000 Face Scans: How China Is Using A.I. to Profile a Minority," *New York Times*, April 14, 2019, https://www.nytimes.com/2019/04/14/technology/china-surveillance-artificial-intelligence-racial-profiling.html; Katie Canales, "China's 'Social Credit' System Ranks Citizens and Punishes Them with Throttled Internet Speeds and Flight Bans If the Communist Party Deems Them Untrustworthy," *Business Insider*, December 24, 2021, https://www.businessinsider.com/china-social-credit-system-punishments-and-rewards-explained-2018-4.

7. Wikipedia, "Algorithm," updated February 8, 2023, https://en.wikipedia.org/wiki/Algorithm; Nicol Turner Lee, Paul Resnick, and Genie Barton, "Algorithmic Bias Detection and Mitigation: Best Practices and Policies to Reduce Consumer Harms," The Brookings Institution, May 22, 2019, https://www.brookings.edu/research/algorithmic-bias-detection-and-mitigation-best-practices-and-policies-to-reduce-consumer-harms/.

8. A History of AI, "Antiquity," accessed January 29, 2023, https://ahistoryofai.com/antiquity/; Wikipedia, "History of Artificial Intelligence," updated February 3, 2023, https://en.wikipedia.org/wiki/History_of_artificial_intelligence; Darrell M. West, "What Is Artificial Intelligence," The Brookings Institution, October 4, 2018, https://www.brookings.edu/research/what-is-artificial-intelligence/; Julianna Photopoulos, "Fighting Algorithmic Bias in Artificial Intelligence," *Physics World*, May 4, 2021, https://physicsworld.com/a/fighting-algorithmic-bias-in-artificial-intelligence/; Stanford University, Human-Centered Artificial Intelligence, "Artificial Intelligence Definitions," September 2020, https://hai.stanford.edu/sites/default/files/2020-09/AI-Definitions-HAI.pdf.

9. Philip Boucher, "Artificial Intelligence: How Does It Work, Why Does It Matter, and What We Do About It," European Parliament Research Service, June 2020, https://www.europarl.europa.eu/RegData/etudes/STUD/2020/641547/EPRS_STU(2020)641547_EN.pdf.

10. Kaya Ismail, "AI vs. Algorithms: What's the Difference," *CMS Wire*, October 26, 2018, https://www.cmswire.com/information-management/ai-vs-algorithms-whats-the-difference/amp/; Emre Kazin and Adriano Koshiyama, "A High-Level Overview of AI Ethics," *ScienceDirect*, September 10, 2021, https://www.sciencedirect.com/science/article/pii/S2666389921001574.

11. Machine learning description from Genevieve Smith and Ishita Rustagi, "Mitigating Bias in Artificial Intelligence," Haas Business School, The Center for Equity, Gender and Leadership, July 2020, https://haas.berkeley.edu/wp-content/uploads/UCB_Playbook_R10_V2_spreads2.pdf; the CEO quoted is Salesforce CEO Marc Benioff, "The AI Revolution Is Coming Fast. But Without a Revolution

in Trust, It Will Fail," World Economic Forum, August 26, 2016, https://www
.weforum.org/agenda/2016/08/the-digital-revolution-is-here-but-without-a
-revolution-in-trust-it-will-fail/; data growth is from European Parliament,
"Artificial Intelligence: Threats and Opportunities," April 5, 2022, https://www
.europarl.europa.eu/news/en/headlines/priorities/artificial-intelligence-in-the
-eu/20200918STO87404/artificial-intelligence-threats-and-opportunities. A
zettabyte equals a thousand billion gigabytes.

12. Technopedia, "Deep Learning," February 23, 2022, https://www.techopedia.com
/definition/30325/deep-learning; Tech Target, "Deep Learning," accessed January
4, 2023, https://www.techtarget.com/searchenterpriseai/definition/deep-learning
-deep-neural-network; MathWorks, "What Is Deep Learning? 3 Things You Need
to Know," accessed January 4, 2023, https://www.mathworks.com/discovery/deep
-learning.html.

13. IBM, "Deep Learning," May 1, 2020, https://www.ibm.com/cloud/learn/deep
-learning.

14. Ines Roldos, "NLP, Machine Learning & AI, Explained," *MonkeyLearn Blog*,
June 9, 2020, https://monkeylearn.com/blog/nlp-ai/.

15. European Parliament, "What Is Artificial Intelligence and How Is It Being Used?"
Most of the example industries listed are from this source.

16. Accenture, "Artificial Intelligence," accessed January 4, 2023, https://www
.accenture.com/us-en/insights/artificial-intelligence-summary-index.

17. Chad Metz and Karen Weise, "A Tech Race Begins as Microsoft Adds A.I. to Its
Search Engine," *New York Times*, February 7, 2023, https://www.nytimes.com
/2023/02/07/technology/microsoft-ai-chatgpt-bing.html.

18. James Eager et al., "Opportunities of Artificial Intelligence," European Parliament,
Policy Department for Economic, Scientific, and Quality of Life Policies, June
2020, https://www.europarl.europa.eu/RegData/etudes/STUD/2020/652713/IPOL
_STU(2020)652713_EN.pdf.

19. Accenture, "Artificial Intelligence."

20. Accenture, "Artificial Intelligence"; European Parliament, "Artificial Intelligence:
Threats and Opportunities."

21. Smith and Rustagi, "Mitigating Bias in Artificial Intelligence"; Accenture,
"Artificial Intelligence."

22. Wikipedia, "List of Cognitive Biases," updated January 4, 2023, https://en
.wikipedia.org/wiki/List_of_cognitive_biases; Jake Silberg and James Manyika,
"Notes from the AI Frontier: Tackling Bias in AI (and in Humans)," McKinsey
Global Institute, June 2019, https://www.mckinsey.com/featured-insights/artificial
-intelligence/tackling-bias-in-artificial-intelligence-and-in-humans; Lee, Resnick,
and Barton, "Algorithmic Bias Detection and Mitigation."

23. Thanks to Airlie Hilliard with Holistic AI for her guidance in helping to define AI
bias; Silberg and Manyika, "Notes from the AI Frontier"; Reva Schwartz et al.,
"Towards a Standard for Identifying and Managing Bias in Artificial Intelligence,"
National Institute of Standards and Technology, *NIST Special Publication 1270*,
March 2022, https://nvlpubs.nist.gov/nistpubs/SpecialPublications/NIST.SP.1270
.pdf; Wikipedia, "Digital Redlining," updated July 4, 2022, https://en.wikipedia
.org/wiki/Digital_redlining.

24. PwC, "Understanding Algorithmic Bias and How to Build Trust in AI," January
18, 2022, https://www.pwc.com/us/en/tech-effect/ai-analytics/algorithmic-bias-and
-trust-in-ai.html; Schwartz et al., "Towards a Standard for Identifying and Managing

Bias"; James Manyika et al., "What Do We Do About the Biases in AI?" *Harvard Business Review*, October 25, 2019, https://hbr.org/2019/10/what-do-we-do-about -the-biases-in-ai.

25. Gartner, "Gartner Says Nearly Half of CIOs Are Planning to Deploy Artificial Intelligence," February 13, 2018, https://www.gartner.com/en/newsroom/press -releases/2018-02-13-gartner-says-nearly-half-of-cios-are-planning-to-deploy -artificial-intelligence.

26. Victoria Shashkina, "What Is AI Bias Really, and How Can You Combat It," *IT Rex Group Blog*, June 4, 2021, https://itrexgroup.com/blog/ai-bias-definition-types -examples-debiasing-strategies/#; Lee, Resnick, and Barton, "Algorithmic Bias Detection and Mitigation."

27. ComputerScience.org, "Women in Computer Science: Getting Involved in STEM," April 28, 2022, https://www.computerscience.org/resources/women-in-computer -science/; Smith and Rustagi, "Mitigating Bias in Artificial Intelligence"; Rebecca Heilweil, "Why Algorithms Can Be Racist and Sexist," *Vox*, February 18, 2020, https://www.vox.com/recode/2020/2/18/21121286/algorithms-bias-discrimination -facial-recognition-transparency; Andrea Kulkarni, "Bias in AI and Machine Learning: Sources and Solutions," *Lexalytics*, June 26, 2021, https://www.lexalytics .com/lexablog/bias-in-ai-machine-learning.

28. Manyika et al., "What Do We Do About the Biases in AI?"; Andrea Kulkarni, "Bias in AI and Machine Learning: Sources and Solutions"; Amazon example is from Lee, Resnick, and Barton, "Algorithmic Bias Detection and Mitigation."

29. Julia Angwin et al., "Machine Bias," *ProPublica*, May 23, 2016, https://www.pro publica.org/article/machine-bias-risk-assessments-in-criminal-sentencing; Silberg and Manyika, "Notes from the AI Frontier"; Equivant, "Response to ProPublica: Demonstrating Accuracy Equity and Predictive Parity," December 1, 2018, https:// www.equivant.com/response-to-propublica-demonstrating-accuracy-equity-and -predictive-parity/.

30. PwC, "Understanding Algorithmic Bias and How to Build Trust in AI"; Photopoulos, "Fighting Algorithmic Bias in Artificial Intelligence"; Jeffrey Dastin, "Amazon Extends Moratorium on Police Use of Facial Recognition Software," *Reuters*, May 18, 2021, https://www.reuters.com/technology/exclusive-amazon -extends-moratorium-police-use-facial-recognition-software-2021-05-18/. It should be noted that a non-profit utilizes Rekognition in its software offering to help law enforcement identify child victims of human trafficking, so the moratorium appears to only be on direct sales. See case study on Amazon Web Services, "Thorn Uses AWS to Help Law Enforcement Identify Child-Trafficking Victims Faster," accessed January 11, 2023, https://aws.amazon.com/solutions/case-studies/thorn/.

31. Manyika et al., "What Do We Do About the Biases in AI?"; Karen Hao, "This Is How AI Bias Really Happens—and Why It's so Hard to Fix," *MIT Technology Review*, February 4, 2019, https://www.technologyreview.com/2019/02/04/137602 /this-is-how-ai-bias-really-happensand-why-its-so-hard-to-fix/; Lee, Resnick, and Barton, "Algorithmic Bias Detection and Mitigation."

32. NATO StratCom COE, "Data Brokers and Security."

33. Bruce Schneier, "The Coming AI Hackers," Harvard Kennedy School, Belfer Center for Science and International Affairs, April 2021, https://www.belfercenter .org/sites/default/files/2021-04/HackingAI.pdf; Natalia Mesa, "Can the Criminal Justice System's Artificial Intelligence Ever Be Truly Fair," *Massive Science*, May 13, 2021, https://massivesci.com/articles/machine-learning-compas-racism-policing -fairness/; Lee, Resnick, and Barton, "Algorithmic Bias Detection and Mitigation."

34. Dave Johnson, "What Is a Deepfake? Everything You Need to Know About the AI-Powered Fake Media," *Business Insider*, January 22, 2021, https://www.business insider.com/what-is-deepfake.

35. Alexandra Benisek, "What Is Revenge Pornography?" WebMD, August 4, 2022, https://www.webmd.com/sex-relationships/revenge-porn.

36. Bobby Allyn, "Deepfake Video of Zelenskyy Could Be 'Tip of the Iceberg' in Info War, Experts Warn," *National Public Radio*, March 16, 2020, https://www.npr.org /2022/03/16/1087062648/deepfake-video-zelenskyy-experts-war-manipulation -ukraine-russia.

37. Zakary Kinnaird, "Dark Patterns Powered by Machine Learning: an Intelligent Combination," UX Collective, October 12, 2020, https://uxdesign.cc/dark-patterns -powered-by-machine-learning-an-intelligent-combination-f2804ed028ce; Dheeraj Khindra, "10 Common Dark Patterns in UX and How to Avoid Them," *Net Solutions Blog*, July 9, 2021, https://www.netsolutions.com/insights/dark -patterns-in-ux-disadvantages/; Katharine Miller, "Can't Unsubscribe? Blame Dark Patterns," Stanford University, Human-Centered Artificial Intelligence, December 13, 2021, https://hai.stanford.edu/news/cant-unsubscribe-blame-dark-patterns; Isabella Kwai, "Consumer Groups Target Amazon Prime's Cancellation Process," *New York Times*, January 14, 2021, https://www.nytimes.com/2021/01/14/world /europe/amazon-prime-cancellation-complaint.html.

38. Miller, "Can't Unsubscribe? Blame Dark Patterns"; Kinnaird, "Dark Patterns Powered by Machine Learning."

39. Alex Engler, "The EU and US Are Starting to Align on AI Regulation," The Brookings Institution, February 1, 2022, https://www.brookings.edu/blog/ techtank/2022/02/01/the-eu-and-u-s-are-starting-to-align-on-ai-regulation/.

40. Intersoft Consulting, "General Data Protection Regulation," accessed January 11, 2023, https://gdpr-info.eu/.

41. Eve Gaumond, "Artificial Intelligence Act: What Is the European Approach to AI?" *Lawfare Blog*, June 4, 2021, https://www.lawfareblog.com/artificial-intelligence-act -what-european-approach-ai.

42. Airlie Hilliard and Emre Kazim et al., "Regulating the Robots: NYC Mandates Bias Audits for Ai-Driven Employment Decisions," *SSRN*, April 27, 2022, https:// papers.ssrn.com/sol3/papers.cfm?abstract_id=4083189; Holistic AI, "What You Need to Know About the Illinois Artificial Intelligence Video Interview Act," June 6, 2022, https://holisticai.com/blog/2022/06/what-you-need-to-know-about-the -illinois-artificial-intelligence-video-interview-act/.

43. Elisa Jillson, "Aiming for Truth, Fairness, and Equity in Your Company's Use of AI," *Federal Trade Commission Business Blog*, April 19, 2021, https://www.ftc.gov /business-guidance/blog/2021/04/aiming-truth-fairness-equity-your-companys-use-ai.

44. Senator Ron Wyden, "Wyden, Booker, and Clarke Introduce Algorithmic Accountability Act of 2022 to Require New Transparency and Accountability for Automated Decision Systems," February 3, 2022, https://www.wyden.senate.gov /news/press-releases/wyden-booker-and-clarke-introduce-algorithmic-accountability -act-of-2022-to-require-new-transparency-and-accountability-for-automated -decision-systems.

45. Adam Connor and Erin Simpson, "Executive Summary: Evaluating 2 Tech Antitrust Bills to Restore Competition Online," *Center for American Progress*, June 7, 2022, https://www.americanprogress.org/article/executive-summary -evaluating-2-tech-antitrust-bills-to-restore-competition-online/.

46. Craig Smith, "Dealing with Bias in Artificial Intelligence," *New York Times*, November 19, 2019, https://www.nytimes.com/2019/11/19/technology/artificial -intelligence-bias.html.

47. Julia Angwin, "How AI Could Undermine an Efficient Market Economy," *The Markup*, June 25, 2022, https://themarkup.org/newsletter/hello-world/how-ai -could-undermine-an-efficient-market-economy.

48. The White House Office of Science & Technology Policy, "Blueprint for an AI Bill of Rights: Making Automated Systems Work for the American People," October 2022, https://www.whitehouse.gov/wp-content/uploads/2022/10/Blueprint-for-an -AI-Bill-of-Rights.pdf.

49. Hilliard, Kazim, et al., "Regulating the Robots"; Dr. Sam De Silva and Barbara Zapisetskaya, "Proposed ISO Standard on Risk Management of AI: What Businesses Should Know," *CMS Law-Now*, May 16, 2022, https://www.cms-lawnow.com /ealerts/2022/05/proposed-iso-standard-on-risk-management-of-ai-what-businesses should-know?cc_lang=en; European Commission, "Ethics Guidelines for Trustworthy AI," April 8, 2019.

50. Smith, "Dealing with Bias in Artificial Intelligence."

51. Bhaskar Chakravorti, "Biden's 'Antitrust Revolution' Overlooks AI—at Americans' Peril," *Wired*, July 27, 2021, https://www.wired.com/story/opinion-bidens-antitrust -revolution-overlooks-ai-at-americans-peril/.

52. Angwin, "How AI Could Undermine an Efficient Market Economy."

Chapter 5

1. Center for Humane Technology, "The Attention Economy: Why Do Tech Companies Fight for Our Attention?" August 17, 2021, https://www.humanetech .com/youth/the-attention-economy and https://socialtruth.humanetech.com/.

2. Marc Andreessen, "Why Software Is Eating the World," *Wall Street Journal*, August 20, 2011, https://www.wsj.com/articles/SB1000142405311190348090457 6512250915629460.

3. Tom Kemp, "The Impact of CCPA & CPRA on Surveillance Capitalism," May 20, 2021, https://tomkemp.blog/2021/05/20/the-impact-of-ccpa-cpra-on-surveillance -capitalism/; Kian Masters and Li Zhang, "Shining a Sustainability Light on the Darker Side of Big Tech," *Harvard Law School Forum on Corporate Governance*, July 19, 2022, https://corpgov.law.harvard.edu/2022/07/19/shining-a-sustainability -light-on-the-darker-side-of-big-tech/.

4. Dentsu Aegis Network, "The Attention Economy: Exploring the Opportunity for a New Advertising Currency," June 2019, https://assets-eu-01.kc-usercontent.com /7bf8ef96-9447-0161-1923-3ac6929eb20f/a5c3d9a2-b1c8-4aee-b899-b24309 52a8e1/The%20Attention%20Economy_Digital%20POV.pdf.

5. Berkeley Economic Review, "Paying Attention: The Attention Economy," March 31, 2020, https://econreview.berkeley.edu/paying-attention-the-attention-economy/.

6. Big Think, "The Eyeball Economy: How Advertising Co-Opts Independent Thought," https://bigthink.com/high-culture/tristan-harris-the-attention-economy-a -race-to-the-bottom-of-the-brain-stem/; Galloway, "WMDs."

7. Galloway, "WMDs"; Center for Humane Technology, "The Attention Economy."

8. Gary W. Small, Jooyeon Lee, Aaron Kaufman, Jason Jalil, Prabha Siddarth, Himaja Gaddipati, Teena D. Moody, and Susan Y. Bookhaimer, "Brain Health

Consequences of Digital Technology Use," *Dialogues in Clinical Neuroscience* 22, no. 2 (June 2020), 179–187, https://www.ncbi.nlm.nih.gov/pmc/articles /PMC7366948/.

9. Hao, "How Facebook Got Addicted to Spreading Misinformation"; Galloway, "TikTok: Trojan Stallion."

10. BJ Fogg, *Persuasive Technology: Using Computers to Change What We Think and Do* (Boston: Morgan Kaufmann Publishers, 2003), 1–2.

11. Roger McNamee, *Zucked: Waking Up to the Facebook Catastrophe* (New York: Penguin Press, 2019), 83.

12. Fogg, *Persuasive Technology*, 6–7.

13. Fogg, *Persuasive Technology*, 7–11.

14. Wikipedia, "Center for Humane Technology," updated January 22, 2023, https:// en.wikipedia.org/wiki/Center_for_Humane_Technology; Ivy Wigmore, "Intermittent Reinforcement," *TechTarget*, May 2018, https://www.techtarget.com /whatis/definition/intermittent-reinforcement.

15. Tristan Harris, "How Technology Is Hijacking Your Mind—from a Magician and Google Design Ethicist," Medium, May 18, 2016, https://medium.com/thrive -global/how-technology-hijacks-peoples-minds-from-a-magician-and-google-s -design-ethicist-56d62ef5edf3.

16. Center for Humane Technology, "Persuasive Technology: How Does Technology Use Design to Influence My Behavior?" August 17, 2021, https://www.humanetech .com/youth/persuasive-technology; Center for Humane Technology, "How Social Media Hacks Our Brains," accessed January 16, 2023, https://www.humanetech .com/brain-science.

17. Harris, "How Technology Is Hijacking Your Mind."

18. Harris, "How Technology Is Hijacking Your Mind."

19. Kinnaird, "Dark Patterns Powered by Machine Learning"; Khindra, "10 Common Dark Patterns in UX"; Sara Morrison, "Dark Patterns, the Tricks Websites Use to Make You Say Yes, Explained," *Vox*, April 1, 2021, https://www.vox.com/recode /22351108/dark-patterns-ui-web-design-privacy.

20. Karen Hao, "The Facebook Whistleblower Says Its Algorithms Are Dangerous. Here's Why," *MIT Technology Review*, October 5, 2021, https://www .technologyreview.com/2021/10/05/1036519/facebook-whistleblower-frances -haugen-algorithms/.

21. Hao, "The Facebook Whistleblower Says Its Algorithms Are Dangerous"; Katharine Trendacosta, "What the Facebook Whistleblower Tells Us About Big Tech," Electronic Frontier Foundation, October 8, 2021, https://www.eff.org /deeplinks/2021/10/what-facebook-whistleblower-tells-us-about-big-tech.

22. Keach Hagey and Jeff Horwitz, "Facebook Tried to Make Its Platform a Healthier Place. It Got Angrier Instead," *Wall Street Journal*, September 15, 2021, https:// www.wsj.com/articles/facebook-algorithm-change-zuckerberg-11631654215.

23. Hagey and Horwitz, "Facebook Tried to Make Its Platform a Healthier Place"; Trendacosta, "What the Facebook Whistleblower Tells Us About Big Tech."

24. Trendacosta, "What the Facebook Whistleblower Tells Us About Big Tech."

25. Hagey and Horwitz, "Facebook Tried to Make Its Platform a Healthier Place."

26. Hao, "The Facebook Whistleblower Says Its Algorithms Are Dangerous."

27. Trendacosta, "What the Facebook Whistleblower Tells Us About Big Tech"; Hagey and Horwitz, "Facebook Tried to Make Its Platform a Healthier Place."

28. Galloway, "WMDs"; Katharina Buchholz, "The Road to One Billion Users"; Scott Galloway, "TikTok Boom," May 20, 2022, https://www.profgalloway.com /tiktok-boom; Galloway, "TikTok: Trojan Stallion."

29. Galloway, "WMDs"; Luiza Jarovsky, "I Was on TikTok for 30 Days: It Is Manipulative, Addictive and Harmful to Privacy," LinkedIn, July 28, 2022, https://www.linkedin.com/pulse/i-tiktok-30-days-manipulative-addictive-harmful -privacy-jarovsky/.

30. Jarovsky, "I Was on TikTok for 30 Days."

31. Galloway, "TikTok Boom."

32. Galloway, "TikTok Boom."

33. Jarovsky, "I Was on TikTok for 30 Days."

34. Galloway, "TikTok: Trojan Stallion"; Manuela Lopez Restrepo, "Why the Proposed TikTok Ban Is More About Politics than Privacy, According to Experts," *National Public Radio*, December 22, 2022, https://www.npr.org/2022/12/22/1144745813 /why-the-proposed-tiktok-ban-is-more-about-politics-than-privacy-according-to-exp.

35. Hao, "The Facebook Whistleblower Says Its Algorithms Are Dangerous"; Center for Humane Technology, "Persuasive Technology"; Center for Humane Technology, "How Social Media Hacks Our Brains."

36. J. Fingas, "Microsoft Study Shows that Tech Is Shortening Your Attention Span," *Engadget*, May 17, 2015, https://www.engadget.com/2015-05-17-microsoft -attention-span-study.html.

37. Center for Humane Technology, "How Social Media Hacks Our Brains."

38. Small, Lee et al., "Brain Health Consequences of Digital Technology Use."

39. Jennifer King, "Do the DSA and DMA Have What It Takes to Take on Dark Patterns," *Tech Policy Press*, June 23, 2022, https://techpolicy.press/do-the-dsa -and-dma-have-what-it-takes-to-take-on-dark-patterns.

40. King, "Do the DSA and DMA Have What It Takes."

41. King, "Do the DSA and DMA Have What It Takes"; Parker Williams Hassard, "What's Not to Like?: The EU's Case Against Big Tech and Important Lessons for the United States," *North Carolina Journal of International Law*, May 1, 2022, https://scholarship.law.unc.edu/ncilj/vol47/iss4/2/.

42. King, "Do the DSA and DMA Have What It Takes."

43. Eugene Kim, "FTC Deepens Investigation into Amazon Prime After Insider Reporting, Sending Out Subpoenas and Other Demands for Information," *Business Insider*, August 4, 2022, https://www.businessinsider.com/ftc-deepens -amazon-prime-probe-sending-subpoenas-issuing-warnings-2022-8; Natasha Singer, "Epic Games to Pay $520 Million Over Children's Privacy and Trickery Charges," *New York Times*, December 19, 2022, https://www.nytimes. com/2022/12/19/business/ftc-epic-games-settlement.html.

44. Senator Mark Warren, "Senators Introduce Bipartisan Legislation to Ban Manipulative 'Dark Patterns'," April 9, 2019, https://www.warner.senate.gov/public /index.cfm/2019/4/senators-introduce-bipartisan-legislation-to-ban-manipulative -dark-patterns; Andrew Blake, "Social Media Bill Would Ban 'Addictive' Features, Outlawing Auto-play and Infinite Scrolling," *Washington Times*, July 30, 2019, https://www.washingtontimes.com/news/2019/jul/30/social-media-bill-would-ban -addictive-features-out/.

45. Cory Doctorow, "How to Ditch Facebook Without Ditching Your Friends," *Pluralistic*, September 19, 2022, https://pluralistic.net/2022/09/19/interoperable -facebook/.

Chapter 6

1. Beeban Kidron et al., "Disrupted Childhood: The Cost of Persuasive Design," 5Rights Foundation, June 2018, https://5rightsfoundation.com/uploads/5rights -disrupted-childhood-digital-version.pdf.

2. Rob Barry et al., "How TikTok Serves Up Sex and Drug Videos to Minors," *Wall Street Journal*, September 8, 2021, https://www.wsj.com/articles/tiktok-algorithm -sex-drugs-minors-11631052944.

3. Common Sense Media, "COPPA 2.0—Fact Sheet," accessed January 4, 2023, https://www.commonsensemedia.org/sites/default/files/featured-content/files /coppa_2.0_one_pager_2021.pdf.

4. Fairplay et al., Letter to US Senate Commerce Committee on Commerce, Science, & Transportation, July 25, 2022, https://fairplayforkids.org/wp-content/uploads/2022 /08/KOSA-COPPA-Letter.pdf; Designed with Kids in Mind, "Why We Need a Design Code," accessed January 16, 2023, https://designedwithkidsinmind.us/why/; Common Sense Media, "COPPA 2.0—Fact Sheet."

5. The statistic that one in three internet users is a child is from Duncan McCann, "I-SPY: The Billion Dollar Business of Surveillance Advertising to Kids," New Economics Foundation, May 2021, https://neweconomics.org/uploads/files/i-Spy __NEF.pdf; children under eight statistic is from Designed with Kids in Mind, "Support the Kids Internet Design and Safety (KIDS) Act," accessed January 16, 2023, https://designedwithkidsinmind.us/wp-content/uploads/2021/11/KIDS-Act -Flyer-FINAL.pdf; tablet and smartphone usage statistics are from Consumer Reports, Letter to California Assemblymember Jesse Gabriel, April 13, 2022, https:// advocacy.consumerreports.org/wp-content/uploads/2022/04/CR-letter-AB-2273 -support-if-amended.pdf; social media usage statistics are from Emily Vogels et al., "Teens, Social Media and Technology 2022," Pew Research Center, August 10, 2022, https://www.pewresearch.org/internet/2022/08/10/teens-social-media-and -technology-2022/.

6. Fairplay et al., Letter to US Senate Commerce Committee; US Surgeon General, "Protecting Youth Mental Health: The US Surgeon General's Advisory," December 7, 2021, https://www.hhs.gov/sites/default/files/surgeon-general-youth-mental-health -advisory.pdf.

7. Fairplay et al., Letter to US Senate Commerce Committee; Ian Russell, "My Daughter Was Driven to Suicide by Social Media. It's Time for Facebook to Stop Monetizing Misery," *Washington Post*, October 25, 2021, https://www .washingtonpost.com/opinions/2021/10/25/facebook-frances-haugen-molly-russell -teen-suicide-social-media-uk/; Zara Abrams, "Why Young Brains Are Especially Vulnerable to Social Media," American Psychological Association, August 25, 2022, https://www.apa.org/news/apa/2022/social-media-children-teens.

8. McCann, "I-SPY."

9. Geoffrey A. Fowler, "Your Kids' Apps Are Spying on Them," *Washington Post*, June 9, 2022, https://www.washingtonpost.com/technology/2022/06/09/apps-kids -privacy/.

10. Common Sense Media, "COPPA 2.0—Fact Sheet"; McCann, "I-SPY"; Designed with Kids in Mind, "Making Sense of Surveillance Advertising (Spoiler: There Is None!)," January 28, 2022, https://designedwithkidsinmind.us/making-sense-of -surveillance-advertising-spoiler-there-is-none/.

11. McCann, "I-SPY."

12. McCann, "I-SPY."

13. Stephanie Nebehay, "Children Prey to Online Ads of Harmful Products, Regulation Needed: UN Study," *Reuters*, February 18, 2020, https://www.reuters.com/article /us-health-children/children-prey-to-online-ads-of-harmful-products-regulation -needed-u-n-study-idUSKBN20C2R0.

14. Sam Levin, "Facebook Told Advertisers It Can Identify Teens Feeling 'Insecure' and 'Worthless'," *The Guardian*, May 1, 2017, https://www.theguardian.com /technology/2017/may/01/facebook-advertising-data-insecure-teens.

15. Rob Barry et al., "How TikTok Serves Up Sex and Drug Videos to Minors."

16. Hao, "How Facebook Got Addicted to Spreading Misinformation"; Georgia Wells et al., "Facebook Knows Instagram Is Toxic for Teen Girls, Company Documents Show," *Wall Street Journal*, September 14, 2021, https://www.wsj.com/articles /facebook-knows-instagram-is-toxic-for-teen-girls-company-documents-show -11631620739.

17. Wells et al., "Facebook Knows Instagram Is Toxic."

18. Wells et al., "Facebook Know Instagram Is Toxic."

19. Wells et al., "Facebook Knows Instagram is Toxic"; Kidron et al., "Disrupted Childhood."

20. Designed with Kids in Mind, "Safer by Design: How the CA Age Appropriate Design Code Would Change Children's Online Experiences," accessed January 15, 2023, https://designedwithkidsinmind.us/wp-content/uploads/2022/06/AADC -How-it-Works.pdf.

21. Kidron et al., "Disrupted Childhood."

22. Kidron et al., "Disrupted Childhood."

23. Wells et al., "Facebook Knows Instagram is Toxic."

24. Kidron et al., "Disrupted Childhood."

25. Clare Morell et al., "Protecting Teens from Big Tech: Five Policy Ideas for States," Institute for Family Studies, August 24, 2022, https://ifstudies.org/blog/protecting -teens-from-big-tech-five-policy-ideas-for-states.

26. Kidron et al., "Disrupted Childhood"; Clare Morell et al., "Protecting Teens from Big Tech: Five Policy Ideas for States."

27. Joel Rosenblatt, "In Dozens of Lawsuits Parents Blame Meta, TikTok for Hooking Kids," *Bloomberg*, September 22, 2022, https://www.bloomberg.com /news/articles/2022-09-22/social-media-addiction-brings-lawsuits-against -youtube-facebook.

28. Gene Johnson, "Seattle Schools Sue Tech Giants over Social Media Harm," *Associated Press*, January 8, 2023, https://apnews.com/article/social-media-seattle -lawsuits-mental-health-965a8f373e3bfed8157571912cc3b542.

29. Rosenblatt, "Dozens of Lawsuits."

30. Audrey Conklin, "Coroner Rules 14-Year-Old Molly Russell's Cause of Death Suicide Resulting from Social Media," *New York Post*, October 1, 2022, https://

nypost.com/2022/10/01/molly-russels-cause-of-death-ruled-a-suicide-resulting-from
-social-media/.

31. 5Rights Foundation, "Friend Suggestions," accessed January 15, 2023, https://www
.riskyby.design/friend-suggestions; 5Rights Foundation home page, accessed
January 15, 2023, https://5rightsfoundation.com/.

32. Designed with Kids in Mind, "How Bad Design Harms Kids," accessed January
16, 2023, https://designedwithkidsinmind.us/how-bad-design-harms-kids/.

33. Common Sense Media, "COPPA 2.0—Fact Sheet."

34. Designed with Kids in Mind, "How Bad Design Harms Kids."

35. Fairplay et al., Letter to US Senate Commerce Committee; 5Rights Foundation,
"New Research Shows Child Accounts Directly Targeted with Graphic Content
Within as Little as 24 Hours of Creating an Online Social Media Account,"
accessed January 15, 2023, https://5rightsfoundation.com/in-action/new-research
-shows-children-directly-targeted-with-graphic-content-within-as-little-as-24
-hours-of-creating-an-online-social-media-account.html.

36. Noah Zon and Adrienne Lipsey, "Children's Safety and Privacy in the Digital
Age," CSA Group, May 2020, https://www.csagroup.org/wp-content/uploads
/CSA-Group-Research-Childrens-Safety-and-Privacy-in-the-Digital-Age.pdf.

37. Zon and Lipsey, "Children's Safety and Privacy in the Digital Age"; Kidron et al.,
"Disrupted Childhood."

38. Cobun Zweifel-Keegan et al., "The Future of Youth Privacy Is Here,"
International Association of Privacy Professionals (IAPP), September 27, 2022,
https://iapp.org/news/a/the-future-of-youth-privacy-is-here/.

39. Zweifel-Keegan et al., "The Future of Youth Privacy Is Here"; The changes are
from the list documented by the 5Rights Foundation, "The California Age
Appropriate Design Code," accessed January 15, 2023, https://5rightsfoundation.
com/uploads/California-Age-Appropriate-Design-Code_short-briefing.pdf.

40. Adam Satariano, "Meta Fined $400 Million for Treatment of Children's Data on
Instagram," *New York Times*, September 5, 2022, https://www.nytimes.com
/2022/09/05/business/meta-children-data-protection-europe.html.

41. The bullets of obligations are from 5Rights Foundation, "The CA Age Appropriate
Design Code: How It Works," accessed January 15, 2023, https://californiaaadc.com
/wp-content/uploads/2022/08/AADC-How-it-Works-FINAL.pdf, and Designed
with Kids in Mind, "Creating a Design Code," accessed January 15, 2023, https://
designedwithkidsinmind.us/how-well-do-it/.

42. Jennifer King, "A Bill Designed to Protect Kids Could Change the Internet for the
Better," *Tech Policy Press*, September 15, 2022, https://techpolicy.press/a-bill
-designed-to-protect-kids-could-change-the-internet-for-the-better/.

43. Evan Symon, "Tech Industry Group Sues AG Rob Bonta & State over New Child
Online Privacy Law," *California Globe*, December 14, 2022, https://californiaglobe
.com/articles/tech-industry-group-sues-ag-rob-bonta-state-over-new-child-online
-privacy-law/.

44. Federal Trade Commission, "Complying with COPPA: Frequently Asked
Questions," accessed January 15, 2023, https://www.ftc.gov/business-guidance
/resources/complying-coppa-frequently-asked-questions.

45. Privo, "History of COPPA Violations," accessed January 15, 2023, https://www
.privo.com/history-of-coppa-violations.

46. Designed with Kids in Mind, "Creating a Design Code"; Geoffrey A. Fowler, "Your Kids' Apps Are Spying on Them."

47. Senator Richard Blumenthal, "The Kids Online Safety Act of 2022," accessed January 7, 2023, https://www.blumenthal.senate.gov/imo/media/doc/kids_online _safety_act_-_one_pager.pdf.

48. Representative Kathy Castor, "Rep. Castor Reintroduces Landmark Kids PRIVCY Act to Strengthen COPPA, Keep Children Safe Online," July 29, 2021, https:// castor.house.gov/news/documentsingle.aspx?DocumentID=403677.

49. Senator Ed Markey, "Senators Markey and Blumenthal, Rep. Castor Reintroduce Legislation to Protect Children and Teens from Online Manipulation and Harm," September 30, 2021, https://www.markey.senate.gov/news/press-releases/senators -markey-and-blumenthal-rep-castor-reintroduce-legislation-to-protect-children -and-teens-from-online-manipulation-and-harm.

50. The White House, "Remarks of President Joe Biden—State of the Union Address as Prepared for Delivery," March 1, 2022, https://www.whitehouse.gov/briefing -room/speeches-remarks/2022/03/01/remarks-of-president-joe-biden-state-of-the -union-address-as-delivered/.

51. US Surgeon General, "Protecting Youth Mental Health: The US Surgeon General's Advisory"; Designed with Kids in Mind, "Why We Need a Design Code"; Designed with Kids in Mind, "How Bad Design Harms Kids."

Chapter 7

1. Barack Obama, "Disinformation Is a Threat to Our Democracy," April 21, 2021, https://barackobama.medium.com/my-remarks-on-disinformation-at-stanford -7d7af7ba28af.

2. Estimated deaths from Anti-Defamation League (ADL), "Murder and Extremism in the United States in 2021," May 3, 2022, https://www.adl.org/murder-and -extremism-2021; "clear nexus" quote from Jonathan Greenblatt, "Congressional Testimony to House Committee on Energy and Commerce, Subcommittee on Consumer Protection and Commerce," December 9, 2021, https://energycommerce .house.gov/sites/democrats.energycommerce.house.gov/files/documents/Witness%20 Testimony_Greenblatt_CPC_2021.12.09_1.pdf.

3. Ryan Mac et al., "The Enduring Afterlife of a Mass Shooting's Livestream Online," *New York Times*, May 19, 2022, https://www.nytimes.com/2022/05/19/technology /mass-shootings-livestream-online.html.; *Gonzalez v. Google LLC*, No. 18016700, United States Court of Appeals, Ninth Circuit, Decided June 22, 2021, in favor of the Defendant.

4. Karen Kornbluh, "Disinformation, Radicalization, and Algorithmic Amplification: What Steps Can Congress Take?" *Just Security*, February 7, 2022, https://www.just security.org/79995/disinformation-radicalization-and-algorithmic-amplification -what-steps-can-congress-take/; David Ingram, "Facebook Says 126 Million Americans May Have Seen Russia-Linked Political Posts," *Reuters*, October 30, 2017, https://www.reuters.com/article/us-usa-trump-russia-socialmedia/facebook -says-126-million-americans-may-have-seen-russia-linked-political-posts -idUSKBN1CZ2OI.

5. Obama, "Disinformation Is a Threat to Our Democracy."

6. Greenblatt, "Congressional Testimony."

7. Obama, "Disinformation Is a Threat to Our Democracy"; Justin Hendrix, "How Social Media Intensifies US Polarization—and What Can Be Done About It," *Tech Policy Press*, September 13, 2021, https://techpolicy.press/how-social-media-intensifies-u-s-polarization-and-what-can-be-done-about-it/.

8. Obama, "Disinformation Is a Threat to Our Democracy."

9. Angwin, "How AI Could Undermine an Efficient Market Economy."

10. Greenblatt, "Congressional Testimony."

11. Obama, "Disinformation Is a Threat to Our Democracy"; Avi Asher, "Big Tech Accused of Failing to Talk US Midterm 'Lies,'" *Reuters*, October 6, 2022, https://www.reuters.com/article/usa-election-tech/big-tech-accused-of-failing-to-tackle-u-s-midterm-lies-idUSL8N30Z6SJ.

12. Obama, "Disinformation Is a Threat to Our Democracy."

13. Ryan Mac and Sheera Frankel, "Internal Alarm, Public Shrugs: Facebook's Employees Dissect Its Election Role," *New York Times*, October 22, 2021, https://www.nytimes.com/2021/10/22/technology/facebook-election-misinformation.html; Nick Statt, "Facebook Reportedly Ignored Its Own Research Showing Algorithms Divide Users," *The Verge*, May 26, 2020, https://www.theverge.com/2020/5/26/21270659/facebook-division-news-feed-algorithms.

14. Hao, "The Facebook Whistleblower Says Its Algorithms Are Dangerous."

15. Eli M. Rosenberg, "Facebook Hit with $2 Billion Lawsuit Connected to Political Violence in Africa," *NBC News*, December 13, 2022, https://www.nbcnews.com/tech/misinformation/facebook-lawsuit-africa-content-moderation-violence-rcna61530.

16. Greenblatt, "Congressional Testimony"; M. Estrada, "Dozens of Spanish-Language Election Fraud YouTube Videos Demonstrate the Platform's Toothless Policies," *Media Matters for America*, October 10, 2022, https://www.mediamatters.org/spanish-language-media/dozens-spanish-language-election-fraud-youtube-videos-demonstrate-platforms.

17. Jeff Horwitz and Deepa Seetharaman, "Facebook Executives Shut Down Efforts to Make the Site Less Divisive," *Wall Street Journal*, May 26, 2020, https://www.wsj.com/articles/facebook-knows-it-encourages-division-top-executives-nixed-solutions-11590507499.

18. Sam Schechner et al., "How Facebook Hobbled Mark Zuckerberg's Bid to Get America Vaccinated," *Wall Street Journal*, September 17, 2021, https://www.wsj.com/articles/facebook-mark-zuckerberg-vaccinated-11631880296.

19. Tech Transparency Project, "Facebook Profits from White Supremacist Groups," August 10, 2022, https://www.techtransparencyproject.org/articles/facebook-profits-white-supremacist-groups; Cristiano Lima, "A Whistleblower's Power: Key Takeaways from the Facebook Papers." *Washington Post*, October 26, 2021, https://www.washingtonpost.com/technology/2021/10/25/what-are-the-facebook-papers/.

20. Jeff Horwitz, "Facebook Says Its Rules Apply to All. Company Documents Reveal a Secret Elite That's Exempt," *Wall Street Journal*, September 13, 2021, https://www.wsj.com/articles/facebook-files-xcheck-zuckerberg-elite-rules-11631541353.

21. Ban Surveillance Advertising, "Real Costs of the Business," accessed January 16, 2023, https://www.bansurveillanceadvertising.com/real-costs-of-the-business.

22. Ban Surveillance Advertising, "Real Costs of the Business."

23. Cristina Tardáguila et al., "How Ad Tech Companies Fund Misinformation," *Poynter*, September 26, 2019, https://www.poynter.org/fact-checking/2019/how-ad-tech-companies-fund-misinformation/; L. Gordan Crovitz, "How Amazon,

Geico, and Walmart Fund Propaganda," *New York Times*, January 21, 2020, https://www.nytimes.com/2020/01/21/opinion/fake-news-russia-ads.html; Issie Lapowsky, "Google Says It's Fighting Election Lies, but Its Programmatic Ads Are Funding Them," *Protocol*, January 14, 2021, https://www.protocol.com/google-programmatic-ads-misinformation.

24. Ban Surveillance Advertising, "Real Costs of the Business"; Mark Sweney, "UK Publishers Losing Digital Ad Revenue Due to Content 'Blacklists,'" *The Guardian*, January 20, 2020, https://www.theguardian.com/media/2020/jan/20/uk-publishers-losing-digital-ad-revenue-due-to-content-blacklists.

25. Anna Edgerton, "Facebook Is the Only Game in Town for Digital Political Ads," *Bloomberg*, October 5, 2022, https://www.bloomberg.com/news/articles/2022-10-05/facebook-is-politicians-last-resort-for-2022-election-ads; Greenblatt, "Congressional Testimony."

26. Greenblatt, "Congressional Testimony."

27. Casey Tolan, "How Political Candidates Are Targeting You on Social Media Based on Your Music Tastes, Shopping Habits and Favorite TV Shows," *CNN*, September 23, 2022, https://www.cnn.com/2022/09/23/business/us-candidates-facebook-ads-targeting-invs/index.html.

28. Jennifer Korn, "Facebook and TikTok Are Approving Ads with 'Blatant' Misinformation About Voting in Midterms, Researchers Say," *CNN*, October 21, 2022, https://www.cnn.com/2022/10/21/tech/facebook-tiktok-misinfo-ads/index.html.

29. Obama, "Disinformation Is a Threat to Our Democracy."

30. Obama, "Disinformation Is a Threat to Our Democracy."

31. Kornbluh, "Disinformation, Radicalization, and Algorithmic Amplification."

32. Meghan Anand et al., "All the Ways Congress Wants to Change Section 230," *Slate*, March 23, 2021, https://slate.com/technology/2021/03/section-230-reform-legislative-tracker.html.

33. Anand et al., "All the Ways Congress Wants to Change Section 230"; Matt Shuman, "Supreme Court to Hear Cases That Could Reel In Social Media Companies' Immunity," *The Huffington Post*, October 3, 2022, https://www.huffpost.com/entry/supreme-court-agrees-hear-cases-social-media-immunity-section-230_n_633b15efe4b02816452c84f6; The White House, "Readout of White House Listening Session on Tech Platform Accountability."

34. Shira Ovide, "What's Behind the Fight over Section 230," *New York Times*, March 25, 2021, https://www.nytimes.com/2021/03/25/technology/section-230-explainer.html; Anand et al., "All the Ways Congress Wants to Change Section 230."

35. Anand et al., "All the Ways Congress Wants to Change Section 230"; Ovide, "What's Behind the Fight over Section 230"; Will Oremus, "How Social Media 'Censorship' Became a Front Line in the Culture War," *Washington Post*, October 9, 2022, https://www.washingtonpost.com/technology/2022/10/09/social-media-content-moderation/.

36. Shuman, "Supreme Court to Hear Cases"; Ben Brody, "The Supreme Court Is Finally Taking Up Section 230," *Protocol*, October 3, 2022, https://www.protocol.com/newsletters/policy/230-scotus-google-algorithms.

37. Brody, "The Supreme Court Is Finally Taking Up Section 230"; Oremus, "How Social Media 'Censorship' Became a Front Line in the Culture War.'"

38. Iris Malone, "Will the EU's Digital Services Act Reduce Online Extremism?" *Just Security*, May 16, 2022, https://www.justsecurity.org/81534/will-the-eus-digital-service-act-reduce-online-extremism/; Adam Satariano, "EU Takes Aim at Social

Media's Harms with Landmark New Law," *New York Times*, April 22, 2022, https://www.nytimes.com/2022/04/22/technology/european-union-social-media-law.html; Kelvin Chan and Raf Casert, "EU Law Targets Big Tech over Hate Speech, Disinformation," *Associated Press*, April 23, 2022, https://apnews.com/article/technology-business-police-social-media-reform-52744e1d0f5b93a426f966138f2ccb52.

39. Lizzie O'Leary, "A Looming Legal Battle Could Change Social Media Forever," *Slate*, September 27, 2022, https://slate.com/technology/2022/09/florida-texas-social-media-laws-supreme-court.html; Brian Fung, "Federal Appeals Court Pauses Texas Social Media Law's Enforcement amid Looming Supreme Court Petition," *CNN*, October 13, 2022, https://www.cnn.com/2022/10/13/tech/texas-social-media-pause/index.html.

40. Fung, "Federal Appeals Court Pauses."

41. Natasha Singer, "Charting the 'California Effect' on Tech Regulation," *New York Times*, October 12, 2022, https://www.nytimes.com/2022/10/12/us/california-tech-regulation.html.

42. Senator Chris Coons, "Coons, Portman, Klobuchar Announce Legislation to Ensure Transparency at Social Media Platforms," December 9, 2021, https://www.coons.senate.gov/news/press-releases/coons-portman-klobuchar-announce-legislation-to-ensure-transparency-at-social-media-platforms.

43. Kornbluh, "Disinformation, Radicalization, and Algorithmic Amplification."

44. Kornbluh, "Disinformation, Radicalization, and Algorithmic Amplification."

45. Obama, "Disinformation Is a Threat to Our Democracy."

46. Greenblatt, "Congressional Testimony."

47. Greenblatt, "Congressional Testimony."

Chapter 8

1. Sara Morrison and Jason Del Rey, "FTC Chair Lina Khan's Plan to Take On Big Tech, in 9 Questions," *Vox*, June 9, 2022, https://www.vox.com/recode/2022/6/9/23160578/lina-khan-ftc-interview.

2. Subcommittee on Antitrust, Commercial, and Administrative Law of the Committee on the Judiciary of the US House of Representatives, *Investigation of Competition in Digital Markets: Majority Staff Report and Recommendations*, by Jerrold Nadler and David Cicilline, CP 117-8 Part I, Washington, Government Printing Office, July 2022, https://www.govinfo.gov/content/pkg/CPRT-117HPRT47832/pdf/CPRT-117HPRT47832.pdf.

3. Subcommittee on Antitrust, *Investigation of Competition in Digital Markets*. Microsoft was the only Big Tech firm not investigated by the subcommittee based on markets selected for review.

4. Subcommittee on Antitrust, *Investigation of Competition in Digital Markets*.

5. Alex Harman, "Big Tech Platforms Stifle Innovation Through Anticompetitive Conduct," *The Hill*, October 23, 2021, https://thehill.com/blogs/congress-blog/technology/578133-big-tech-platforms-stifle-innovation-through-anticompetitive/; Subcommittee on Antitrust, *Investigation of Competition in Digital Markets*.

6. The Organization for Economic Cooperation and Development (OECD), "Competition Policy in the Digital Age," February 23, 2022, https://www.oecd.org/daf/competition

-policy-in-the-digital-age/; Harman, "Big Tech Platforms Stifle Innovation"; Subcommittee on Antitrust, *Investigation of Competition in Digital Markets*; David Streitfeld, "Amazon's Antitrust Antagonist Has a Breakthrough Idea," *New York Times*, September 7, 2018, https://www.nytimes.com/2018/09/07/technology /monopoly-antitrust-lina-khan-amazon.html.

7. Subcommittee on Antitrust, *Investigation of Competition in Digital Markets*; Charlotte Slaiman, "Antitrust Bills Will Unleash America's Innovation Economy," *Tech Policy Press*, July 25, 2022, https://techpolicy.press/antitrust-bills-will -unleash-americas-innovation-economy/; Doctorow, "How to Ditch Facebook Without Ditching Your Friends."

8. Streitfeld, "Amazon's Antitrust Antagonist"; Lina Khan, "Amazon's Antitrust Paradox," *The Yale Law Journal*, January 2017, https://www.yalelaw journal.org/note/amazons-antitrust-paradox.

9. Khan, "Amazon's Antitrust Paradox"; Subcommittee on Antitrust, *Investigation of Competition in Digital Markets*; Streitfeld, "Amazon's Antitrust Antagonist."

10. Streitfeld, "Amazon's Antitrust Antagonist."

11. Khan, "Amazon's Antitrust Paradox"; Shira Ovide, "Amazon Prime: Loved at Almost Any Price," *New York Times*, January 12, 2022, https://www.nytimes.com /2022/01/12/technology/amazon-prime-price.html; Subcommittee on Antitrust, *Investigation of Competition in Digital Markets*.

12. Khan, "Amazon's Antitrust Paradox"; Subcommittee on Antitrust, *Investigation of Competition in Digital Markets*.

13. Khan, "Amazon's Antitrust Paradox"; Subcommittee on Antitrust, *Investigation of Competition in Digital Markets*.

14. Subcommittee on Antitrust, *Investigation of Competition in Digital Markets*.

15. Ben Lovejoy, "iPhone US Market Share Hits an All-Time High, Overtaking Android; Dominates Global Premium Sales," *9to5Mac*, September 2, 2022, https://9to5mac.com/2022/09/02/iphone-us-market-share/.

16. Subcommittee on Antitrust, *Investigation of Competition in Digital Markets*; Wikipedia, "Supra-competitive Pricing," updated December 10, 2020, https:// en.wikipedia.org/wiki/Supracompetitive_pricing.

17. Sarah Perez, "Apple Dropping App Store Fees to 15 Percent for Small Businesses with Under $1 Million in Revenues," *TechCrunch*, November 18, 2020, https:// techcrunch.com/2020/11/18/apple-to-reduce-app-store-fees-for-small-businesses -with-under-1-million-in-revenues/; Subcommittee on Antitrust, *Investigation of Competition in Digital Markets*.

18. Tripp Mickle, "Spotify Wants to Get Into Audiobooks but Says Apple Is in the Way," *New York Times*, October 25, 2022, https://www.nytimes.com/2022/10/25 /business/spotify-apple-audiobooks-app.html; Subcommittee on Antitrust, *Investigation of Competition in Digital Markets*.

19. Coalition for App Fairness, "Issue: A Broken Marketplace," accessed January 15, 2023, https://appfairness.org/issues/broken-marketplace/.

20. Coalition for App Fairness, "Issue: A Broken Marketplace"; Mickle, "Spotify Wants to Get Into Audiobooks."

21. Subcommittee on Antitrust, *Investigation of Competition in Digital Markets*.

22. Tripp Mickle, "Apple Dominates App Store Search Results, Thwarting Competitors," *Wall Street Journal*, July 23, 2019, https://www.wsj.com/articles /apple-dominates-app-store-search-results-thwarting-competitors-11563897221; Subcommittee on Antitrust, *Investigation of Competition in Digital Markets*.

23. US Department of Justice, "Amended Complaint of US and Plaintiff States vs. Google LLC," January 15, 2021, https://www.justice.gov/atr/case-document/file /1428271/download; Sara Morrison, "How Much Longer Can Google Own the Internet?" *Vox*, May 20, 2022, https://www.vox.com/recode/23132580/google -antitrust-search-android-mobile-ads; Slintel, "Market Share of Google DoubleClick," August 3, 2022, https://www.slintel.com/tech/ad-exchange/google -doubleclick-market-share; Subcommittee on Antitrust, *Investigation of Competition in Digital Markets*.

24. Subcommittee on Antitrust, *Investigation of Competition in Digital Markets*.

25. Morrison, "How Much Longer Can Google Own the Internet?"; Subcommittee on Antitrust, *Investigation of Competition in Digital Markets*.

26. Subcommittee on Antitrust, *Investigation of Competition in Digital Markets*.

27. Subcommittee on Antitrust, *Investigation of Competition in Digital Markets*.

28. Subcommittee on Antitrust, *Investigation of Competition in Digital Markets*.

29. US Department of Justice, "Justice Department Sues Monopolist Google for Violating Antitrust Laws," October 20, 2020, https://www.justice.gov/opa/pr /justice-department-sues-monopolist-google-violating-antitrust-laws.

30. John Koetsier, "Google Antitrust: The 14 Most Explosive Allegations," *Forbes*, February 4, 2022, https://www.forbes.com/sites/johnkoetsier/2022/02/04/google -antitrust-the-14-most-explosive-allegations; Subcommittee on Antitrust, *Investigation of Competition in Digital Markets*.

31. Texas Attorney General Ken Paxton, "Paxton Files Third Amendment in Antitrust Lawsuit Against Google," November 16, 2021, https://www.texasattorneygeneral .gov/news/releases/paxton-files-third-amendment-antitrust-lawsuit-against-google; David McCabe and Tripp Mickle, "Justice Dept. Said to Conduct New Interviews in Inquiry into Google's Ad Tech," *New York Times*, August 9, 2022, https://www .nytimes.com/2022/08/09/technology/justice-dept-google-ad-tech.html; Miles Kruppa et al., "Google Offers Concessions to Fend Off US Antitrust Lawsuit," *Wall Street Journal*, July 8, 2022, https://www.wsj.com/articles/google-offers-concessions -to-fend-off-u-s-antitrust-lawsuit-11657296591.

32. David McCabe and Daisuke Wakabayashi, "Dozens of States Sue Google over App Store Fees," *New York Times*, July 7, 2021, https://www.nytimes.com/2021/07/07 /technology/google-play-store-antitrust-suit.html.

33. Cecilia Kang, "A Facebook Antitrust Suit Can Move Forward, a Judge Says, in a Win for the FTC," *New York Times*, January 11, 2022, https://www.nytimes.com /2022/01/11/technology/facebook-antitrust-ftc.html.

34. Shirin Ghaffary and Sara Morrison, "Can Facebook Monopolize the Metaverse?" *Vox*, February 16, 2022, https://www.vox.com/recode/22933851/meta-facebook -metaverse-antitrust-regulation; Subcommittee on Antitrust, *Investigation of Competition in Digital Markets*; Federal Trade Commission, "FTC Sues Facebook for Illegal Monopolization," December 9, 2020, https://www.ftc.gov/news-events /news/press-releases/2020/12/ftc-sues-facebook-illegal-monopolization.

35. Federal Trade Commission, "FTC Sues Facebook for Illegal Monopolization."

36. Federal Trade Commission, "FTC Sues Facebook for Illegal Monopolization"; Federal Trade Commission, "FTC Alleges Facebook Resorted to Illegal Buy-or-Bury Scheme to Crush Competition After String of Failed Attempts to Innovate," August 19, 2021, https://www.ftc.gov/news-events/news/press-releases/2021/08/ftc-alleges -facebook-resorted-illegal-buy-or-bury-scheme-crush-competition-after-string-failed; *FTC vs. Facebook, Inc.*, Case No.: 1:20-cv-03590-JEB, Filed January 13, 2021,

https://www.ftc.gov/system/files/documents/cases/051_2021.01.21_revised_partially
_redacted_complaint.pdf.

37. *FTC vs. Facebook, Inc.*, Case No.: 1:20-cv-03590-JEB.

38. Cecilia Kang, "Judge Throws Out 2 Antitrust Cases Against Facebook," *New York Times,* June 28, 2021, https://www.nytimes.com/2021/06/28/technology/facebook -ftc-lawsuit.html; Kang, "A Facebook Antitrust Suit Can Move Forward, a Judge Says, in a Win for the FTC."

39. Federal Trade Commission, "Monopolization Defined," accessed January 16, 2023, https://www.ftc.gov/advice-guidance/competition-guidance/guide-antitrust-laws /single-firm-conduct/monopolization-defined; Sara Morrison, "Microsoft Avoided the Latest Round of Big Tech Antitrust Scrutiny. Then It Bought a Company for $69 Billion." *Vox,* January 27, 2022, https://www.vox.com/recode/22893117/microsoft -activision-antitrust-big-tech.

40. Morrison, "Microsoft Avoided the Latest Round of Big Tech Antitrust Scrutiny"; Subcommittee on Antitrust, *Investigation of Competition in Digital Markets.*

41. Subcommittee on Antitrust, *Investigation of Competition in Digital Markets.*

42. Evgeny Obedkov, "FTC Has 'Significant Concerns' About Microsoft's Acquisition of Activision Blizzard, Ruling to Come in November," *Game World Observer,* October 5, 2022, https://gameworldobserver.com/2022/10/05/ftc-ruling-microsoft-activision -blizzard-concerns-deadline; Morrison, "Microsoft Avoided the Latest Round of Big Tech Antitrust Scrutiny"; Karen Weise and David McCabe, "FTC Sues to Block Microsoft's $69 Billion Acquisition of Activision," *New York Times*, December 8, 2022, https://www.nytimes.com/2022/12/08/technology/ftc-microsoft-activision.html.

43. The Kauffman Foundation, "The Share of Private Sector Jobs Held at Firms Aged 0-1 Year Old," accessed January 17, 2023, https://indicators.kauffman.org/indicator /contribution; Gené Teare, "Decade in Review: Trends in Seed and Early Stage Funding," *Crunchbase*, March 13, 2019, https://news.crunchbase.com/venture /decade-in-review-trends-in-seed-and-early-stage-funding/.

44. Subcommittee on Antitrust, *Investigation of Competition in Digital Markets.*

45. Subcommittee on Antitrust, *Investigation of Competition in Digital Markets.*

46. Chakravorti, "Biden's 'Antitrust Revolution' Overlooks AI"; Schwab, "The Fourth Industrial Revolution: What It Means, How to Respond."

47. Subcommittee on Antitrust, *Investigation of Competition in Digital Markets.*

48. Subcommittee on Antitrust, *Investigation of Competition in Digital Markets*; Pew Research Center, "Newspaper Fact Sheet," June 29, 2021, https://www.pewresearch .org/journalism/fact-sheet/newspapers/.

49. Subcommittee on Antitrust, *Investigation of Competition in Digital Markets.*

50. Cecilia Kang et al., "Tech Giants, Fearful of Proposals to Curb Them, Blitz Washington with Lobbying," *New York Times,* June 22, 2021, https://www.nytimes .com/2021/06/22/technology/amazon-apple-google-facebook-antitrust-bills.html; Subcommittee on Antitrust, *Investigation of Competition in Digital Markets.*

51. European Commission, "Questions and Answers: Digital Markets Act: Ensuring Fair and Open Digital Markets."

52. European Commission, "Questions and Answers: Digital Markets Act: Ensuring Fair and Open Digital Markets." All bullets are paraphrased from the DMA Questions and Answers document.

53. European Commission, "Questions and Answers: Digital Markets Act: Ensuring Fair and Open Digital Markets."

54. Mark Gurman, "Apple to Allow Outside App Stores in Overhaul Spurred by EU Laws," *Bloomberg*, December 13, 2022, https://www.bloomberg.com/news/articles /2022-12-13/will-apple-allow-users-to-install-third-party-app-stores-sideload-in -europe; Jon Porter, "Amazon and EU Reach Agreement to Try to Level the Playing Field for Third-Party Sellers," *The Verge*, December 20, 2022, https://www.theverge .com/2022/12/20/23518569/amazon-european-union-eu-antitrust-third-party-sellers.

55. Khari Johnson, "Europe Prepares to Rewrite the Rules of the Internet," *Wired*, October 28, 2022, https://www.wired.com/story/europe-dma-prepares-to-rewrite -the-rules-of-the-internet/.

56. Bullet list compiled from the following two sources: Coalition for App Fairness, "Tell Your Lawmakers: Stand Against App Store Monopolies and Support the Open App Markets Act!" accessed January 16, 2023, https://actnow.io/RelFQaN and Sara Morrison, "How Much Control Should Apple Have over Your iPhone?" *Vox*, December 8, 2021, https://www.vox.com/recode/22821277/apple-iphone-antitrust -app-store-privacy.

57. Antoine Prince Albert III, "Big Tech, Big Problems, & Big Solutions: The Legislative Package to Reinvigorate Platform Competition," *Public Knowledge*, September 15, 2021, https://publicknowledge.org/big-tech-big-problems-big-solutions-the -legislative-package-to-reinvigorate-platform-competition/.

58. Khan, "Amazon's Antitrust Paradox"; Doctorow, "How to Destroy Surveillance Capitalism."

59. Subcommittee on Antitrust, *Investigation of Competition in Digital Markets*.

60. Doctorow, "How to Destroy Surveillance Capitalism"; Subcommittee on Antitrust, *Investigation of Competition in Digital Markets*; Keach Hagey and Tripp Mickle, "Google Charges More Than Twice Its Rivals in Ad Deals, Unredacted Suit Says," *Wall Street Journal*, October 22, 2021, https://www.wsj.com/articles/google-charges -more-than-twice-its-rivals-in-ad-deals-wins-80-of-its-own-auctions-court-documents -say-11634912297.

61. Subcommittee on Antitrust, *Investigation of Competition in Digital Markets*.

62. Cory Doctorow, "At the FTC, a Quiet, Profound Shift on Antitrust," *Pluralistic*, May 9, 2022, https://pluralistic.net/2022/05/09/rest-in-piss-robert-bork/.

63. Slaiman, "Antitrust Bills Will Unleash America's Innovation Economy"; Subcommittee on Antitrust, *Investigation of Competition in Digital Markets*; Wikiquote, "Louis Brandeis," updated December 29, 2022, https://en.wikiquote.org /wiki/Louis_Brandeis.

Conclusion

1. Subcommittee on Antitrust, *Investigation of Competition in Digital Markets*.

2. Share prices from Yahoo! Finance, accessed October 31, 2022, https://finance.yahoo .com/; Scott Galloway, "Elephants in the Room," November 4, 2022, https://www .profgalloway.com/elephants-in-the-room/.

3. Mark Zuckerberg, "Mark Zuckerberg's Message to Meta Employees," Meta Newsroom, November 9, 2022, https://about.fb.com/news/2022/11/mark -zuckerberg-layoff-message-to-employees/.

4. Galloway, "Elephants in the Room"; Cal Newport, "TikTok and the Fall of the Social-Media Giants," *New Yorker*, July 28, 2022, https://www.newyorker.com /culture/cultural-comment/tiktok-and-the-fall-of-the-social-media-giants.

5. Apple, "If an App Asks to Track Your Activity," accessed January 4, 2023, https://
    support.apple.com/en-us/HT212025; Jerath, "Mobile Advertising and the Impact of
    Apple's App Tracking Transparency Policy"; Flurry, "App Tracking Transparency
    Opt-In Rate—Monthly Updates"; Leswing, "Facebook Says Apple iOS Privacy
    Change Will Result in $10 Billion Revenue Hit This Year"

6. Eric Seufert, "Meta Q3 2022 Earnings: 'Those Who Are Patient and Invest with
    Us Will End Up Being Rewarded,'" Mobile Dev Memo, October 27, 2022, https://
    mobiledevmemo.com/meta-q3-2022-earnings-those-who-are-patient-and-invest
    -with-us-will-end-up-being-rewarded/.

7. Adam Satariano, "Meta Fined $275 Million for Breaking EU Data Privacy Law,"
    New York Times, November 28, 2022, https://www.nytimes.com/2022/11/28
    /business/meta-fine-eu-privacy.html.

8. Adam Satariano, "Meta's Ad Practices Ruled Illegal Under EU Law," New York
    Times, January 4, 2023, https://www.nytimes.com/2023/01/04/technology/met
    a-facebook-eu-gdpr.html; Schechner, "Meta Fined Over $400 Million in EU for
    Serving Ads Based on Online Activity"; Jason Kint (@jason_kint), "Oomph.
    Reminder: EU is closing in on Facebook's . . . ," Twitter, October 3, 2022, 8:47
    a.m., https://twitter.com/jason_kint/status/1576962040639258624.

9. Ben Thompson, "Meta Myths," Stratechery, October 31, 2022, https://stratechery
    .com/2022/meta-myths/.

10. Thompson, "Meta Myths."

11. Karen Weise, "Amazon Expands Corporate Layoffs to 18,000 Jobs," New York
    Times, January 4, 2023, https://www.nytimes.com/2023/01/04/business/amazon
    -corporate-layoffs.html; Macrotrends, "Microsoft: Number of Employees 2010–
    2022 | MSFT," accessed January 20, 2023, https://www.macrotrends.net/stocks
    /charts/msft/microsoft/number-of-employees; Macrotrends, "Meta Platforms:
    Number of Employees 2010-2022 | META," accessed January 20, 2023, https://
    www.macrotrends.net/stocks/charts/meta/meta-platforms/number-of-employees;
    Macrotrends, "Amazon: Number of Employees 2010-2022 | AMZN," accessed
    January 20, 2023, https://www.macrotrends.net/stocks/charts/amzn/amazon
    /number-of-employees; Macrotrends, "Alphabet: Number of Employees 2010-2022 |
    GOOG," accessed January 20, 2023, https://www.macrotrends.net/stocks/charts
    /goog/alphabet/number-of-employees; Dave Lee, "Big Tech Groups Disclose $10bn
    in Charges from Job Culls and Cost Cutting," Financial Times, February 3, 2023,
    https://www.ft.com/content/9daf27f6-dde7-40d8-b01d-33b70844aa69; Subrat
    Patnaik, "Meta Evokes Big Tech's Glory Days with Biggest Surge Since 2013,"
    Bloomberg, February 2, 2023, https://www.yahoo.com/now/meta-stock-market
    -rebound-surpass-112630251.html.

12. Slaiman, "Antitrust Bills Will Unleash America's Innovation Economy."

13. Matt Krantz, "13 Firms Hoard $1 Trillion in Cash (We're Looking at You Big
    Tech)," Investor's Business Daily, February 3, 2022, https://www.investors.com
    /etfs-and-funds/sectors/sp500-companies-stockpile-1-trillion-cash-investors-want
    -it/; Richard Waters and Kadhim Shubber, "Google Invests $300mm in Artificial
    Intelligence Start-Up Anthropic," Financial Times, February 3, 2023, https://www
    .ft.com/content/583ead66-467c-4bd5-84d0-ed5df7b5bf9c.

14. US Department of Justice, "Attorney General Eric Holder Speaks at the Sherman
    Act Award Ceremony," April 20, 2010, https://www.justice.gov/opa/speech
    /attorney-general-eric-holder-speaks-sherman-act-award-ceremony.

Appendix 1

1. Michael Muchmore, "Stop Trackers Dead: The Best Private Browsers for 2022," *PCMag*, April 1, 2022, https://www.pcmag.com/picks/stop-trackers-dead-the-best -private-browsers; Apple, "We're Committed to Protecting Your Data," accessed January 16, 2023, https://www.apple.com/privacy/features/.

2. Federal Trade Commission, "How to Protect Your Privacy Online," accessed January 16, 2023, https://consumer.ftc.gov/articles/how-protect-your-privacy-online; Bennett Cyphers, "How to Disable Ad ID Tracking on iOS and Android, and Why You Should Do It Now," Electronic Frontier Foundation, May 11, 2022, https:// www.eff.org/deeplinks/2022/05/how-disable-ad-id-tracking-ios-and-android-and -why-you-should-do-it-now.

3. Apple, "If an App Asks to Track Your Activity"; DuckDuckGo, "App Tracking Protection Beta Is Now Available to All Android Users," November 15, 2022, https://spreadprivacy.com/app-tracking-protection-open-beta/.

4. Vivian McCall and Barbara Smith, "What Is Signal? How the Popular Encrypted Messaging App Keeps Your Texts Private," *Business Insider*, October 19, 2021, https://www.businessinsider.com/signal-app.

5. Apple, "Use Mail Privacy Protection on iPhone," accessed January 16, 2023, https://support.apple.com/guide/iphone/use-mail-privacy-protection-iphf084865c7 /ios; IronVest, accessed January 17, 2023, https://ironvest.com/.

6. Grauer, "Big Ass Data Broker Opt-Out List," GitHub, accessed January 26, 2023, https://github.com/yaelwrites/Big-Ass-Data-Broker-Opt-Out-List.

7. Grauer, "Big Ass Data Broker Opt-Out List."

8. Consumer Reports, "California Consumer Privacy Act: Are Consumers' Digital Rights Protected?" October 1, 2020, https://advocacy.consumerreports.org/wp -content/uploads/2021/05/CR_CCPA-Are-Consumers-Digital-Rights-Protected _092020_vf2.pdf; Kaveh Waddell, "California's New Privacy Rights Are Tough to Use; Consumer Reports Study Finds," Consumer Reports, March 16, 2021, https:// www.consumerreports.org/privacy/californias-new-privacy-rights-are-tough-to -use-a1497188573/.

9. The author made an angel investment in Atlas Privacy in 2021.

10. Brian X. Chen, "The Default Tech Settings You Should Turn Off Right Away," *New York Times*, July 27, 2022, https://www.nytimes.com/2022/07/27/technology /personaltech/default-settings-turn-off.html.

11. Thorin Klosowski, "Why You Should Enable Apple's New Security Feature in iOS 16.2 Right Now," *New York Times*, December 14, 2022, https://www.nytimes.com /wirecutter/reviews/how-to-set-up-apples-new-icloud-encryption-security-feature/.

12. Heather Kelly, "Amazon Privacy Settings to Change Now," *Washington Post*, September 23, 2021, https://www.washingtonpost.com/technology/2021/09/23 /amazon-privacy-settings/.

13. Kelly, "Amazon Privacy Settings to Change Now."

Appendix 2

1. The bullets are from Tom Kemp, "Comparing Consumer Rights: GDPR vs. CCPA vs. CPRA," May 30, 2020, https://tomkemp.blog/2020/05/30/comparing -consumer-rights-gdpr-vs-ccpa-vs-cpra/.

2. Information Commissioner's Office, "Rights Related to Automated Decision
-Making Including Profiling," accessed January 4, 2023, https://ico.org.uk
/for-organisations/guide-to-data-protection/guide-to-the-general-data-protection
-regulation-gdpr/individual-rights/rights-related-to-automated-decision-making
-including-profiling/.

3. The bullets are from Tom Kemp, "Comparing Business Obligations: GDPR vs.
CCPA vs. CPRA" and from Tom Kemp, "Is CPRA Actually Stronger than the
ADPPA?" August 12, 2022, https://tomkemp.blog/2022/08/12/not-so-fast-is-cpra
-actually-stronger-than-adppa/.

4. EPIC, "Comparison of American Data Privacy and Protection Act vs. California
Privacy Laws," July 28, 2022, https://epic.org/wp-content/uploads/2022/07
/ADPPAvCCPA-07282022.pdf.

5. EPIC, "Comparison of American Data Privacy and Protection Act vs. California
Privacy Laws."

6. The bullets are from Tom Kemp, "Comparing Enforcement: GDPR vs. CCPA vs.
CPRA," June 4, 2020, https://tomkemp.blog/2020/06/04/comparing-enforcement
-gdpr-vs-ccpa-vs-cpra/.

Index

Note: References followed by "n" refer to endnotes.

Facebook Files, 101, 102, 116, 117, 118, 134–135
Facebook Messenger, 22
Fair Credit Reporting Act (FCRA), 34, 89
Fair Housing Act (FHA), 75
Fast Company, 53
FCRA. *See* Fair Credit Reporting Act
FDA. *See* Food and Drug Administration
fear of missing out (FOMO), 117
Federal Aviation Administration (FAA), 73, 178
Federal Trade Commission (FTC), 43, 51, 143, 156, 157, 170, 199
  antitrust lawsuit against Meta, 158
  antitrust lawsuit against Microsoft, 159–160
  charges against Meta, 63–65, 67–69, 158
  concerns on data brokers, 43, 52–53, 57–58
  Do Not Call registry, 59, 190
  enforcement policy against using dark patterns, 108, 109
  FCRA enforcement, 89
  FTC Act, 89, 91
  regulation for AI-based services, 91
  regulations concerning kids' online privacy, 124–125
feedback loop, 101, 119
finance, AI in, 80
Firefox browser (Mozilla), 155
First Amendment of United States, 124, 140–141
Fischer, Deb, 108
flawed data sampling, 84–85
Fog Data Science, 54
Fogg, BJ, 98
Food and Drug Administration (FDA), 91, 109, 143, 178, 199
Ford, 2
Fourth Amendment Is Not For Sale Act, 58
Fourth Amendment of United States, 12, 54
FTC. *See* Federal Trade Commission

G

Galloway, Scott, 97, 104
Gates, Bill, 26
GDPR. *See* General Data Protection Regulation
Gebru, Timnit, 90
General Data Protection Regulation (GDPR), 7, 33, 71, 88, 123, 169
General Motors (GM), 2–3
Genetic Information Nondiscrimination Act (GINA), 35
GLBA. *See* Gramm–Leach–Bliley Act
Global Disinformation Index (GDI), 136
Global Privacy Control (GPC), 199
Gmail (Google), 18–19
Goldman Sachs, 168
Gonzalez, Nohemi, 129–130
Google, 2, 6, 16, 37, 60, 201n5. *See also* Amazon; Android; Apple; Meta; Microsoft; YouTube
  acquisitions, 18–19
  algorithmic amplification in, 132–133
  anticompetitive practices of, 153–157
  app tax, 161
  data breaches, 62
  data collection and monetization, 5, 14, 20–21
  digital surveillance business model, 17–18, 63, 96, 113, 177
  dominance in digital markets, 145–146
  dot-com crash impact, 16–17
  extending tendrils, 19–20
  as gatekeeper of digital markets, 146–147
  online advertising, 13, 15
  product settings, 192–193
  users of products, 3–4
Google Maps (Google), 18
Gramm–Leach–Bliley Act (GLBA), 34, 35
Grassley, Charles, 167
Grauer, Yael, 190
Gretzky, Wayne, 92
Guardian, 136